KEEPERS OF THE GATE

KEEPERS OF THE GATE

A History of Ellis Island

THOMAS M. PITKIN

Formerly Supervising Historian
National Park Service

NEW YORK: NEW YORK UNIVERSITY PRESS
1975

Figures 1 through 4 were reproduced from photographs in the General Research and Humanities Division, The New York Public Library, Astor, Lenox and Tilden Foundations

Figures 5 through 7 were reproduced from photographs in the Economic and Public Affairs Division, The New York Public Library, Astor, Lenox and Tilden Foundations

Figures 8 through 10 were reproduced from photographs in the William Williams Scrapbooks, Manuscripts and Archives Division, The New York Public Library, Astor, Lenox and Tilden Foundations

Library of Congress Catalog Card Number: 74-21686
ISBN: 0-8147-6562-9

Manufactured in the United States of America

To the Memory of Al Hurst

CONTENTS

PREFACE

Ellis Island has for generations been to the American public the symbol of immigration, as was Castle Garden on the Battery before it. Many millions of immigrants arrived in America under state auspices before the first federal immigration station was established on tiny Ellis Island in New York Harbor. Later, millions more came through other ports. But the great drama of immigration reached its climax during the years 1901 to 1914, when Ellis Island was the principal gateway to America. In this period, as in the 1890s, approximately three-quarters of all immigrants passed through the Port of New York.

For most new Americans, their passage through the station was a brief experience. Yet it was very likely the great dividing point in their lives. For the growing nation, the island was the principal testing ground for immigration policy. This work is not primarily the story of the immigrants. Rather, it is an attempt to tell the administrative side of the Ellis Island story, to account for its place in legend, and to bring out from the shadows some of the men who were responsible for receiving and processing the great tide of newcomers. Not a band of unsung heroes, perhaps, they were nevertheless for the most part able and conscientious men faced with problems of great complexity, working under heavy pressure and in the often scorching heat of public criticism, in a post that probably attracted more hostile voltage than any other except the presidency itself. They were often embroiled in controversy and continually had to deal with problems stemming from corruption and from improper treatment of immigrants. During the busiest years the commissioners were caught in the middle between those who favored increasingly restrictive immigration policies and those who vehemently opposed them. Increasingly, they had to contend with the onerous task of overseeing deportation of undesirables. Whatever position the commissioner took, however honest and competent he might be, he was always a good target for the press.

Ellis Island's early history is interesting only as it occasionally reflects in miniature the life of the growing Port of New York. When the great European wars that followed the French Revolution threatened, time and again, to involve the United States, its position facing the ship channel came to be regarded as strategically important and it was fortified. The fort later became a munitions depot and a subject of recurrent alarm to nearby cities. When the secretary of the treasury was looking for an isolated site on which to place the first federal immigration station, to replace state-operated Castle Garden, Congress presented him—to his dismay—with Ellis Island. Not only was it tiny, it was so low that it barely rose above high tide, and it was situated in very shallow water. The secretary much preferred Bedloe's Island or Governor's Island, but he had to accept Ellis Island nonetheless.

The first immigration station on Ellis Island was hastily built of wood. It was opened at the beginning of 1892 and burned down one night in the summer of 1897. Plans for a fireproof station to replace it took some time to execute; meanwhile, immigrants were received in cramped quarters at the Barge Office on the Battery. There the conditions that had given Castle Garden a bad name prevailed, and the Barge Office quickly became known for corruption and brutality. When the new station on Ellis Island was opened at the end of 1900, the staff that returned there from the Battery brought with them some sinister habits.

Reform of the new station, which was becoming notorious as a den of thieves, was undertaken early in the administration of President Theodore Roosevelt, and after 1902 the island was administered honestly and efficiently, but its problems increased with a rising tide of newcomers. The plant had been designed to handle only the modest immigration of the depression-haunted 1890s. A new burst of national prosperity brought eager immigrants from the far corners of Europe, and, time and again, they almost swamped the little island. The station was never quite adequate to meet the needs of receiving, examining, sorting out, and admitting, detaining, or excluding the vast numbers of immigrants that came.

As the immigration laws grew stricter and the men at Ellis Island tried to enforce them, howls of anguish rose from the foreign language press, as many were detained and turned back; congressmen with immigrant constituencies took up the refrain. There were numerous investigations of Ellis Island, which was charged with many crimes, up to and including murder. A rising nativist movement, on the other hand, sought stricter control of the flood of immigration. Immigrants were coming increasingly from southern and eastern Europe, and were compared unfavorably with the previous immigrants who had come largely from the north and west. The administrators of Ellis Island, through which most of the immigrants had to pass, were freely belabored by the nativists if they did not demonstrate that they were enforcing the exclusion provisions of the law to the limit.

Equally difficult was their task of trying to protect the immigrants from robbery and abuse. To the commissioner of immigration at the island, it seemed that the whole business community, from steamship lines through boarding-houses and hotels to railroads, was in league against the newcomers to snatch away their meager savings and to humiliate them. Powerful interests were involved, and tremendous pressure could be brought to bear on the man who guarded the nation's gateway. When he was adamant, the pressure switched to Washington, and he was often overruled.

The island was relieved of the great tide when World War I erupted in Europe, but other pressures mounted as byproducts of the war. As one wave of hysteria after another swept the country, depositing unwanted aliens on Ellis Island for deportation, the island again became a focus of controversy. At the same time, the army and navy were using most of the buildings as hospitals and barracks. When the war was over and the deportation fever subsided, the trained staff of the immigration station had been widely dispersed and the buildings were in bad condition.

Into the debilitated station there shortly began pouring a new tide of aliens from war-stricken Europe. Many of them were virtually refugees and without funds, and had to be detained in the island's crowded dormitories. During these immediate postwar years, the physical facilities of Ellis Island were at their worst. Congress, stung by floods of criticism at home and abroad, finally voted funds for basic improvements. It moved, also, to cut down the flood of immigrants. The war had brought a revulsion against all things European. Immigration was cut sharply by the first quota immigration law of 1921. This law brought little relief to Ellis Island, however, as under its terms the immigrants came in great spurts at the beginning of each month of the heavy travel season. In 1924 the second quota law not only cut immigration further and spread the flow more evenly throughout the year but also provided for the examination of prospective immigrants at American consulates overseas.

Ellis Island thus lost the principal function for which it had been established. It became primarily a center for the assembly and deportation of aliens who had entered the United States illegally or had violated the terms of their admission. Fewer and fewer new immigrants, all of whom had received a final inspection on the ships coming up the bay from Quarantine, were sent to Ellis Island because their papers were not in order or because they needed medical treatment. The great assemblage of buildings, once overcrowded almost beyond endurance, came to be half empty. The station, increasingly expensive to maintain in the light of its reduced functions, was finally closed in 1954.

After a long period of indecision as to its fate, during which a great variety of plans for the island were offered, interest began to grow in Ellis Island in terms of its association with the dramatic story of immigration. In 1965, by proclamation of the president, it became a part of Statue of Liberty National

Monument and was placed under the administration of the National Park Service. Plans for its development for public use are under way.

This book is the outgrowth of a report prepared for the National Park Service in 1966, after Ellis Island had been placed under its administration. I wish to acknowledge the support of that agency in my further research on the subject and its endorsement of publication. Much of the material in the present work appeared in *The New-York Historical Society Quarterly* in October 1968. Permission to republish has been graciously granted. My thanks for active assistance in pursuing research relating to Ellis Island are due to many people, including both librarians and public officials. They include personnel of the National Park Service, the National Archives, the U.S. Immigration and Naturalization Service, the Library of Congress, the New York Public Library, the New-York Historical Society, Columbia University Libraries, Yale University Library, and Cornell University Library. Editing by the New York University Press has improved the manuscript at a number of points.

ILLUSTRATIONS

Immigrants under interrogation by immigrant inspectors in 1903. They are burdened with hand luggage which they have carried up a long flight of stairs.
—Courtesy of the New York Public Library

CHAPTER I

YEARS OF OBSCURITY

Ellis Island is one of the islets off the New Jersey shore of the Upper Bay of New York. These tiny islands, including Liberty Island (formerly known as Bedloe's) and a now-submerged reef, are all in the shallow waters west of the ship channel, sometimes called the Jersey Flats. In colonial times they were often referred to in a group as the Oyster Islands, and the waters around them were known as the Oyster Bank. Nomenclature was flexible, however. The largest of the Oyster Islands came to be known as Bedloe's Island, from an early owner. Ellis Island, called by the Indians Kioshk, or "Gull Island," from its only inhabitants, was later labeled Dyre's Island, Bucking Island, and Gibbet Island before the name of Samuel Ellis, its only known eighteenth-century owner, was firmly fixed to it.[1]

The island was a tiny bank of mud and sand, mixed with oyster shells, about three acres in extent and scarcely rising above the water at high tide. It was a singularly uninviting piece of terrain, useful only because of its position in the midst of rich oyster beds and as a fine place from which to stake out nets during the spring run of shad.[2] It had none of the attractions of its somewhat larger neighbor, Bedloe's Island, which was closer to deep water, had some vegetation and a pleasing elevation at the end toward the channel, and boasted a supply of good fresh water.

In 1629 the Dutch West India Company created the patroon system to stimulate settlement and development of the colony of New Netherland. Under this system, lands and extensive feudal privileges were granted to company directors who would bring in settlers. Michael Paauw (or Paw) was one of the first patroons. He received a grant of land on the west bank of the North River opposite New Amsterdam, including the site of present-day Hoboken. This land was purchased for him from the Indians by the director general and council of the colony on July 12, 1630, the compensation being "certain cargoes, or parcels of goods." [3]

To this purchase there was shortly added Staten Island, and some time afterward the intervening tract including the site of Jersey City. The patroonship was called Pavonia, from a play on Paauw's name in Latin, and in it were the first white settlements in the later state of New Jersey. It presumably included the later Ellis Island. Washington Irving, in his fanciful account of the assembling of the Dutch colonial forces to attack the Swedes on the Delaware, speaks of the vassals of "that renowned Mynheer, Michael Paw, who lorded it over the fair regions of ancient Pavonia, and the lands away south even unto the Navesink mountains, and was moreover patroon of Gibbet Island." [4]

Paw could not have taken part in this muster himself, since he never left the comforts of Amsterdam for the crude colony overseas, and he had, in any case, sold Pavonia to the company long before the Swedes threatened the Dutch control of the Delaware. Nevertheless, Irving's assumption that the patroonship of Pavonia had included Gibbet (Ellis) Island seems sound. It is quite likely that the later Bedloe's Island was regarded as part of his domain as well. Both islands huddled close to the shore of Pavonia. Communipaw ("Paw's Community"), just opposite Ellis Island on the mainland, was one of the first permanent settlements in the tract. There was a trading house there as early as 1634, and a town, later absorbed by Jersey City, was laid out in 1660.[5]

The first supposed reference to the later Ellis Island is found in a court case of 1661, in which a missing boat was discovered undamaged "on Oyster Island." Why it has been assumed that this was Ellis Island and not Bedloe's Island is not clear. It could have been either, more likely Bedloe's, the larger and more inviting of the two. The first certain reference is in an undated grant by Governor Edmund Andros to William Dyre, his collector of customs, of "Little Oyster Island." The grant was made at some time between 1674 and 1680. A few years later, in 1686, William Dyre and Mary, his wife, conveyed to Thomas Lloyd lands on Manhattan, "and alsoe a certaine Island Scituate and lyeing in Hudson River to the Westward of Manhattans or York Island and north of Bedloes Island Commonly called or knowne by the name of Dyre's Island or Oyster Island." Lloyd in turn conveyed the island to Enoch and Mary Story.[6] Here the trail of ownership breaks off for nearly a century.

In 1691 the island was formally included within the boundaries of New York County. An act of that year divided the colony into counties, each county being bounded and described: "The city and county of New York to contain all the Island commonly called Manhattan's-Island, Manning's-Island, the two Barn Islands, and the three Oyster-Islands; Manhattan's Island, to be called the City of New-York, and the Rest of the Islands, the County." [7]

The charter granted to the city of New York by Governor John Montgomerie in 1730 referred to the island as Bucking Island and included it within the city's boundaries, which were "to include Nutten Island, Bedlow's Island, Bucking Island, and Oyster Island, to low water mark on the west side of the North River." The name Bucking Island, of unknown origin, was applied to the island during a good part of the eighteenth century. In 1757, when the city council was seeking a site for a pesthouse, it appointed a committee "to view and Examine Buckin Island." The committee's report, not found, was evidently negative, for in the next year Bedloe's Island was purchased for the purpose.[8]

The name Gibbet Island has been traced to an event of 1765. A pirate by the name of Anderson, captured in the West Indies, was returned to New York, the port from which his ship had sailed, tried, and executed "upon an Island in the Bay, near the city, which, from that circumstance, has ever since been called, Anderson's or Gibbet Island." Other hangings took place there, and Washington Irving, writing early in the following century, consistently used the name Gibbet Island. The British army during the American Revolution, however, in its military cartography, used the name Bucking Island on one map and Oyster Island on another, to designate the later Ellis Island.[9]

Private ownership of the island reappears in 1785 with the advertisement for sale by one Samuel Ellis of "that pleasant situated Island, called Oyster (now Ellis) Island, lying in New York Bay, near Powles Hook." How he obtained his title is unknown, but it seems not to have been challenged. No sale followed the advertisement. Samuel Ellis died in 1794, and by his will of the same year the island, "with all the buildings and improvements thereon," was bequeathed to the child of his daughter Catherine Westervelt, with which she was then pregnant, if it should be a son. He also wished the son to be named Samuel Ellis. If the child should be a daughter, his estate was to be divided among Catherine's children equally.

Catherine dutifully produced a son, who was named Samuel Ellis as his grandfather had wished. But the boy died in infancy, and letters of administration were granted to his mother. At this point the title becomes confused. Samuel Ellis Ryerson, son of another daughter of Samuel Ellis, and his wife Rachel deeded the island and property in Manhattan to John A. Berry in 1806.[10] When Lieutenant Colonel Jonathan Williams, U.S. Army chief of engineers, wanted the island shortly afterward for the construction of fortifications, he found that there were several claimants.

There had been a battery on Ellis Island for some years before Williams cast his eye upon it. In 1794 there was a serious threat of war with Great Britain because of her interference with American trade in the French West Indies. The long European conflict that followed the French Revolution was under way, and England and France were beginning their titanic twenty-year struggle. The War Department sent engineers to the chief coastal cities to prepare defenses against the British fleet. Charles Vincent was sent to New

York, to make a plan on a very limited budget. At about the same time the state of New York appropriated funds for the same purpose and appointed a commission, including Governor George Clinton, with full powers to erect forts "at or near the city and port of New-York."

Vincent submitted a plan including outer works on the Narrows and an inner defense based on the triangle of Bedloe's, Governor's, and "Oyster" islands. In the same year he reported the works on all three islands as under construction. Governor Clinton's commission, being informed that "the President of the United States had appointed Mr. Vincent a French Engineer of experience to examine the Harbour of New York and form a plan for its fortification," had accepted Vincent as its own engineer. Since the appropriated federal funds were entirely inadequate, the commission voted to use the funds appropriated by the state for the forts that he was to design and construct under its direction.[11]

Considerable work was done, mostly in the form of earthworks and largely with state money. The city of New York deeded Bedloe's Island, which it owned, and the "soil from high to low Water mark around the Isle called Ellis's Isle," which it evidently claimed under a liberal interpretation of the Montgomerie charter, to the state for purposes of fortification. The state prepared to buy the island itself, and a deed was drawn up for the purpose, but Ellis died and the deed was not executed. The works built there in the 1790s were actually on private property, so far as they rose above high tide.[12]

Further work was done on the fortifications in the harbor in 1798, when a threat of war with France developed. This was under the direction of Ebenezer Stevens, a veteran officer of the Continental artillery, acting as "agent for the Department of War." Ellis Island, Stevens reminded the secretary of war after this work was done, "is private property and . . . I think something ought to be done with respect to purchasing it and the State will cede the jurisdiction to the Federal Government." Nothing was done about purchasing the island, but in 1800 the state of New York passed an act ceding jurisdiction over all three of the fortified islands—Governor's, Bedloe's, and Oyster (Ellis)—to the United States.[13] The United States government has since held Governor's and Bedloe's islands continuously. Ellis Island remained disputed territory.

The successive threats of war and bursts of fortification fever had not brought the works in New York Harbor to completion. Major Decius Wadsworth, reporting on the state of the forts there in 1802, found the fort on Ellis Island unfinished and with its guns unmounted. Ellis Island, though it lacked good fresh water, he thought "a very proper position for batteries to defend the harbor of New York against an attack by sea." Only part of the island had been purchased for public use, he noted, and he recommended that the rest of it be acquired.[14]

There seems to have been no permanent garrison on the island at this time and Washington Irving, describing a walk on the Battery in 1804, depicted it as a quiet place, concerned only with the surrounding oyster beds: "the fleet of canoes, at anchor between Gibbet Island and Communipaw, slumbered on their rakes, and suffered the innocent oysters to lie for a while in the soft mud of their native banks." Presently a storm came up, and "the oyster-boats that erst sported in the placid vicinity of Gibbet Island, now hurry affrighted to the land." [15]

The War Department used the name Gibbet Island occasionally. When Lieutenant Colonel Williams was sent to New York in 1805 to survey the harbor for further fortification, he was instructed, among other things, to measure "the distance from Governor's Island to the Island near Gibbet Island." In his report on this mission, however, Williams used the modern designation. He noted that "the forts at Bedlow's and Ellis's Islands are dismantled and totally out of repair." Like Vincent, Stevens, and Wadsworth before him, Williams approved of the position of Ellis Island, if not of its other characteristics. He dreamed of erecting there a three-tiered circular work of many guns. "Ellis's Island appears to me a proper place for such a battery," he stated, "since it could fire in a sweep of ¾ of a circle from Paulus Hook to the Narrows to the extent of cannon shott." [16]

Under the pressure of fund limitations and other considerations, he had eventually to forgo his tower on Ellis Island and content himself with a very modest battery. But for a time he was unable even to work on the island because of lack of title. His plan of harbor fortification, approved in the summer of 1807, called for "a casemated Battery" to be erected on Ellis Island and urged that "a purchase should be made of the part now belonging to citizens." Governor Daniel Tompkins of New York had assured him that the title to the land between high and low water was in the hands of the state and would be conveyed to him, but that he would have to get a deed for the island as a whole. The works that had been built there were "occupied merely by the permission of the owner." [17]

Williams ran into "all manner of difficulties" about the title and decided to ask the state of New York to give the federal government title and buy up the different claims. The necessary legislation was forthcoming, calling for condemnation by a special jury. The jury priced the island at $10,000, and Williams was outraged. They had "estimated capabilities instead of real estate," he wrote Secretary of War Henry Dearborn, "taking into consideration the advantage of setting fish nets on the flatts all around, letting rakes to the oystermen, & keeping a house of entertainment for all these amphibious customers." It was a very high price to pay for "2¾ acres of sand bank." But Governor Tompkins assured the secretary that the island couldn't be had for less. He concluded the purchase on behalf of the state, making the payment out of his own pocket as there was no appropriation. A deed was then executed, June 30, 1808, conveying the state's title to the United States.[18]

At the end of the construction season, Williams reported on the progress of fortification in the harbor of New York. As for "Ellis's or Oyster Island," its position was so advantageous that "it would be desirable to erect a castle here," similar to the one then under construction on Governor's Island. However, the island was of so spongy a nature that no foundation could be made without filling and without entirely removing the old fort, since there was no space for a new site. For these reasons, and because funds were running low, the secretary had ordered him to make "an open barbette battery here for about twenty guns on one platform." This was nearly completed. In spite of this optimistic report, work on the little fort lagged, other projects in the harbor receiving priority in the construction program. At the end of the season of 1811, it still lacked a magazine and adequate barracks. In the following spring, only a few months before the outbreak of the War of 1812, this construction was directed and presumably completed.[19]

During the second conflict with Great Britain, the battery on Ellis Island was manned by a small garrison, and a few British prisoners were also confined there from time to time. Like the other forts that Jonathan Williams built in New York Harbor, it saw no action with the enemy. Like those forts, however, it no doubt helped to discourage a British naval attack on New York, such as those that were made in the course of the war on Baltimore and Washington. In the fall of 1814 Governor Tompkins briefly took command of the Third Military District, which included New York and the forts in the harbor. One of his first acts was to give names to the forts on Bedloe's and Ellis islands. The works on Bedloe's were named Fort Wood, and those on Ellis were named Fort Gibson, in honor of two gallant and distinguished American officers who had recently been killed at the battle of Fort Erie.[20]

Fort Gibson's peacetime history thereafter was relatively uneventful. In the 1830s the island came into use again as a place of execution, and several pirates were hanged there. In the 1830s, also, the states of New Jersey and New York came to an agreement on a boundary dispute that had flared up from time to time and involved Ellis Island. New York claimed the waters of Hudson River and New York Bay to high water mark on the New Jersey shore, while New Jersey contended that her sovereignty extended to the middle of the river. In 1833 commissioners of the two states met in New York City and entered into a compact later ratified by the legislatures of both states and approved by Congress in 1834.

Under this compact the boundary line between New York and New Jersey was declared to be the middle of the Hudson River through Upper New York Bay, but Staten Island was recognized as part of New York, and it was further declared that "The state of New York shall retain its present jurisdiction over Bedloe's and Ellis's Islands." The state of New York was to have exclusive jurisdiction over the waters of the Bay of New York to low water mark on the New Jersey side, except that "The state of New Jersey shall have the exclusive right of property in and to the land under water lying west of the middle of the bay of New York." New Jersey retained jurisdiction over wharves and docks on its shore and had exclusive right of regulating the fisheries on the westerly side of the river.[21] This complicated arrangement, needless to say, has since given rise to considerable litigation in the busy harbor and has left jurisdictional ghosts that apparently have not yet been laid.

Fort Gibson was used for a time as a recruit depot, but by 1835 it had been turned over to the Navy Department for use as a powder magazine. It was returned to army jurisdiction in 1841, the navy reserving "the entire control over the Naval Magazine there and the rights and privileges incident thereto." The army made extensive repairs to the fort in the next year, including the construction of a hotshot furnace. By 1843 Fort Gibson was reported as "armed and equipped" since its return by the navy. Interestingly, in the light of its later use, the New York State commissioners of emigration, then newly created, wrote to Secretary of War William Marcy in 1847 inquiring whether Ellis Island might not be available for use by "the Convalescent Emigrants." The request was denied. "Ellis' island," it was stated, "is very small; it is the site of a naval magazine, containing large supplies of ammunition; the government has not heretofore allowed any person, other than a proper guard, to reside on the island." [22]

The army, after repairing and modernizing Fort Gibson (shortly reduced in rank to Battery Gibson, as a new Fort Gibson had been built in the West), had put no garrison in it but allowed the navy to maintain Ellis Island under a small guard to protect its munitions. This odd arrangement continued. During the Civil War the navy built extensive additional magazines there. At the same time the army was installing heavy new guns in the fort. There was some friction evident between the two services on the tight little island at this time, and small wonder. The engineer officer from Governor's Island reported unhappily to his chief that the navy had put some of its magazines so close to the hotshot furnace that it could not be used, and he could not learn what else the navy was up to. "The Gunner in charge states that the Chief of the Naval Ordnance Dept. contemplates erecting another building; information with respect to its location could not be definitely obtained by me." Shortly after the war, the navy was left in sole possession, and it continued to maintain large stocks of munitions on Ellis Island.[23]

A few years after the end of the war, the presence on Ellis Island of all these explosives gave rise to alarm. The New York *Sun*, corroborated by *Harper's Weekly*, "called attention to the startling fact that New York, Brooklyn, Jersey City, and the numerous villages on Staten Island, are now, and have been for a long time, in imminent peril of being at once destroyed by the explosions of the magazines on Ellis's Island." *Harper's* sent over a reporter and an artist who made a sketch of these sinister structures. There were six of the buildings, "built of solid masonry with slate roofs." They had a combined capacity of 5,000 barrels of powder. At the moment, it was said, they held about 3,000 barrels and "a very large number of shells." While elaborate precautions were taken to prevent any accident on the island, "still the greatest of precautions are sometimes in vain." There was not the slightest necessity for accumulating this amount of powder "in such close proximity to the most populous city in the country," it was argued, and *Harper's* demanded that Secretary of the Navy Welles should at once remove it.[24]

Having given their readers a few chills, *Harper's* and the *Sun* apparently let the matter drop. The subject was revived in 1876, when Congressman Hardenburgh of New Jersey offered in the House a resolution that Ellis Island in New York Harbor be abandoned as a site for a powder arsenal. "If it were struck by lightning," he said, "the shock would destroy Jersey City, Hoboken, and parts of New York." [25] Nothing came of this, and the navy still maintained a powder magazine on Ellis Island at the beginning of 1890.

There was still opposition to its presence, however. The Johnstown flood in 1889 had reminded Jersey City of its own local peril, and the subject had been brought up in a meeting of the Board of Trade. A member warned that the powder magazine might blow up at any time and that "such an explosion might sacrifice more lives and destroy more property than the flood did in the Conemaugh Valley." A resolution was adopted requesting the removal of the powder magazine from Ellis Island and putting the New Jersey senators and the Jersey City congressman on notice "to use their best efforts to that end." [26] As the need for a federal immigration station developed in the following year, this action drew attention to the island as a possible site for it.

CHAPTER II

THE FIRST IMMIGRATION STATION

Except for the counting of immigrants as they arrived, and some limitation on the packing to which they could be subjected on shipboard, the federal government left the control of immigration largely in the hands of the states until 1875. In that year a federal law dealing primarily with problems of the Oriental coolie traffic excluded criminals and forbade the importation of women for purposes of prostitution. Enforcement was left to the collectors of the ports, who were to make their inspections aboard ship and forbid the landing of the proscribed classes. While this law was narrow in scope, it did forecast federal control and restriction of the whole movement. The Supreme Court had for some time been moving in the same direction, and shortly after the law of 1875 was passed it declared unconstitutional the law of New York State requiring steamship companies to post a bond in the amount of $300 or else pay a poll tax for each immigrant. The court said that it thought that the subject had been confided to the Congress by the Constitution, and recommended national legislation covering all ports and all vessels.[1]

This decision left New York and other maritime states without means to care for sick and indigent immigrants except by taxation and hastened the movement toward federal control. In 1882 a more comprehensive statute excluded "any convict, lunatic, idiot or any person unable to take care of himself or herself without becoming a public charge." A separate law excluding Chinese laborers was passed in the same year. The secretary of the treasury was charged with the execution of the general exclusion law, but he was authorized to work through state boards or officers in its actual administration. The law provided for a head tax of 50 cents on immigrants, to be used to defray the expenses of examination of passengers on their arrival and for the relief of those in distress. New York had long been the principal port of immigration, and since 1855 the state had received immigrants at Castle Garden on the Battery. Under the new law, the secretary made a contract with the New York State commissioners of emigration to carry it out as far as that port was concerned.[2]

Another piece of federal legislation in 1885 marked a further step in the direction of national control and restriction of immigration. This was the Alien Contract Labor Law, passed under pressure from organized labor, making it unlawful to import aliens for labor under contract. This law did not provide any administrative machinery, but it was later placed under the administration of the secretary of the treasury. While he was authorized to administer this law also by contract through state agencies, federal contract labor inspectors were afterward assigned to Castle Garden to supplement the state examining staff. Labor unions had complained that the New York State commissioners of emigration were making no effort to enforce the law, arguing that enforcement of this law was not in their contract.[3]

For several years the reception of immigrants at New York and elsewhere was handled by this mixed federal-state system. The arrangement proved unsatisfactory, and pressure mounted for full federal control. In 1887 Joseph Pulitzer's New York *World* attacked the management of Castle Garden vigorously, as one of its crusading ventures. The secretary of the treasury directed David Okey, a departmental official, to investigate. Consequently, extensive hearings were held in New York, at which varied charges of mismanagement, abuse of immigrants, and evasion of the laws were aired. Okey's report was not made public, but it undoubtedly influenced the Treasury Department toward a decision to abrogate the contract and take full charge of immigrant reception at the Port of New York. Charges of lax enforcement of the immigration laws and of abuse of immigrants continued in the columns of the *World*. Other New York journals expressed alarm at what they considered the deteriorating quality of the arriving immigrants, who were coming increasingly from southern and eastern Europe.[4]

In the summer of 1888 Congressman Melbourne Ford of Michigan offered a resolution in the House calling for a select committee to investigate the administration of the immigration laws at New York and elsewhere. The resolution was approved, and Ford was made chairman of the committee. The committee, with the power of subpoena, spent several weeks in New York and later visited Boston, Pittsburgh, and Detroit. Ford presented his report to the House in the following January, together with a bill designed to tighten the immigration laws. The committee had conducted more extended investigations at New York than elsewhere, he said, because the great majority of the immigrants landing in the United States were received there. During the fiscal year 1888, there were 546,889 immigrants landed at the various ports; of these, 418,423, or about 76 percent, came to New York. The greater portion of them came between the months of April and September. As for their reception at that port, he reported:

> The committee visited Castle Garden on several occasions, and witnessed the arrival and inspection of immigrants, and it was very obvious to them that it was almost impossible to properly inspect the large numbers of persons who arrive daily during the immigrant season with the facilities afforded; and the testimony taken puts it beyond question that large numbers of persons not lawfully entitled to land in the United States are annually received at this port. In fact, one of the commissioners of immigration himself testified that the local administration of affairs at Castle Garden, by the method and system now followed, was a perfect farce.

Ford's bill, which he put into the hopper at the same time, called for a number of additional prohibited classes, provided severe penalties for evasion, tightened the terms of the contract labor law, raised the head tax to $5, and provided for legal examination of prospective immigrants at United States consulates in Europe. The enforcement of the immigration laws, Ford recommended, should be entrusted to the federal government and not to the states.[5]

The country was far from ready for such drastic immigration control as Ford proposed, but Castle Garden had been given a drubbing from which it never recovered. Secretary of the Treasury William Windom in the same year reported "grave difficulties in the execution of the law through State agencies," which were not subject to effective control. There were jurisdictional disputes and "serious differences in the settlement of the accounts of certain State commissions." The secretary recommended that the whole business of immigration control be assumed by the federal government.[6]

A few months later he sent W. P. Hepburn, the departmental solicitor, to New York to investigate the differences which existed between the Treasury and the New York State commissioners of emigration over the handling of immigration matters under the existing contract. Following his investigation, Hepburn submitted a report which included a detailed description of the operation of Castle Garden and of the immigrant hospital which the commissioners maintained on Ward's Island in the East River. In his view, the insufficiencies of the local administration and their differences with the Treasury Department were such as to call for termination of the contract. The required sixty days' notice should be given the commissioners, he recommended, after which the department should itself receive the immigrants, either at Castle Garden or at the nearby Barge Office. After consultation with the collector of customs at New York, on February 15, 1890, Secretary Windom sent a letter to the commissioners revoking the contract, effective April 18.[7]

While he recognized that temporary quarters would have to be occupied, at Castle Garden or elsewhere, Windom was resolved to build a new station that would be isolated and completely under federal control. One of the islands in the Upper Bay, all of which were federally owned, seemed best suited to the purpose. The secretary came to New York and made a reconnaissance even before he notified the state commissioners officially of the contract termination. His first choice was Bedloe's Island. At once the New York *World*, which had a few years before led the campaign to raise money for the pedestal of Bartholdi's Statue of Liberty there, began a vigorous protest. The island, which it said, "was to have been made into a beautiful park as a fit setting for the great Statue," was now "to be converted instead into a Babel."

The *World* for weeks kept up a drumfire of agitation against the proposed use of what it called "Liberty Island," insisting that the decision was "universally deprecated by those who look with pride upon Liberty's imposing beacon." It not only marshaled the support of American admirers of the Statue of Liberty but also sought out Auguste Bartholdi, its creator, in Paris. Bartholdi was properly horrified. The proposal to move the immigration station to Liberty Island, he said, was "a monstrous plan" and a "downright desecration." [8]

Even before Secretary Windom's decision had been made known, the *World* had called attention to the availability of Ellis Island for immigration purposes. Senator John R. McPherson of New Jersey early in the year had introduced a joint resolution simply calling for the removal of the powder magazine there, citing petitions from the Jersey City Board of Trade and other groups around the harbor. This resolution had been referred to the Committee on Naval Affairs. After the *World*'s campaign of protest against the use of Bedloe's Island for the immigration station had gathered sufficient momentum, this resolution became the vehicle for placing that facility on Ellis Island in place of the powder magazine.

A temporary joint committee on immigration had been formed in the meantime, under the chairmanship of Senator William E. Chandler of New Hampshire, a convinced immigration restrictionist, to investigate the workings of the immigration laws and of the contracts made by the secretary of the treasury under the law of 1882. As amended in the House, Chandler's resolution on the subject called for the review of Windom's selection of Bedloe's Island as the committee's first task. The committee came to New York and inspected Bedloe's Island, Governor's Island, and Ellis Island. The military gentlemen quartered on Governor's Island, under the command of General O. O. Howard, were a unit in opposing the use of any part of the choice army reservation there for immigration purposes. Senator William Evarts of New York, who had been a principal promoter of the Statue of Liberty, gave the committee an impassioned plea against the use of Bedloe's Island. In this situation the choice of Ellis Island, where the navy's powder magazine was under attack and where there was no powerful sentiment to be overridden, was natural. On its return to Washington the committee, with only two opposing votes, approved the selection of Ellis Island as the site for the new immigration station.

Meanwhile, Senator McPherson's resolution for the removal of the powder magazine there had been brought out of committee and passed by the Senate with an amendment appropriating $75,000 "to enable the Secretary of the Treasury to improve said Ellis Island for immigration purposes." This resolution was taken up by the House, passed with only brief debate, and signed by President Benjamin Harrison on April 11.[9]

This action had not been taken without protest. One of the members of the joint committee had based his opposition on the statement of Secretary Windom, who had looked at Ellis Island, among other localities in New York Harbor, and rejected it as a possible site on what he considered good and sufficient grounds. He had told the committee:

> We also tried to reach Ellis Island. We were on a little revenue cutter, and asked the officer to take us to Ellis Island. He said he could not get the boat there, because the water was not deep enough. I told him then to take us as near to it as he could; and he went within 30 rods of it, I should think, or perhaps less. The difficulty of reaching it and the observations we had at that distance from us, where it seemed to be almost on a level with the water, presented so few attractions for an immigrant depot that we steamed away from it under the impression that even if we could get rid of the powder magazine which is there now, and could secure the island, it was not a desirable place; and we were so advised by the collector of customs of New York and some others who were with us.[10]

Whether he liked it or not, Ellis Island was the place presented to the secretary for the building and operation of the first federal immigration station. It was transferred to the Treasury Department for this purpose, the powder having been removed to Fort Wadsworth on the Narrows, on May 24, 1890. Planning got under way almost at once in the office of the superintendent of repairs of United States buildings in New York. The secretary's report for the fiscal year indicated that the work of construction was already "being prosecuted with vigor," with hopes that the new plant would be ready for occupation in the following April.

The work going forward consisted of the dredging of a channel to a depth of 12 feet or more, 200 feet wide and 1,250 feet long; the building of 853 feet of docks, with 860 feet of additional crib work (to contain fill enlarging the island); the construction of a large two-story wooden building, with a small separate hospital group, a boiler house, laundry, and electric light plant; and the digging of artesian wells and construction of cisterns.[11] As might have been expected, such a formidable program was not completed by the following April; it was the beginning of 1892 before the Ellis Island station, still far from complete, could be put into use for the reception of immigrants.

The termination of the contract between the secretary of the treasury and the New York State commissioners of emigration went into effect, as scheduled, on April 18, 1890, and Castle Garden was closed. The commissioners, in a resentful mood, had refused to permit its use by the Treasury Department while the Ellis Island station was under construction. A temporary immigration station was found in the Barge Office, at the southeast corner of Battery Park, not far from Castle Garden. The Barge Office got its name from the fact that there had been in the vicinity a landing place for barges plying to and from Governor's Island from colonial times to the Civil War. The building then existing under that name, near the Staten Island ferry, was a granite structure with a corrugated iron annex, completed in 1883 for the use of the Customs Bureau. It was intended as a central landing place for steamship cabin passengers and their baggage, to simplify customs inspection. The plan had not worked, as both passengers and steamship companies had objected strenuously. In 1890 the building, which was a Treasury Department facility, was largely idle.[12]

The quarters at the Barge Office were cramped, and immigration was on an upward curve and heavily concentrated at New York. In the two and one-half months remaining in the fiscal year 1890, 118,819 immigrants were landed and examined at this temporary station. In the following full year, 405,664 immigrant aliens were received there, of a national total of 516,253, or approximately 80 percent. The secretary of the treasury put a good face on the situation, reporting that though the place was "not entirely satisfactory," his expectations that "the Department could administer the service with greater economy and efficiency through agencies under its own control" had been fully realized.

The department had no staff of its own, except for a few contract labor inspectors, ready and trained to take over this sudden and serious responsibility. The organization at the Barge Office was made up largely of former Castle Garden employees, under the general direction of a superintendent subject to the control of the collector of customs. Many former New York State immigrant examiners (or "registry clerks" as they were long called in accordance with their actual functions) served not only there but also later at Ellis Island. There was at first no bureau in Washington charged with responsibility for immigration matters. For the time being, the Port of New York was the only one at which immigration was handled directly by the Treasury Department. Existing contracts with state authorities at the ports of Portland, Boston, Philadelphia, Baltimore, Key West, New Orleans, Galveston, and San Francisco remained in force.[13]

In the following year, however, the federal government assumed full responsibility for the reception of all immigrants. For a long period after the Civil War the immigrant had been generally welcomed in the rapidly expanding United States, but latent nativism revived in the troubled 1880s. As the stream of migration shifted increasingly from northern and western Europe to southern and eastern Europe, hostility to the immigrant, at first undifferentiated, gradually took on a geographical character. The Italians, Slavs, and Russian Jews who formed the bulk of the new migration were often, by western European standards, "educationally deficient, socially backward, and bizarre in appearance," arousing instant dislike. They were compared unfavorably with the Germans, the Irish, the British, and the Scandinavians who had led the procession into the early 1880s. Prejudice against them was soon strengthened by racial theories imported from northern Europe or of native manufacture. Senator Chandler intended his joint committee to bring about thoroughgoing and effective federal control, and then, if possible, sharp restriction, of immigration.[14]

After the decision to build the new station at Ellis Island had been reached, Chandler's committee held extensive hearings at New York and elsewhere. Castle Garden clerks described the hasty examination procedure which they employed: it was little more than a matter of registering the incoming immigrants and ordinarily took about thirty seconds. Terence V. Powderly, head of the Knights of Labor, testified at length about the deteriorating quality of immigrants and the lack of enforcement of the contract labor law. Hungarians and Lithuanians, who "herded together like animals and lived like beasts," were crowding Americans out of the coal fields of Pennsylvania, he charged. Edgar L. Ridgway, president of the board of state commissioners, also testified that the immigration was getting worse. He held that the Russians and the Italians were "the most undesirable immigrants" and argued for further restrictions on immigration. The *New York Times* hoped that something better than Ford's idea of a consular examination to screen out undesirables would come about. The *Times* maintained that the consular examination was unworkable, but it thought that a head tax of $25 would be a good idea. "Such an expedient would undoubtedly attain both the object of lessening the bulk of immigration and the object of raising its quality." [15]

While the restrictionists did not have things altogether their own way in the next winter's session of Congress, the immigration act that was passed at its close did provide some further restrictions and laid a permanent administrative foundation for national control of immigration. The law of 1891 placed immigration wholly under federal authority. It set up a practical method of enforcement of exclusion regulations by compelling steamship companies to carry back to Europe all passengers rejected by U.S. inspectors. Since it was expected that the companies would hold their ticket agents responsible for the cost of the return passage, this provision would, in effect, make these agents overseas immigrant inspectors. The law contained the first effective provisions for deporting undesirable aliens; those who entered illegally, or who became public charges from causes existing prior to landing, might be expelled within one year. It added to the exclusion categories polygamists and "persons suffering from a loathsome or dangerous contagious disease." It also broadened the contract labor law to make employers' advertisements directed at would-be immigrants illegal.[16]

The act created the office of Superintendent of Immigration in the Treasury Department. The superintendent was required to report annually to the secretary on the work of his office. In accordance with the provisions of the act, the Bureau of Immigration was established in the department on July 12, 1891.

A commissioner of immigration was installed at each major port. Colonel John B. Weber, a Buffalo businessman and former member of Congress, who was already superintendent of the Barge Office, was the first appointee at New York. His staff was made up almost entirely of former Castle Garden employees. Weber and his principal assistants, the *New York Tribune* noted with satisfaction when the temporary station at the Barge Office went into operation, were all good Republicans.[17]

While Weber was chosen in the first instance by the New York Republican machine of Boss Tom Platt, he seems to have been an able and conscientious administrator. An early investigation of the Barge Office by the House Committee on Immigration—inspired by a somewhat hysterical missionary—cleared him of charges of abusing the immigrants. Its report to the House declared that the treatment of immigrants by Weber and his staff was "humane and kind." The *American Hebrew*, highly sensitive to the treatment of Russian Jewish immigrants fleeing from Czarist oppression, found him "an excellent disciplinarian" and remarkably efficient, but also a man with a heart.[18]

In the summer of 1891 Weber headed a commission sent to Europe by the secretary of the treasury to investigate the problems of contract labor, other forms of assisted immigration, and the principal causes of emigration to the United States in general. European countries were believed to be unloading paupers, criminals, and other undesirables on this country by paying their passage, and many other artificial stimuli to emigration were suspected. The new law took a dim view of "assisted immigrants," and any immigrant who did not pay his own passage had to prove he was not a member of one of the excluded classes. Weber's commission traveled extensively throughout Europe for several months.

The group was sharply divided in its views, and several individual reports were submitted. The principal report, signed only by Weber and one other member, gave little comfort to the restrictionists. It found that 60 percent of the immigrants came on prepaid tickets or on money sent by friends or relatives already in America. They were technically assisted immigrants, but they were not undesirables being expelled. They came in search of better living conditions and greater freedom. Emigration from Russia was a special case; savage official and unofficial oppression of the Jews there was producing a mass movement. They were being assisted by wealthy coreligionists in other countries, a fact that Weber apparently took in stride. Steamship companies, Weber found, were not stimulating immigration in the aggressive manner forbidden by the law. The existing laws had, moreover, virtually stopped contract labor engagements, and there was no evidence of systematic dumping of criminals or insane persons. The report opposed consular inspection of immigrants as likely to be expensive and inefficient. It approved immigration in general and favored only limited new legislation tightening up deportation procedures, making paupers and criminals subject to expulsion up to the time of acquiring citizenship. Weber a few months later also expounded these views in the *North American Review*, no doubt to the irritation of his superiors in Washington; they ran counter to views strongly held there.[19]

The secretary's report for 1891 stated somewhat optimistically that "The new and commodious Immigrant Station on Ellis Island, in New York Harbor, is practically completed, and the business of receiving and inspecting immigrants will be transferred thither from the Barge Office as soon as certain details are arranged." There would be a regular ferry maintained between Ellis Island and the Barge Office, it said, and the annex forming part of the latter was to be used as a final landing place for those immigrants going to New York and nearby points. Officials at New York were obviously close to desperation because of their limited quarters and their overwhelming responsibilities, and they looked forward to the move eagerly. "The new receiving station," it was affirmed, "besides adding vastly to the comfort, convenience, and sanitary well-being of the arriving immigrants, will enable the inspection officers to perform their duties much more thoroughly, effectively, and expeditiously." [20]

Not long before Ellis Island opened as an immigrant station, an enthusiastic writer described the new plant in admiring detail in *Harper's Weekly*. It was apparent, he said, that "the Federal government does not appear to be overestimating its needs so much as to be putting to shame the neglectful State officials who previously mismanaged the business." The new main building looked like "a latter-day watering place hotel, presenting to the view a great many-windowed expanse of buff-painted wooden walls, of blue-slate roofing, and of light and picturesque towers." It was 400 feet long, 150 feet wide, and two stories high, and would permit the handling of 10,000 immigrants in a day. In the baggage room on the first floor there was room to store and handle the baggage of 12,000 immigrants. Elsewhere on the island, which had been practically doubled in size, there were, either finished or under construction, hospital buildings, bathhouse, powerhouse, kitchen and restaurant, and doctors' quarters.

Steerage passengers, *Harper's* explained, would be landed in barges at Ellis Island and ascend to the second story for medical inspection and interrogation. Some would be detained for further physical examination; the others would continue on into the main second-story room, where they would be separated into ten lines and march down aisles "between the desks of the so-called 'pedigree clerks,' who will cross-examine them as the law requires." Beyond these aisles were two great pens or enclosures. Into one of them would go those destined to New York and its vicinity; into the other would be put the greater number who were about to begin another journey to distant states and territories. On this second floor also were spaces for the railroad ticket sellers, the clerks of the information bureau, the telegraph and money exchange counters, and the lunch stand. "Colonel John B. Weber, the Commissioner of Emigra-

The first immigration station at Ellis Island in 1896. These buildings were all burned in the following year.

—*Courtesy of the New York Public Library*

tion, will have his office in one corner on that floor, and General O'Beirne, the Assistant Commissioner, will occupy a similar office in another corner." [21]

The station was opened with some formality on January 1, 1892. Annie Moore, a young Irish girl from County Cork, was the first immigrant to step ashore from the landing barge, and Commissioner Weber presented her with a ten-dollar gold piece. "The newcomers trooped into the big depot," the New York *World* reported; "everything worked like a charm, and the prediction was general that under the new conditions the comfort and safety of the immigrants will be all that can be desired." The cost of the plant up to that time was about $500,000. In addition to the new construction, which was wholly of wood, there was then and later considerable remodeling of the brick and stone barracks of old Fort Gibson, as well as of the heavy masonry structures built by the navy for the storage of explosives. Some of the magazines were converted into vaults for the storage of immigration records. Other old buildings were used for various purposes. One of them, enlarged and extended, formed part of an extensive two-story dormitory for detained immigrants. The hospital buildings, which were new, were built with sheltered verandas, arranged in a quadrangle.

A medical officer who served at Ellis Island during this period recalled that the main building was closer to the water than the later structure, "in fact directly along the ferry slip." Its functional arrangement forecast that of the later main building, but it "was built largely of Georgia pine" and the interior was finished in the natural wood. The greater part of the second story was open to the roof. The floor was of pine, and an effort was made to keep it looking like the wooden deck of a ship. Numerous tall windows running to the eaves let in abundant light and sunshine. "On the whole," he said, "the former building at Ellis Island impressed the visitor with its cleanliness, light and airiness." [22]

To some extent, perhaps, this cleanliness was made possible by the falling off of immigration. The tide was still rising when the new station opened for business. Fiscal year 1892 saw 445,987 immigrants admitted through the Port of New York. Germany, Ireland, England, Sweden, and Norway, the leading emigration nations of the recent past, were still sending considerable numbers of their sons and daughters, but Italy, Russia, Poland, Hungary, and Austria were sending more. The change from the "old" immigration to the "new" immigration, about which nativists then and later were greatly concerned, was continuing. As the New York *World* noted the rising clamor for restriction, which at the moment was taking the form of a proposed head tax "heavy enough to keep poor men and their families out," it observed that it might be well to consider where the necessary supply of unskilled labor was to come from before taking any such drastic action. The Irish had replaced the Germans in the field, and now the Italians had elbowed out both. Each group in its turn had come under abuse. "The German peasant and the Irish bogtrotter have had their day of distrust and contumely, but have had time to demonstrate how little they deserve it. The turn has come of the Italian, the Slovak and the Russian Hebrew. The accents of alarm are pitched in the old familiar key. The question to be resolved is whether they have any better cause."[23]

In the latter part of the calendar year, both old and new immigration dropped off sharply. In August there was a cholera scare emanating from European ports, and President Harrison ordered a strict quarantine of twenty days' duration on all vessels carrying immigrants from foreign ports. Many steamship companies thereupon refused to embark emigrants. The scare continued through the autumn, and Commissioner Weber was notified separately when each arriving vessel had completed its quarantine and its immigrants could be landed. Before the railroads would accept him for further transportation, each immigrant clearing through Ellis Island had to be certified as free of cholera by the Marine Hospital Service, which had charge of the medical inspection there. Revenue from the head tax, which supported the Immigration Bureau, declined markedly. The staff at the island was reduced, and Weber offered his resignation in the interest of economy.[24]

Senator Chandler saw an opportunity in this situation to achieve some really drastic immigration restriction. He summoned the Senate Committee on Immigration to meet and hold hearings in New York City. Commissioner Weber testified that cholera had not reached Ellis Island, but Chandler, with some medical backing, professed fear that the disease would reappear in 1893. A suspension of immigration would help to keep it out, he was told, and he determined to seek a total suspension of immigration from Europe for one year. On his return to Washington, he introduced a bill to this effect, approved by his committee.

Chandler did not succeed in stampeding Congress into passing his bill. Instead, there was an act giving the president the authority to suspend immigration in case of an epidemic if he deemed the existing quarantine procedures inadequate. Neither Harrison nor any of his successors ever invoked this power. Chandler had hoped to get a strong permanent restrictionist bill passed at the same time. This proved impossible, but an administrative measure was passed, providing machinery for the enforcement of the immigration law of 1891, which many believed would have a powerful restrictionist effect. The experience of the next few years seemed to bear them out.

Colonel Weber had felt that detailed information on the individual immigrant should be supplied by the steamship companies to facilitate inspection, and had so recommended in his report after his return from Europe. While the cholera scare was still on, he met with steamship agents in New York to try to work out a suitable questionnaire. By the immigration act passed in the following winter, detailed ships' manifests somewhat along the lines that Weber had proposed were required. The measure did not exclude any additional categories of would-be immigrants, but it gave immigration officials for the first time a detailed body of information on each immigrant which could serve as the basis for a cross-examination. As the information covered all the proscribed and doubtful categories, it was assumed that the ticket agent would conduct a preliminary examination along its lines before selling a ticket, if only for his own protection. The steamship company would have to conduct another examination, since ships' officers were required to sign the manifest sheets and certify to their correctness. Self-interest, it was believed, would keep out undesirables as described in the law of 1891. The new act also called for the establishment of boards of special inquiry at the immigration stations, to pass on doubtful cases sent to them by the medical officers or the immigration inspectors.[25]

Immigration revived briefly in the spring of 1893. But at the same time there was a financial panic, followed by years of severe and nationwide depression. Immigration figures went down again accordingly, reaching a low point in 1898 of 229,299, of which New York's share was only 178,748. The first immigration station at Ellis Island was at times a very busy place, but it was not tested to its full capacity for protracted periods. When it was destroyed by fire and plans were made to rebuild it, calculations were based on the experience of the recent past rather than on an imaginative projection of future needs. The Port of New York had never been called upon to receive more than 500,000 immigrants in a year, and in the mid-1890s immigration officials, though acknowledging the existence of a depression, thought that the transatlantic movement of population had passed its crest because of the effect of the immigration laws of 1891 and 1893. When Superintendent Herman Stump of the Bureau of Immigration was asked in 1894 why more Europeans were leaving the country than were arriving, he attributed it to "our laws regulating immigration and their rigid enforcement." As he saw it, "Every immigrant returned hinders a hundred from coming, as they are told of the rigors of the law. It is having a most wholesome effect." "With the present law energetically enforced," the commissioner-general of immigration reported in 1897, just after the Ellis Island station had burned, "I do not apprehend that immigration will ever reach the volume of past years, notwithstanding the most prosperous conditions in our country." There was never a poorer prophecy, but the new station was designed in accordance with such thinking.[26]

Grover Cleveland, a Democrat, became president in 1893 and appointed Dr. Joseph H. Senner as new commissioner of immigration at the Port of New York. Of German-Austrian background, Dr. Senner had a doctor of laws degree from the University of Vienna and had been on the editorial staff of some of the leading German language newspapers in the United States. The editor of the *New–Yorker Staats-Zeitung* was his principal sponsor, but he had also done good service to the Cleveland ticket in speaking before voters of German background. His appointment was closely scrutinized on political grounds, the Democratic party in New York State then being badly torn by faction, and his administration of Ellis Island was minutely inspected early in his term by the Senate Committee on Immigration. But the staunchly Republican *New York Tribune* viewed his appointment with respect, and the momentarily Democratic *Sun* praised him warmly when he had been in office only a few weeks. "The new Commissioner of Immigration at Ellis Island, Dr. Senner, has already introduced there better business methods than those which have existed for years past," said the *Sun*. "He gives personal attention to all the details of the business of the island. He enforces the laws more strictly than they were ever enforced by any of his predecessors. He is vigilant in the performance of all his duties." Later he was to be attacked vigorously in the New York press, and the *Sun* even ridiculed his accent, but he was undoubtedly a man of integrity and ability, intent on improving the service at the island.[27]

Senner entered on duty at Ellis Island at the beginning of April, and the new administrative law went into effect with the arrival of the first ship bearing immigrants that had left port beginning May 3. He therefore had an opportunity to compare the old system of inspection, largely a hangover from Castle Garden practice, with the new. Under the old system, he declared later, inspection "had become very nearly a mere matter of census-taking." Now a hitherto unknown examination was required by the steamship companies in the preparation of the detailed manifests, and the inspection by federal officers was vastly improved. The inspector had in his hand a written record on the immigrant he was inspecting and, asking the same questions over again, could compare the oral statements with it. If any discrepancy aroused his suspicion, he could have the alien detained for a board of inquiry hearing. Senner thought that government officials were "sufficiently enabled by the provisions of the latest immigration law to protect this country from an influx of any considerable number of undesirable immigrants without excluding desirable and welcome additions to our population." [28]

The law also began providing the government for the first time with some reasonably reliable immigration statistics. Up to 1893, for instance, Senner testified before the Industrial Commission some years later, no one had ever asked an immigrant whether he had ever been in the United States before. Thus a man might be counted two or three times. This contributed to the fact that there were wide discrepancies between old immigration statistics and census reports. The immigration station at New York probably had the best statistics on immigrants. Nevertheless, he found that under the old system, most statistical figures there were based on guesswork. He had found, on checking old records, that while "the few registry clerks in the office were supposed under the old law to take a statement from the immigrants about their nationality, destination, and ages," as a matter of fact "whole pages did not contain any reply to any of these points. They were nothing more than an index of names of people arriving at the port." This was especially true of the old Castle Garden records, which had been stored at Ellis Island while he was in charge there, and which he had time to examine before they were all burned in the fire that destroyed the station. It was, he said, "a matter of impossibility to rely in any way on these old statistics." As for statistics taken since 1893, he stated modestly that "They are vastly improved." [29]

The preliminary screening by the steamship companies in the preparation of the manifests no doubt did to some extent cut down the percentage of inadmissible aliens received at United States ports in the years that followed, but manifests were often carelessly or fraudulently prepared. Immigrants constituted a highly profitable self-loading cargo, and shipowners tended to count on mass movement for their profit, taking chances on rejections and complaining vociferously when rejections mounted. The manifest became the basic record on the individual immigrant. Copies of ships' manifests accumulated at Ellis Island in enormous bulk and number. They were used in the compilation of immigration statistics and became invaluable references under legislation involving naturalization and deportation.

Under the laws of 1891 and 1893, which provided the basic procedures for a generation and more, the admissibility of an alien on arrival was determined by a medical examination, an interrogation of each passenger by an immigration inspector armed with a copy of the manifest sheet bearing his name, and the consideration of any information furnished by the medical examiner. The passenger was to be admitted to the United States forthwith if he was, in the opinion of the inspector, "clearly and beyond doubt entitled to land." If not, the law required that he be held for investigation by a board of special inquiry, composed of four (later three) qualified officials. An adverse decision of this board formally excluded the immigrant, but appeal was allowed through the commissioner to the secretary in Washington. The secretary's decision was final.

The procedures of the Bureau of Immigration in cases of exclusion and deportation were administrative and not judicial. The law of 1882 gave the secretary of the treasury authority to make such rules and regulations "as he shall deem best calculated for carrying out the provisions of this act and the immigration laws of the United States." It was under such rules, and not under normal court procedures, that the boards of special inquiry operated. The practice was confirmed by the Supreme Court in 1893. The court held that deportation was not a punishment for crime but merely an administrative process for the return of unwelcome and undesirable aliens to their own countries. Aliens were deported on the grounds of expediency and not of crime, because their presence was "deemed inconsistent with the public welfare." A few years later a federal judge in New York, in dismissing a writ of habeas corpus presented on behalf of an alien about to be deported, said that the immigration authorities had decided that the alien was to be deported and that he could do nothing about it. "The courts," he said, "have decided that over and over again." "If the Commissioners," he added ironically, "wish to order an alien drawn, quartered, and chucked overboard they could do so without interference."

The guarantees of the Bill of Rights, intended to protect persons accused of crime, did not apply to aliens as far as their right to enter or remain in the United States was concerned. The hearings of the boards of inquiry were conducted in a manner best calculated to elicit the desired information. Due process of law, as applied to criminal cases, was at a minimum. Counsel was not permitted to the alien under examination, and he was not permitted to confer with friends and relatives until after the decision of the board. Nor was bail permitted pending a decision on appeal. Counsel was permitted in the appeal process, however, and many decisions were appealed. Such appeals were frequently sustained by the secretary. The secretary also had power, often used, to direct the landing of an immigrant, otherwise excludable, under bond not to become a public charge.[30]

A series of struggles with the steamship lines—a prominent feature of Ellis Island's operation in the years to come—was forecast during Dr. Senner's administration. The use of the ships' manifest, with its detailed information on the individual immigrant, had tightened the inspection process greatly. Now detentions, pending decisions of boards of inquiry or the arrival of friends or money, were much more numerous than they had been before. Some detainees were debarred from landing and ordered returned to Europe by the lines that had brought them. The far greater proportion were finally permitted to enter.

The steamship lines, finding their expenses increased, began protesting that they should not pay for the maintenance at Ellis Island of those detained but eventually landed. Some of the companies undertook a "strike" against this procedure, arguing that the charge should be against the immigrant fund provided by the head tax. When Senner reported this development to Washington, he and the companies got an emphatic ruling on the subject. "The Immigrant Fund, created by the Act of 1882, for the care of immigrants arriving in the United States, and for the relief of those in distress," Superintendent Stump declared, "has been used for their benefit after being landed, which means after examination and discharge, and not to relieve steamship lines of any liability prior to such landing . . . the steamship companies are liable for all expenses incurred in guarding and lodging and feeding detained immigrants pending the decision of the Immigration Officials." Along with this declaration, Senner received orders to form boarding parties and examine on board ship all immigrants arriving on the vessels of the protesting companies. This, of course, would have caused great confusion and delay, and the companies quickly gave in.[31]

One of the relatively few riots among detained immigrants at Ellis Island took place while Dr. Senner was commissioner. As a general rule, detainees were so mixed in nationality that cooperation among them was unlikely. Assaults by individuals on guards and fights among the detainees were not uncommon, but violent group protest was rare. In the mid-1890s and for years thereafter, however, the Italian immigrants were in particular disfavor, as the Irish had been a generation or so before. In the spring of 1896, in spite of the lingering depression in the United States, there was a considerable influx of Italians, nearly all men and mostly penniless. Both New York newspapers and immigration officials attributed this to an effort to evade military service, Italy being at the time at war (disastrously) with Abyssinia. Boards of special inquiry at Ellis Island, working overtime, freely ordered detentions and deportations under the "pauper" clause of the immigration law. The limited detention quarters on the island soon overflowed, and Senner feared an epidemic.

To the detainees already on the island there were soon added 531 more Italians from the steamers *Bolivia* and *Alesia*, who had been ordered deported almost en masse. As there was no day space for them in the regular detention quarters, a "temporary detention pen" was fitted up in an open space on the island. One afternoon a crowd of them rushed the fence and began tearing off the pickets. The guards succeeded in beating them back with considerable difficulty. Senner, fearing more trouble, telegraphed Washington asking permission to employ armed constables on the island during the congestion there. In response to his alarm, the Washington office appealed to the navy for protection at Ellis Island and received a promise to send marines from the Brooklyn Navy Yard on call.

The *New York Tribune* sent over a reporter to follow up the story. "A forlorn-looking lot they are," he said of the deportees in the outdoor detention pen, "restless, depressed, degraded and penniless, and it is pitiable indeed to watch their longing looks, hoping against hope as they do, for freedom. The most sympathetic, however, could but exclaim, as they looked upon the groups, 'we don't want them; send them back!' " [32]

This episode, and the rush of Italian immigration that had produced it, were investigated with Senner's cooperation by Prescott F. Hall and Robert DeCourcy Ward of the new Immigration Restriction League. This Boston organization, in collaboration with Senator Henry Cabot Lodge of Massachusetts, had chosen a literacy test as the best method of cutting down immigration from southern and eastern Europe. Ward's account of the Ellis Island affair gave considerable impetus to the literacy test immigration bill then before Congress. Most of the Italians then coming in were illiterate, and, it was reasoned, they and other unpopular groups could be excluded by such a test. The bill to this end, amended in debate to apply to Russian Jews who might be literate in Yiddish or Hebrew but not in their national language, was passed in the following year. President Cleveland vetoed it in a vigorous message just before he left office. It was a radical departure from our national policy, he pointed out. Heretofore we had welcomed all except those whose moral or physical condition or history threatened danger to the national welfare and safety. "It is said," the president reminded Congress, "that the quality of recent immigration is undesirable. The time is quite within recent memory when the same thing was said of immigrants who, with their descendants, are now numbered among our best citizens." Senner had been quoted during the fracas on the island as making uncomplimentary remarks about the Italian immigrants, and the Italian ambassador had protested. Senner hastily made amends in an article in the *North American Review*, in which he minimized the troubles at Ellis Island and disavowed any hostility to Italians as a group.[33]

Under Dr. Senner's administration most of the procedures used at Ellis Island throughout its great period as an immigrant receiving station took form, and many of its persistent problems were foreshadowed. Many physical improvements were made, including extensive repairs to the hastily built wooden buildings and new construction, and the island was enlarged several acres to accommodate them. Senner's reports were replete with recommendations, not always acted upon, for the betterment of the Immigration Service. But the days of the first immigration station, like those of Senner's tenure of office, were numbered. On June 14, 1897, shortly after midnight, fire broke out, "and in one hour's time scarcely a vestige was left of these pine buildings."

The plant had been finished only the day before, with the completion of cables to New York City for telegraph and telephone communication via Governor's Island. The fire was discovered almost at once, but "all efforts to extinguish it were unavailing." It was of mysterious origin, and a later investigation failed to trace its cause. There were a good many immigrants on the island at the time, some in the hospital and others in the detention dormitory. The medical staff and the night guard force acted promptly, and all were evacuated safely to New York by ferry. The sick were transferred to Bellevue Hospital before sunrise. In some respects, the destruction of the station was a relief to its administrator. While he did not include the language in his official report, Commissioner Senner spoke freely to a *New York Tribune* reporter after the fire. "Ever since I have been in office," he said, "the fear of something like this fire has haunted me, and now that it has come and no lives were lost I am glad of it. A row of unsightly, ramshackle tinderboxes has been removed, and when the Government rebuilds it will be forced to put up decent fireproof structures."[34]

The wooden buildings were eventually replaced with more permanent and fireproof structures, but the lost records were irreplaceable. The immigration records of Castle Garden, from 1855 to 1890, had been turned over to the Ellis Island authorities only the year before and had been placed in some of the old navy powder magazines for safekeeping. The intense heat of the fire cracked and crumbled these heavy vaults, and all the state records on immigration, together with most of those since accumulated at the Barge Office and the island, were destroyed. The absence of records prior to the middle of

June 1897 was a continuing handicap in the years that followed, particularly in the verification of immigrant landings.

The Barge Office was at once reactivated to receive immigrants. Pending its use, the Washington office directed that examinations be done aboard ship, but the steamship agents offered the use of their piers. Several ships with large numbers of steerage passengers arrived the day after the fire, and inspection was carried out on that and succeeding days "with the same scrutinizing care employed on the island." The Customs Bureau vacated the annex of the Barge Office, and it was immediately set aside for the use of detained immigrants. As this space was inadequate, two large houses on State Street, facing Battery Park, were leased and fitted up for use as detention quarters and a hospital.[35]

This emergency arrangement was modified a few months later. An old passenger steamer, the *Narragansett*, was brought into service. It was tied up at Ellis Island. Landing and inspection of immigrants took place at the Barge Office, which also housed the administrative offices, and detainees were ferried over to the *Narragansett* as fast as they accumulated. The steamer furnished sleeping accommodations for eight hundred, as well as quarters for a matron, physician, and attendants. The sick were sent to local hospitals under contract. Operations in the "very inconvenient and cramped accommodations of the old Barge Office," with a necessarily reduced staff, were reported in the following year as progressing "uninterruptedly and satisfactorily." [36]

In spite of this cheerful official note, trouble was brewing at the Barge Office. The return to the Battery removed whatever protection to the immigrant the isolation of Ellis Island had afforded. Steerage passengers arrived in "the old Castle Garden environment." Thomas Fitchie replaced Dr. Senner as commissioner of immigration for the Port of New York soon after the fire. Fitchie was a New York Republican politician who had loyally supported William McKinley in his successful campaign for the presidency in 1896. His assistant was Edward F. McSweeney, who had served Senner in the same capacity. Fitchie was generally regarded as a man of high character, but was getting on in years and lacked executive force. Consequently, McSweeney became the active directing power at the immigration station under the very difficult prevailing conditions.

The new head of the Bureau of Immigration in Washington was Terence Powderly. He had resigned as general master workman of the fading Knights of Labor, but still had influence in labor circles, though opposed by the rising American Federation of Labor. Powderly, too, had assisted McKinley in the campaign of 1896. All three men—Powderly, Fitchie, and McSweeney—were active politicians while in office. It was not long before friction—not uncommon in the relationship between the head of a Washington bureau and a principal subordinate in the field—developed into a serious feud. This split the force at the Barge Office into factions, one loyal to the commissioner, another currying favor with the commissioner-general (this title had now replaced that of superintendent of immigration), and another waiting to see which way to jump. There was also infighting at the level of the Treasury Department, where Fitchie and McSweeney had friends and Powderly had enemies.[37]

One particular point of friction between Powderly and McSweeney concerned the contract labor inspectors. The contract labor law had been passed at the behest of craft unions, supported by the Knights of Labor, who were at the height of their power in the 1880s and acting in the belief that foreign labor was imported in large numbers under contract to break strikes and hold down wages. Actually, big industrialists and mine owners did not ordinarily have to bother with making such contracts. They hired their unskilled foreign labor from agencies (usually known as "padrones") in New York and elsewhere in the United States. Skilled craftsmen, however, were imported under contract in considerable numbers both before and after the law was passed. Evasion of the law was comparatively easy: workmen were provided with cabin tickets. The examination of cabin passengers was a mere formality; only steerage passengers were automatically sent to Ellis Island for closer scrutiny. Only when a tip came from a craft union, that specific contract workmen were coming in, were such passengers likely to be apprehended and detained at Ellis Island. When they were discovered, the courts were reluctant to prosecute the manufacturers that had hired them.

Unskilled laborers, on the other hand, arriving by steerage, were often detained and deported when it was found that they had made some arrangement with relatives or labor agencies to provide them with jobs on their arrival. It became an article of faith with the American Federation of Labor, which succeeded the Knights of Labor, that foreign contract labor was a serious threat, and the terms of the contract labor legislation were tightened again and again by an obliging Congress to balance off the tariff protection afforded the manufacturers.

To enforce this legislation, which the state authorities had declined to do, federal contract labor inspectors had been appointed to work with them at Castle Garden. When the federal government assumed full responsibility for immigrant reception, they were continued as a separate class of inspectors, and their numbers were increased under Powderly's administration of the Bureau of Immigration. Their attitude toward their immediate superiors, a carry-over from Castle Garden days, was independent and sometimes insubordinate. Some were corrupt. As they were permitted to interview suspected contract laborers *in camera*, and report their findings to the boards of inquiry in the form of affidavits, the opportunities for blackmail were considerable. Fitchie and McSweeney sought to get rid of them as a class by combining the registry clerks and the contract labor inspectors in a single class of "immigration inspectors." This reform eventually took place, but Powderly resisted it bitterly.[38]

Dr. Senner had not been happy with the quality of his politically-appointed staff at Ellis Island and had urged that the Immigration Service be placed under civil service regulations. This was done in 1896, as part of a general extension of the classified service by an executive order of President Cleveland, but incumbents became classified civil service employees without examination. It was some time before a register of eligibles based on a formal examination was established for immigration inspectors, and only four appointments were made from this list before 1900. Meanwhile, appointments seem to have been made by mere certification by the Civil Service Commission on the strength of recommendations by politicians. While, under the depressed conditions of the mid-1890s, good men who would not otherwise have entered federal service came to work at Ellis Island and the Barge Office, the quality of the staff was distinctly mixed.

At the Barge Office, where the waterfront harpies swarmed, temptations and opportunities for graft were abundant. It was not long before there were charges of brutality and corruption. Press attacks were redoubled, culminating in a serious scandal involving the improper landing of immigrants in 1899. The commissioner-general conducted a full-scale investigation of the Barge Office. Extensive hearings were held in New York City in the following year, and a report was submitted to the department in June, implicating a number of officials. This report was bottled up by Powderly's superiors in the Treasury Department, who were critical of the manner in which the hearings had been conducted, but charges were brought against a number of men, mostly of subordinate grades, and some of them were dismissed from the service.[39]

There was no thorough house cleaning at the Barge Office, however, and the sorry mess was carried over, still stewing, to the rebuilt immigration station at Ellis Island. With returning prosperity, immigration was reviving, and the Barge Office was, aside from its other troubles, overwhelmed with business. The commissioner-general's report for the fiscal year expressed the hope "that before the close of the calendar year 1900, the contractors will have completed the new buildings and turned them over for the occupancy of the immigration force at the barge office, thus relieving a tension that had become almost unendurable." [40]

CHAPTER III

HIGH TIDE

Ellis Island, newly incarnated in 1900, got off to a bad start. It was poorly administered, and corruption was rampant. The staff that operated the station, being essentially the same group that had served at the Barge Office, included a certain percentage of "worthless and dishonest characters." The employees of the various concessionaires, and the concessionaires themselves, averaged higher in knavery. To Ellis Island were also drawn, in spite of its isolation, many of the varied types of sharpers that had preyed upon the immigrant since Castle Garden days. As a veteran medical officer in immigrant inspection service observed in this connection many years later, "wherever one finds ships he will find at least an attenuated form of piracy . . . and wherever one sees travelers he can find extortion and robbery." [1]

"Roughness, cursing, intimidation and a mild form of blackmail prevailed to such a degree as to be common," a well-informed traveler and observer of immigrant conditions stated. The commissioner in charge at the time was "far above all this," but was seemingly powerless to discharge dishonest employees or in any way to improve the morale of the place. It was still operated largely on the spoils system. Those who did their full duty smarted under the wrongs done to the weak and helpless mass of immigrants. He recalled the time "when the restaurant was a den of thieves, in which the immigrant was robbed by the proprietor, whose employees stole from him and from the immigrant also." As an experiment, he changed a twenty-mark gold piece at the exchange concession and was robbed of nearly 75 percent of his money.

On another occasion he was approached by an inspector who, in a very friendly way, intimated that he might have difficulty in being permitted to land. Money judiciously placed might accomplish something, the inspector suggested. A Bohemian girl he had met on the steamer came to him with tears in her eyes. One of the inspectors had promised to pass her quickly, she said, if she would promise to meet him at a certain hotel. "Do I look like that?" she asked. His complaints were treated with the same neglect as were those of others, "until with the coming in of the Roosevelt administration they had their resurrection." [2]

The physical facilities of the new station on Ellis Island—by and large judged adequate at the time—were ready for occupancy on December 17, 1900. Commissioner Fitchie and his staff moved in with little ceremony and received the first shipload of immigrants. It consisted of 654 Italians from the steerage of the *Kaiser Wilhelm II.* Other steerage passengers came in during the day from the *Victoria,* the *Vincenzo Florio*, and the *Umbria,* making a total of 2,251.

"The impression of the way things are done in the United States made upon the immigrant who arrived to-day," the *New York Tribune* commented, "will be a more favorable one than that made upon his brother who arrived here a week ago. He will enter this country by the gateway of the new immigration station on Ellis Island, instead of the grimy, gloomy Barge Office—more suggestive of an inclosure for animals than a receiving station for prospective citizens of the United States." A few days after the new station opened, Secretary of the Treasury Lyman Gage and a large party made an official inspection. They were entertained at lunch in the commissioner's office. The secretary congratulated Fitchie and his staff on their new home, which, he said, "with its companion buildings will form what the Treasury Department set out to make it, the model immigration station of the world." [3]

The new group of buildings had been authorized within little over a month after the fire. It was the first important government architecture to be designed by private architects under award following competition, in accordance with the recent Tarsney Act providing such procedure. The New York firm of Boring and Tilton won the contract, awarded in 1898, in a competition entered by a number of eminent firms. The problem to be solved, as called for by the government's program, *Harper's Weekly* explained at the time of the award, lay in planning a fireproof structure which would keep immigrants free from all outside interference until discharged, while affording means for relatives and friends to communicate with them at the proper time. Suitable facilities were also needed for the officials of the Immigration Bureau in the discharge of their duties. The new station must be adapted to the shelter and dispatching of several thousand immigrants, together with the countless relatives and professed friends who would flock to the island with the arrival of each new shipload. To serve these purposes, *Harper's* noted, there were to be waiting rooms, dormitories, a restaurant, a hospital, transportation facilities, post office and customhouse branches, and a telegraph station. There were also to be "numberless" administrative offices, and space for charitable enterprises, "besides baths, lavatories, and abundant toilet facilities, and all the other needs of this greatest of caravanseries perched on an island of diminutive size." [4]

The main building was in the center of the island, approximately on the site of the old wooden one. It was 385 feet long, 165 feet wide, and 62 feet high, with four corner towers reaching to a height of 100 feet. There were massive triple-arch entrances on the east and west sides, the arches reaching well into the second story. The material was brick laid in Flemish bond over a steel frame, with limestone trim. The largest room in the building was the registry room, or examination hall, on the second floor, 200 feet long, 100 feet wide, and 56 feet high. Most of its floor space was divided into narrow alleys by iron railings. Down these passages the immigrants marched in the examination process, after having landed from barges, entered, and climbed the stairs. Here both medical and legal examinations to determine their right to enter took place. It was calculated that 5,000 immigrants could be examined here with ease in a day, and many more in an emergency.[5]

North of the main building were a large restaurant and laundry building, with a bathhouse capable of bathing 8,000 in a day under showers, and a power house. On a separate new island across the ferry slip from the main building was the hospital. At the time the new station was opened, it was estimated that $1 million had been spent in its construction, and an additional appropriation was necessary to complete it. The final cost was about $1.5 million. Auxiliary structures were largely completed in 1901; the hospital was not opened until the following year.[6]

After the station had been in operation for some time and most of its elements had been completed, the *Architectural Record* bestowed its professional approval. The problem here, as the *Record* saw it, had been to meet the requirements of "both a hospice and a hospital," and also essentially that of a railroad station, the requirement of landing, collecting, and distributing great and sudden crowds with a minimum of confusion and delay. This last requirement the designer had met successfully, having provided for a continuous human flow that had already handled more than 6,500 arriving immigrants in one day. The *Record* believed that "the general composition of the central building, the distribution of its masses and the treatment of them," were "thoroughly admirable." The character of the detail aroused less enthusiasm; it was "scarcely worthy of the real nobility of the general composition." Molding could have been used to good effect to soften the harshness of rectilinearity. "But these," it concluded, "are mere blemishes upon a capital piece of work." [7]

Physical attributes did not offset the inept administration and the corruption-prone activities of officials and others dealing with immigrants, however. A scandal broke in the summer of 1901, involving frauds in the landing of immigrants direct from steamships, bypassing Ellis Island altogether. Fraudulent American citizens' certificates, permitting them to land at the piers, were supplied to steerage immigrants for a fee, which was split between ships' officers and immigrant boarding inspectors. It was believed that the practice had gone

Immigrants in front of the main building. The steel and glass canopy, built in 1903, remained in place until 1931.
—*Courtesy of the U.S. Immigration and Naturalization Service*

on for years, and that possibly 10,000 immigrants had been landed in this way at an average fee of $5 a head. While Commissioner Fitchie directed an investigation of the matter by members of his own staff, and a number of charges were filed as a result, his administration had been badly compromised. The charges were reminiscent of those made the year before, in fact practically a continuance of them, the *New York Tribune* noted. In spite of Commissioner-General Powderly's protests, no action had been taken at that time against Assistant Commissioner McSweeney and other important officials who had been named as involved in fraud and misconduct. "The careers of Fitchie and McSweeney in office have been fruitful of official squabbles and scandals," said the *Tribune*. "It has long been predicted that a thorough overhauling of the New-York immigrant station was to be effected." [8]

Within the first month after he succeeded William McKinley as president of the United States, Theodore Roosevelt began moving to clean up the situation at Ellis Island. Writing to Nicholas Murray Butler on October 9, 1901, he noted that "As for Fitchie, there is a consensus of testimony to his utter inefficiency," and "Every really good man whom I have met who knows anything about that office has agreed in believing McSweeney to be corrupt." His own friends had been united in telling him that Powderly was a good man, but some question had come up about him, too. Roosevelt had already determined to replace Fitchie, and probably to make a clean sweep of the Immigration Bureau. He asked Butler for suggestions for possible successors to all three men, adding, "I am more anxious to get this office straight than almost any other."

This was not easy, for Roosevelt had to contend with politically powerful forces. All three men had strong backing, and McSweeney, in particular, whom Roosevelt saw as the prime villain, was strongly intrenched in New York, Connecticut, and Massachusetts politics, and had friends among the steamship companies and the missionaries. Fitchie's term of office conveniently expired, and the removal of Powderly was made easy by replacing him with another respected labor man, Frank P. Sargent, chief of one of the railroad brotherhoods. Despite loud protests from high sources in the Republican party, Roosevelt also forced the resignation of McSweeney, whose position was in the classified civil service.[9]

After a long search for the right man, the president chose William Williams, a young Wall Street lawyer of good standing with some experience in government legal service and a commendable record in the recent war with Spain, as commissioner of immigration at Ellis Island. Williams, who did not know Roosevelt and was satisfied with the practice of his profession, was taken by surprise at a sudden call to the White House and was at first reluctant to accept the appointment. But Roosevelt assured him that he should take it "because it is the most interesting office in my gift," that nearly a million immigrants a year were passing through Ellis Island, and that "they were being improperly inspected, robbed and abused." He challenged Williams by pointing out that it was a very hard office to administer.

The president's characterization of the job was accurate. The commissioner of immigration at Ellis Island had to cope not only with processing large numbers of immigrants and with a variety of corrupt practices but with a press ever ready to publicize administrative shortcomings. He was also subject to partisan political attacks. Perhaps more important, during the flood years he was—whatever his own position—the man in the middle of an intermittently resurgent national debate between restrictionists and antirestrictionists. Roughly grouped on one side were nativists in favor of further restriction, including intellectuals carrying on an active propaganda through the Immigration Restriction League, many officials of charitable and law enforcement agencies, a number of leading sociologists and biologists, organized labor, and a variety of patriotic societies. Opposing further restriction, and sometimes urging repeal of restrictive legislation already on the books, were numerous ethnic societies, the steamship companies, the railroads, and the manufacturers. They were aided after 1906 by the National Liberal Immigration League, organized by foreign-born groups but enlisting the support of a number of native American intellectuals, which sought to offset the Immigration Restriction League with a powerful counterpropaganda. The commissioner was often under bombardment from one side or the other, sometimes from both at once. Each side had spokesmen in Congress, and each was willing and able to make life difficult for the "Man at the Gate" whenever it found his administration of the immigration laws displeasing.

Williams went home to New York to consider President Roosevelt's offer. He learned all he could about Ellis Island, read the immigration law, and after thinking it over, accepted. He was to serve twice as one of the island's two dedicated commissioners during the years of heaviest immigration. The *Commercial Advertiser,* whose editor was close to the president and probably had a hand in the appointment, hailed it with enthusiasm. "Mr. Williams has precisely the qualities needed for the place," it affirmed. "He has had experience in many fields of activity in which he has demonstrated his possession of administrative capacity, . . . and he has the force of character essential to the most efficient performance of its duties." New life and energy were much needed at Ellis Island. Williams would supply them and "rid the service of some long-standing causes of complaint and in every way . . . increase its efficiency." [10]

Joseph E. Murray, Roosevelt's oldest political friend, who had gotten him his first nomination and election to the New York State Assembly, became Williams's assistant. Murray's appointment to a position which was in the classified civil service was made without examination, under a special rule of the Civil Service Commission obviously dictated by the president. Aside from saddling him with an assistant whom he soon found unwilling or unable to carry his share of the load, Roosevelt gave Williams a free hand. Williams, as commissioner, was the actual as well as the nominal chief of Ellis Island, and "a place which had been a political snug harbor was swept, garnished, and set in running order on a strict merit basis," as a Roosevelt admirer proclaimed.[11]

Politically motivated sniping at Williams soon began, as he antagonized influential New York Republicans by his award of contracts for money exchange, food, and baggage concessions at Ellis Island. In the past these had gone to deserving Republicans who found them highly profitable. Williams, with the approval of the Washington office, awarded them to firms that seemed to offer the best service to immigrants. In the case of the money exchange privilege, he urged and promptly got the annulment of the contract before it actually expired. The concessionaire, he charged, had been defrauding the immigrants for a long time, and he wanted to make an example of him. Roosevelt, bracing himself for a powerful onslaught, asked Williams for all the facts regarding the contracts and then stood by his new man. "The management of the Ellis Island business has been rotten in the past," he told New York Governor Benjamin Odell, "and Williams has got to make a thorough sweeping out." It was evident, the *Tribune* noted approvingly, after describing the changes taking place at the island, that immigrants were to receive the first consideration. In making the new awards, said the *Commercial Advertiser*, Williams had "broken up a nest of patronage that has long been perpetuated there, and which for years has been a smoldering public scandal." [12]

Even before the concession contracts came up for renewal at the end of the fiscal year, Williams had set the tone of his administration. Three days after taking office he wrote sharply to a ships' agent in the matter of incomplete and improperly prepared immigrant manifests. Steamship companies were not only often careless in the preparation of these important documents, but tended to neglect it altogether in the case of cabin passengers. The agent to whom Williams wrote seemed surprised and hurt, as though a very cozy arrangement had suddenly been disturbed. Quite likely it had; fines could be imposed for improperly prepared manifests, but they could be ignored by accommodating officials. A few days later Williams preferred charges against a clerk, a Civil War veteran who had gone on a four-day drunk. Veteran's status gave him preference in getting a government job, Williams noted, but gave him no special privilege afterward. Two weeks later he wrote to Senator Platt of New York declining to promote a gateman to the grade of inspector, as the senator had asked, because the man was "not fitted either by temperament or training" for a better position, and his promotion "would be detrimental to the best interests of the service." [13]

Williams entered on duty April 28, 1902, so that his first annual report as commissioner of immigration covered only two months of his own administration. Nevertheless, he had already uncovered a good bit of corruption and inefficiency and had instituted a good many reforms. When he took office, he reported, he found conditions in the new plant far from the ideal predicted by his predecessor. He discovered that immigration inspectors often signed blank detention cards and detailed unqualified employees, including interpreters or even laborers, to make the actual inspections. The chief inspector was in the habit of marking "Hold" against the names of immigrants having considerable sums of money as shown on the ships' manifests, thus having them brought to him for inspection. Boards of special inquiry, which determined admissibility in doubtful cases, were by statute independent tribunals but frequently rendered decisions directed by the executive office, including the admission of immigrants certified by the medical staff as incapacitated. Some officials themselves examined detained immigrants and discharged them or put them back in detention, bypassing the boards of inquiry. "The resulting power of blackmail," the commissioner observed, "will be readily seen."

The general treatment accorded immigrants before the change in administration "was not calculated to make upon them a favorable impression at the time of their first contact with the institutions of this country," Williams reported. They were hustled about and addressed in rough language. The detention quarters were formerly called "pens" and were in filthy condition. He mentioned particularly the dining room, "the floor of which was allowed by the former privilege holder to remain covered with grease, bones, and other remnants of food for days at a time." He himself saw in the first days of his administration that immigrants were fed without knives, forks, or spoons. The same bowls were used over and over without washing. At the food stands an employee of the concessionaire wearing a cap with a gilt eagle compelled immigrants to buy bags of food, even when they were bound for New York. The prices were in many cases exorbitant. In the kitchen immigrants "were frequently compelled to perform service."

"The influence exerted here by the former holder of the feeding privilege in the face of such facts," Williams professed to believe, "is incomprehensible." The former commissioner, he said, could have had the contract canceled immediately by reporting the conditions to the secretary. Actually, Williams had been told before he entered on duty that the food concessionaire was a mere front for Charles A. Hess, former Republican leader of the 25th Assembly District, "one of the most unmitigated scoundrels in this city," according to Herbert Parsons, leader of the New York Republican reform element. It had been made clear to him that his own appointment had been in good part the work of Parsons's group, and that one of the things they wanted was to have Hess's contract taken away from him.[14]

While the administration of the office was still in a state of transition, many evil practices had been abolished or would be soon, Williams assured the secretary of the treasury. Inspection had been made "more conscientious"; detained immigrants could no longer be discharged except by specified inspectors, and all data on detention cards were now made in ink to prevent alterations; detention time was being reduced; a notice had been posted requiring that all immigrants be treated with "kindness and consideration," with severe penalties imposed for violations. The practice by the railroad companies, represented at Ellis Island, of issuing passes to Immigration Service officials "to a demoralizing extent," had been abolished. No favors were to be accepted from railroad or steamship companies, since their interests "obviously demand liberal immigration laws and a liberal execution of the same." Some of the steamship companies had been bringing in cases of favus and trachoma, contagious diseases easily detected. This had been taken up with the companies "in very plain language," and some improvement had resulted. Violations of the law requiring that all aliens appear on ships' manifests had been constant. Fair warning followed by fines which he had been authorized to impose at his discretion had, Williams believed, largely cleared up this practice.[15]

The most important official remaining at Ellis Island from the old regime was John Lederhilger, chief of the Registry Division. Serious charges had been made against him in the 1900 investigation of the Barge Office, but no action had been taken in his case. As Williams familiarized himself with the organization, he found that Lederhilger dominated the boards of special inquiry and exercised undue and pernicious influence throughout the staff. Lederhilger was placed on enforced leave of absence during an investigation of his records. In spite of the fact that many possibly incriminating records had been destroyed, the result was that he was dismissed on a variety of charges. Commissioner-General Sargent backed up Williams heartily, saying: "I do not believe in allowing rascals to go out of the service by resignation with letters of indorsement of good character and faithful service, when we know them to be unprincipled scoundrels." Two other employees were soon suspended on charges, and others were expected to follow, with some cases to be presented to a federal grand jury, as Williams sought to root out corruption, brutality, and lax performance of duty.[16]

The Williams regime won enthusiastic approval from *Leslie's Weekly* only a few months after it had begun. All records for immigration had been broken in the fiscal year ending June 30, 1902, but in spite of this rising tide at Ellis Island, "the aliens are now treated in the main quite as considerately as would be crowds of like size and character in the heart of the city." There had been advantage taken of them in the past and they had been "misused and fleeced by dishonest employees of the bureau," but the new commissioner, *Leslie's* said, was "a thorough, resourceful, and hard-working executive," who, with his able associates, was doing his best to make the conduct of affairs "more honest, efficient, and humane."[17]

There is no doubt of the almost revolutionary character of the changes that Williams brought about with the vigorous support of the president and of his immediate superiors in Washington. "Indeed, it was amazing," reported the *Outlook* after one of its staff visited Ellis Island, "to see how, in spite of the routine that is necessary in managing hundreds and sometimes thousands every day, each official seemed actuated by the human more than the professional motive. The visitor to Ellis Island would have to be of very callous heart not to be conscious of the real tenderness with which helplessness is there treated." [18] Whatever their real feelings toward the immigrants may have been, Williams had evidently put the fear of God into the staff.

Jacob Riis, an immigrant of the Castle Garden days, author of the famous study of the slums, *How the Other Half Lives,* an old friend of Roosevelt's and intimately associated with him as adviser during his term as police commissioner of New York City, visited Ellis Island a few months later. He thought that the quality of the immigrants coming in was not what it had once been, but he saw and approved the new regime in action. "The law of kindness rules on Ellis Island; a note posted conspicuously invites every employee who cannot fall in with it to get out as speedily as he may." But this law was sometimes put to a severe strain. Not one in a thousand landing at Ellis Island needed harsh treatment, Riis believed, but rather advice and help. This did not prevent the thousandth case from receiving its full due. He saw Williams himself "soak" a Flemish peasant twice his size for beating and abusing a child. The man turned and towered over the commissioner, "but the ordinarily quiet little man presented so suddenly a fierce and warlike aspect that, although neither understood a word of what the other said, the case was made clear to the brute on the instant, and he slunk away." [19]

While Williams was thus himself capable of taking physical action against an alien when he thought the occasion demanded it, his law of kindness was no scrap of paper. He was a strict disciplinarian and worked hard and long to break up the vicious habits that had grown up among the staff under his predecessors. "I was very much displeased at the rough and unkind manner in which I heard you address two immigrants in the Discharging Bureau this afternoon," he warned an employee. "Do not let this occur again." "For having used vulgar antd abusive language this morning to an immigrant," he informed a gateman, "I have suspended you from duty for two weeks, and shall recommend to the Department that during this time you receive no pay." "Not long ago I summoned you to my office," he admonished another employee, "and warned you that it would be necessary for you to alter your manner toward immigrants while assisting in grouping them." But only the day before he had noticed that the man's manner was very objectionable. If he could not conform to the rules of the office, particularly those made for humanitarian purposes, Williams warned him, "you will be compelled to sever your connection therewith." This warning was routed through the man's superiors, presumably for their benefit as well.[20]

After Williams had left Ellis Island, the *Outlook*'s "Spectator" columnist went over to inspect the station once more. He "came away impressed by the order, the system, the wisdom, and the kindness which America shows in receiving immigrants at her greatest port." While improvements were still going on, his official guide pointed out that it was Commissioner Williams who had "brought order out of chaos" and instituted the basic reforms. "The Spectator takes off his hat to ex-Commissioner Williams, who has made it what it is, and hopes that the present Commissioner will be an equally able and benevolent despot." While Williams had been bitterly attacked in the interim by Jewish and other groups, the well-informed *American Hebrew* noted at the time of his resignation: "It would not be fair to Mr. Williams to allow him to retire without a word of praise for his efficient administration. He has transformed the internal affairs at Ellis Island to such an extent that visitors to-day will find very few of the evils complained of before he came. . . . His retirement will be a distinct loss to the immigration department." [21]

Williams, having forced a showdown with President Roosevelt in an effort to get rid of his assistant, Joe Murray, resigned early in 1905 and returned to his neglected law practice. Murray, whom Williams considered lazy, stupid, and inefficient, had been a thorn in his side from the beginning of his term. When he finally insisted that Murray be replaced with a man of his own choosing, the president was in a quandary but refused to abandon Murray and reluctantly accepted Williams's resulting resignation. The president "could not be dictated to," he told the *Outlook*'s representative in Washington.[22]

Williams was succeeded by Robert Watchorn, a career Immigration Service officer, also handpicked by Roosevelt. Watchorn, then serving at Montreal, where with the cooperation of Canadian authorities he had been attempting to seal the whole border against illegal Chinese immigration, was highly gratified at his appointment to the important Ellis Island post, but expressed his regret at Williams's resignation. He had served at the island under the old regime and knew what had since taken place there. "You have dispersed and routed the derelicts and knaves which at one time made Ellis Island a byword and a reproach," he wrote Williams. "You have reduced to order, discipline and decency that which was chaotic and sinful, and the best thanks of the nation are due you because of your great and worthy achievement . . . all the good you have accomplished will be conserved by the course I shall pursue. No backward steps will be taken." [23]

The *Outlook*, which had praised Williams's administration highly, became equally enthusiastic over Watchorn. "For nearly three years," it reported at the end of 1907, "the country has been fortunate in having in command of the sentinel forces at Ellis Island a man who combines with the force of character and the executive ability necessary for a rigid administration of the immigration laws, a broad human sympathy which insures to the incoming alien not only justice but kindliness, not only a stern protection of his rights but a warmhearted care for his comfort." After a year in office, Secretary of

Commerce and Labor Oscar S. Straus wrote to Watchorn in terms of the highest praise. Of the twelve bureaus in his department, he said, the Immigration Bureau was the most trying to administer. "The difficulties surrounding the administration of that Bureau, which throbs with tearful tragedies," he told Watchorn, "are greatly lightened by the fact that at the port where more than eighty per cent of the aliens arrive, I have the satisfaction of knowing that the Department is represented by a man possessing extraordinary qualifications of head and heart for tempering justice with mercy." Edward Steiner, close student of immigration, dedicated one of his books to Watchorn. "He knows no nationality nor race," said Steiner, "his business is to guard the interests of his country, guarding at the same time the rights of the stranger." Work of this kind could not be done without friction, Steiner noted, "for intense suffering follows many of his decisions. Yet I have found no one closely acquainted with the affairs of the island, who does not regard the 'man at the gate' as the right man in the right place." [24]

Watchorn carried on the Williams tradition of honesty, efficiency, and kindness for a four-year term, and then in 1909 Williams returned to Ellis Island, at the earnest request of President William H. Taft. He served again as commissioner of immigration there until the middle of 1913, a year before the outbreak of World War I. He was succeeded by his trained assistant, Byron H. Uhl, who served for the following year as acting commissioner.[25] During Ellis Island's busiest period as an immigrant receiving station, it was, once the pattern of politics and corruption had been broken in 1902, probably run as efficiently, as honestly, and with as much consideration for the immigrants as its overwhelming problems and the frailty of human nature would permit.

Ellis Island was under constant criticism as long as it was in operation, in this period largely because of the determined efforts made by its administrators to carry out the laws passed by Congress—laws steadily tending toward immigration restriction. As one shrewd observer put it: "Immigration laws must be characterized as unpopular. They may be endorsed in the abstract, but the public will always be found against their enforcement in concrete cases." An alien excluded by a board of special inquiry would often have his appeal filed by a society devoted to the interests of his ethnic group, and some of the "missionary" societies represented at Ellis Island were founded primarily to prevent the exclusion of members of one ethnic group or another. The society's representative at the island would notify a congressman with a constituent who was a relative of the excluded one. This gentleman, who had as likely as not voted cheerfully to exclude all aliens with similar disabilities, would bring pressure to bear to have the appeal sustained and this particular alien admitted. Attendant publicity in the press would stress a separated family or the unfeeling rigidity of the boards of special inquiry. The public would be sympathetic.[26]

The belief that the "new" immigration from southern and eastern Europe, which had for years been replacing the "old" immigration from northern and western Europe, was inferior and unassimilable, had been growing since the late 1880s, stimulated after the organization of the Immigration Restriction League by an adroit and persistent propaganda. Efforts to translate this belief into legislation, centering around Senator Lodge's literacy test proposal, were thwarted for years to come, but it was frequently aired. Hostility to the new immigration was less clamorous in the prosperous 1900s than it had been in the depressed 1890s, but it was nevertheless widespread and destined to grow. *Leslie's Weekly*, viewing Ellis Island and praising its new management in 1902, gave vent to an almost classic statement of the nativist dogma. Describing the landing of bargeloads of immigrants at the island, it reported:

> Those of the poorer class are often grimy and strangely and shabbily dressed, although numbers of the women wear bright and picturesque costumes. These include Italians, Russian Jews, and several other nationalities. They appear generally to be of a low order of knowledge, if not intelligence, as well as of physical development. The better class, comprising natives of Great Britain, Germany, and Scandinavia, frequently are as well attired as are average Americans. Better developed physically, and mentally superior to the former class, they are more desirable acquisitions to American citizenship.

"Once the stream came mainly from the North of Europe," the *World's Work* noted in the same year; "now it comes chiefly from the South—from the undesirable countries." [27]

Williams shared this view and expressed himself freely on the subject, while insisting that all who came to Ellis Island received equal treatment. "The constantly deteriorating quality of the recent immigration is a well-established fact," he declared in his first annual report as commissioner at Ellis Island, "and calls for the execution of the existing laws in the most stringent manner." He thought, too, that a stated sum should be set for immigrants to possess, to indicate that "clearly and beyond a doubt" they would not become public charges. Commissioner-General Sargent in Washington felt the same way, but while upholding Williams's stated views on the need of screening out paupers, he introduced a note of caution: "I have in mind sturdy Scotchmen, Irishmen or Germans, who land at Ellis Island with but a few dollars. When they are permitted to enter they immediately find employment and earn their livelihood. In such cases, usually, we are never appealed to by relatives or others in their behalf." In his judgment, such a class of aliens should not be debarred simply because they did not have a certain sum of money in their possession. "There are other nationalities who are not of that type and who should not be permitted to enter unless they produce satisfactory proof of their ability to work and support themselves, and pending the time of their finding employment, have a sufficient amount of money to support them so that they will not become public charges." [28] Given such views on the part of their superiors, complete objectivity among the immigrant inspectors at the island must have been a difficult attitude to achieve.

The tide of immigration mounted higher in the spring of 1903. "Commissioner Williams and Commissioner General Sargent held an informal conference last week on the influx of immigrants," the *New York Tribune* noted early in April. "It has astonished them, in view of the greater stringency of the immigration laws and the more rigid enforcement." A few weeks later Williams told a *New York Times* reporter that about 800,000 immigrants would be landed at the Port of New York in the fiscal year, and that this was about 300,000 too many. There had been no restrictive legislation since 1891 and 1893 until the law just recently passed, he said, and since that time the character and nationalities of the incoming aliens had changed. "The present predominating immigration from southern and eastern Europe is inferior on the whole to the old north European immigration. It contains many undesirable and unintelligent people." Too many of them became public charges; there were too many with poor physique; there were too many diseased. He thought that the literacy test would probably be the best means of keeping out undesirable immigrants; along with the illiterate, those with poor physique should be excluded. "Aliens have no inherent right to land on American soil," he concluded.[29]

Williams unquestionably sought by all means within the law to keep the new immigration at a minimum. While new categories of excludable aliens were established from time to time, as in 1903 and 1907, and administrative procedures were tightened, only a very small percentage of those who actually arrived at Ellis Island could ultimately be excluded. How many were discouraged from leaving Europe by his policy can never be known. Such discouragement was a conscious part of that policy. Since the Jewish immigration of the period was largely from eastern Europe and much more impoverished on the whole than the older Jewish immigration from Germany and the west had been, many Jews were detained at Ellis Island and quite a number of them were excluded. Open attacks on Williams from German, Jewish, and other sources diminished for a time after a presidential investigating commission of 1903 made its report. The *American Hebrew*, which had taken no part in these attacks and, in fact, had discouraged them, nevertheless warned its brethren abroad "that the American immigration laws are very strict, and that, in truth, they are being rigidly enforced by the officials." Those whose passage had been prepaid by another, or who came with the promise in advance of work, would be turned back, "nor will the Jews here raise a hand to stay the acts of the authorities. The law is there and must be enforced." [30]

But the *American Hebrew* did not represent the dominant opinion on this point within its own group. The New York Jewish community had theretofore concerned itself chiefly with social service to the immigrant. Now an organization was formed primarily for the purpose of getting him past the gates. In 1904 the Hebrew Immigrant Aid Society, organized two years before, found a very able man as its representative at Ellis Island. This was Alexander Harkavy, writer and lecturer in Hebrew and Yiddish. He worked at the island for a number of years, together with representatives of other Jewish societies, and enjoyed the confidence of Commissioner Williams and later that of Watchorn. With his coming to the station, "the lot of the Jewish immigrant improved greatly," according to the historian of the organization. His principal task was "to intervene with the Board of Inquiry in behalf of immigrants slated for deportation," assisting them in overcoming language barriers and legal formalities that hampered them in defending themselves. With Harkavy's retirement in 1909, his functions were taken over by Irving Lipsitch. The society also had a strong representative in Washington in the person of Simon Wolf.[31]

One center of controversy was the boards of special inquiry: their intelligence, their fairness, and their independence were often challenged. Boards of special inquiry, established in 1893, were made up of immigration inspectors designated by the commissioner. Immigration inspectors, who might serve on the line one day and on a board of inquiry the next, though the general practice was to leave the boards intact, were appointed after civil service examination. They were expected to be thoroughly familiar with the immigration laws and regulations, but were not ordinarily men of legal training. They were, however, under the close supervision of the station's legal staff, which offered instruction in examination technique and followed up questionable testimony presented to the boards. The legal staff also assisted the commissioner in reviewing appeals from board decisions.[32]

Critics of Ellis Island often assailed the boards, charging that they were too bound by the letter of the law and were dominated by the commissioner, and pointing out that nearly 50 percent of appeals from their decisions were sometimes sustained. On one such occasion early in 1911, in the heat of debate, Secretary of Commerce and Labor Charles Nagel admitted that better boards were needed. "I do think," he told the Council of the Union of American Hebrew Congregations, "that the system under which we work is at fault and not equal to the situation. . . . Aliens come, often 3,000 a day. We have a limited force and only limited compensation to pay. We need competent boards and enough boards, who can, as a good Judge should, be appealed to by the individuality of every alien instead of falling into the rut of merely asking the specified questions." As for the percentage of reversals of board decisions, he advised his hearers "not to be tinkering with that phase of the question." He passed on every appeal case personally, he asserted. Under the law he was required to hear an appeal based only on the record. "If I had not the right to go beyond the record, however, to get the atmosphere of each individual case . . . it wouldn't take more than half an hour to sign all the cases before me."[33]

Williams defended his inspectors vigorously in his next annual report, holding that as a whole they were conscientious, intelligent, and industrious. Their task was unusually difficult, "for they are constantly called upon to work rapidly, and yet to exercise sound judgment in applying indefinite tests to human beings." The magnitude and difficulty of their work were often overlooked by those who found fault with decisions in isolated cases. "Last year they decided 70,829 cases," he pointed out, "rendering admitting decisions in a great majority of them, but excluding from admission a great deal of the riffraff and scum which is constantly seeking to enter." He thought that the work of the boards of inquiry at Ellis Island compared favorably with that of other similar bodies, whether executive or judicial. As for the high percentage of reversals on appeal, he argued that the board members' discretion was necessarily more limited than that of their superiors. They were not called upon to take chances, and "if admission is to occur through mercy shown in cases close to the line it is proper that this be done by the highest authorities." [34]

The National Association of Manufacturers, interested in an abundant supply of cheap labor, devoted much of its annual meeting in 1911 to the subject of immigration. Its committee on immigration, quoting the recently-published report of the Immigration Commission, pointed out that the immigration inspectors were without judicial or legal training; that, as they were selected by the commissioner under whom they served, their decisions were influenced by the views of their superiors; and that a high percentage of the cases appealed were reversed. "In justice to the immigrant and to the country as well," the report read, "the character of these boards should be improved. They should be composed of men whose ability and training fit them for the judicial functions performed, and the provision compelling their hearings to be separate and apart from the public should be repealed." The New York *World*, though traditionally favorable to the immigrant, took issue at once. "It is true that these boards often make harsh rulings," said a *World* editorial, "but always in the 'judicial function' of trying to obey the law. It is true that Washington often reverses them, but Washington is usually wrong in doing so, because Washington doesn't see the applicants and the men of horse sense and great experience in the special boards do see them." For American manufacturers, at a time when business was dull and many honest men were out of work, "to demand that the bars be lowered which keep out unfit or doubtful immigrants —this is merely another instance of customary and consummate cheek." [35]

President Taft came to share the view that the men at the island were better judges of the cases that came before them than an outsider could be. When a delegation of foreign language newspaper editors came to him to complain about Williams's harsh deportation policy, he told them about his own visit to Ellis Island a few months before. He had listened to a number of cases brought to Williams from the boards of inquiry for review. "I interested myself once or twice," Taft said, "the statements made having worked upon my compas-

President Taft and party at Ellis Island in 1910. Secretary Nagel stands at his right and Commissioner Williams at his left.

—Courtesy of the New York Public Library

sion, and I indicated an opinion to the commissioner once or twice where I rather think he would have taken a different course but for my suggestion. I have since followed these cases in which I influenced him against his better judgment, and I am obliged to make the humiliating confession to you that the outcome vindicated him and showed that my judgment was at fault for lack of experience." [36]

The island was always fair game for the press, if not for corruption, then for inhumane conditions; if not for lenient immigration practices, then for strict ones. It was right on the doorstep of the New York metropolitan newspapers, a numerous and lively group in those days. It was a government institution—and one duty of the press in a democratic society is admittedly to keep public servants in their place. It was also rich in human interest. There was always a good story to be had at the island, and if it involved a dishonest employee or some pathetic case of exclusion, so much the better. Reporters were not dependent on official channels for their information. Steamship lines and missionaries were fruitful sources; minor employees enjoyed attention from the press and were hard to muzzle. The attitude of the big-city newspapers was often highly critical, but it generally fell within the limits of legitimate news gathering and editorializing.

The foreign language press, on the other hand, sensitive to every exclusion within its several groups, was likely to be shrill and vituperative, freely charging the Ellis Island authorities with perpetrating brutalities, atrocities, and even murder. An Ellis Island veteran with considerable knowledge of European tongues declared, probably with some exaggeration, that he had never read a newspaper article concerning the island that did not make the staff there appear "stupid fools." Able and honest administrators though they were, Williams and Watchorn were both frequently under attack. Press attacks were often followed by official investigations. After he had left the island, Watchorn told a *New York Times* reporter: "There has always been trouble down at that place and always will be," adding, with evident relief, "I'm out of it." Edward Corsi, browsing through the old files during his term as commissioner in the early 1930s, thought that "It would take a special volume to fully chronicle the investigations of Ellis Island and their repercussions across the nation." [37]

In an interview for the *Commercial Advertiser* reviewing the accomplishments of his first year at Ellis Island, Williams frankly took most pride in the fact that deportations had nearly doubled under his administration. He had not been in office many months before he was subjected to a vicious campaign of abuse by the *Staats-Zeitung*. The articles concentrated on his treatment of aliens, particularly in matters of detention and deportation. According to this leading German language daily, Ellis Island was a hell on earth, where only the knout was lacking to make it a Czarist prison camp. German friends of the president expressed to him concern at the possible effect on his administration of these attacks, and Roosevelt instructed Williams to confer with them. "As you know," he reminded the commissioner, "I have backed you, and will continue to back you, in every way, against politicians of every degree. Now we are dealing not with politicians, not with demagogues or dishonest men." He wanted Williams "to be able to show them that my administration is acting in a spirit of the utmost fairness and justice toward all immigrants: that we desire to aid the immigration of all those fit to come; that we are simply warring against the morally and physically unfit." [38]

Whatever may have taken place at this conference, it did not stop the attacks in the *Staats-Zeitung*, and other German language papers began to join in. President Roosevelt, who was highly aware of the importance of the German vote, finally appointed an investigating commission. It was headed by Arthur von Briesen, a prominent New York German-American, but included representatives of Jewish and Irish groups. The president announced the commission during a whirlwind visit to the island. It was assumed, according to the *New York Times*, that his action had been brought about by New York German-American newspapers, "which for some time have been printing editorials making charges of various sorts involving the management of the Immigration Station." [39]

The charges that had been made in a long series of articles by Leopold Deutschberger, the Ellis Island correspondent of the *Staats-Zeitung*, were not sustained in the hearings. Deutschberger submitted a set of clippings containing the charges. He swore that they were factual but admitted that much of his evidence was second hand and refused, with the backing of his editor, to divulge his sources or to submit to cross-examination. The verbal charges that he made to the commission were much more subdued in tone than his articles had been, and he seems to have made a poor impression generally. Commissioner Williams appeared before the commission and denied the charges in detail. He gave the facts in a number of cases to which misleading interpretations had been given, but agreed that there was congestion and discomfort on the island and admitted that mistakes might have been made. A few other witnesses were heard, some urging changes in procedure and others defending Williams. Representatives of the missionary societies generally approved of his administration, noting great improvement on the island recently, but agreed that the facilities there were too limited.

The commission's report stated that charges of improper detention of large numbers of immigrants, of deportation of large numbers of immigrants who should have been landed, of too severe an interpretation of the law by the officers at Ellis Island, and of a general animus against immigration were unfounded or had not been sustained by evidence. Neither had charges of uncleanliness in and about the buildings there, nor charges that immigrants detained in the hospital had been required to do menial work, been sustained. The board found that immigrants in detention had been refused permission to leave the island until their relatives were heard from, as charged, but approved the policy, "as every effort is made to protect immigrants from falling into evil hands."

The report did make a number of recommendations in regard to procedure, however. Some of these were suggested by Williams himself, notably one proposing that the commissioner be empowered to hear and determine appeals from boards of inquiry, his decision to be final upon the approval of the secretary. Other recommendations called for enlargement and improvement of the physical facilities of Ellis Island, a program with which Williams was most heartily in accord. But Williams viewed some recommendations with less enthusiasm. One suggested the representation of transportation companies and of the immigrants themselves at board hearings, which Williams felt would give too much opportunity for coaching the detainees. Another called for the enforcement of the equal liability of contractors and aliens in cases under the contract labor law, which would tend to fill Ellis Island with detainees during protracted legal proceedings, since the immigrants would have to be held as witnesses. And the commission suggested limiting of the liability of steamship companies for the maintenance of detained aliens. Williams held that these companies were chiefly responsible for the detentions because they brought in immigrants who did not meet the legal requirements.[40]

At the time, Williams believed that the *Staats-Zeitung*'s campaign of vilification had been the work solely of its Ellis Island reporter, who had been closely associated with the old regime on the island. He thought that Deutschberger's motive had been partly political and partly the result of the fact that the government had, since May 1902, "deprived a number of his friends of the opportunities which they formerly enjoyed of abusing immigrants and profiting improperly at their expense." He asked permission to bar the man from the island. This newspaper, however, remained his bitter critic, and its attacks rose to new heights during his second administration. The movement spread in 1911 through much of the German press of the United States, greatly puzzling Williams and Secretary of Commerce and Labor Nagel, then his superior in Washington. Williams, who had received part of his education in Germany and spoke the German language fluently, was hurt as well. "If this hostility were confined to papers representing south Europeans," he told Nagel, "I could at least understand the philosophy of it all. But we are so fond of Germans, so anxious to have them come here, and we send back and detain such a negligible quantity of those who arrive, that we must look for this hostility elsewhere than in the application of the immigration law to Germans." Secretary Nagel, himself of German background and closely tied to the big German community of St. Louis, was also at sea. Both suspected that one of the great German steamship lines, which brought immigrants from all parts of Europe and were naturally interested in the most liberal interpretation of the immigration laws, might be in back of the campaign. Steamship advertising was an important source of revenue to most of the foreign language press.[41]

The attacks continued and were taken up by the Hearst press, first in its German language *Morgen Journal*, which launched a systematic campaign against Williams. "A call in tones of thunder is heard throughout the ranks of the German press of the country," it declared: "Away with Czarism at Ellis Island." Almost every exchange received in the editorial offices of the paper contained articles in protest against "the cruel treatment of the new arrivals at the Isle of Tears." Twenty-two German language papers, most in the Middle West, had joined the *Morgen Journal*'s protest by the middle of April 1911, and the list was growing. The Columbus *Express-Westbote* condemned "the cruelties which are perpetrated daily at Ellis Island"; the *Demokrat* of Evansville expressed "indignation at the treatment of immigrants at Ellis Island"; the Cincinnati *Volksblatt* said that "The manner in which immigrants are treated in New York gives the United States the reputation of surpassing even Russia in cruelty and despotism." [42]

Hearst had long posed as the champion of the foreign born. Presently the attack was taken up in his influential *New York Journal*, edited by Arthur Brisbane. "Brutality at Ellis Island" was Brisbane's lead editorial on May 24, 1911, and it thundered out a series of sensational charges against Williams. New York Congressman William Sulzer was induced to take up the crusade, and he conducted hearings before the House Rules Committee on his resolution aimed at an investigation of Williams's administration by the Committee on Immigration and Naturalization. At these hearings a variety of charges were presented by representatives of various German language newspapers and organizations in New York and New Jersey, of the National German-American Alliance, as well as of the Jewish *Wahrheit* of New York. Other witnesses included a former Ellis Island employee and a New York congressman. The charges were reminiscent of those made in 1903, centering on unfair interpretation of the "likely to become a public charge" clause of the law, abuse of immigrants, and crowded and unsanitary conditions at Ellis Island. But there were also attacks on the law itself. "Mr. Watchorn," said one witness, "was not such an enemy to decent immigration; but the present commissioner has an especial antipathy to all those who come from any other shore to this country, and his administration is scandalous and a stench in the nostrils of the Nation."

Secretary Nagel was troubled, as the campaign put him distinctly in the middle, but he resolved to defend Williams. He examined the record of every case brought to his attention, he told a correspondent, but pointed out that he could not waste time answering general charges. He came to the conclusion that the campaign was "reckless and extravagant." When Williams got a copy of the committee hearings he was furious; he was "outraged by the falsehoods told about my administration," he wrote Nagel. "These criticisms pass the bounds of decency and in some manner the persons making them ought to be told what decent people think about them." Nagel counseled patience: "I am satisfied that our time will come," he told Williams, "and I do not think that in your place I would go into the discussion at all until I was prepared to enter into it fully." A further hearing before the Rules Committee was arranged, and Williams and Nagel, armed to the teeth with factual data, appeared and refuted the charges in detail to the evident satisfaction of the committee. Sulzer's resolution was not acted upon, though Williams openly welcomed an investigation. "I do not think any investigation is necessary," the chairman of the Immigration Committee said during the hearings, "and none should be ordered." When Secretary Nagel said flatly that the charges of brutality were false, "Mr. Sulzer acquiesced." [43]

The agitation continued and was taken up by some Italian and Hungarian papers. Not all the foreign language press joined the chorus, however, and Williams had his defenders within its ranks. Williams had been exonerated from the charges of being "inhuman, incompetent, and partial," said the *Slovak National News* of Pittsburgh, "charges brought by the motherly benevolence of the care-worn Germans, the Jews and the 'in their train limping' Magyars." The whole thing was plain, said this Slovak journal. Most of the immigrants were brought to this country by steamship companies owned or controlled by German capital. Everybody knew that immigration from Germany was slight, and consequently the Germans were not concerned so much with German immigrants as they were with German capital, for which they wanted big dividends. "And because Commissioner Williams, being independently rich and a gentleman, cannot be bribed, and more, because he would not submit to political influence, therefore and for that reason only have the German societies and the German papers started this crusade. There is where the dog is buried!" [44]

Whatever the impetus for the attacks on Williams in the German press, and on Nagel for supporting him, they continued. Both men were bitterly assailed in the annual convention of the National German-American Alliance. So vehement was the hostility toward Nagel that a motion inviting him to address the convention was withdrawn before a vote was taken, and a resolution calling for Williams's dismissal from office was adopted. In 1912 the *Morgen Journal* sought to revive the nationwide assault of the previous year, declaring: "The removal of Williams from office would be the most crushing defeat which could be inflicted on the nativists. Therefore the slogan of the German-Americans is: Williams Must Go!" At the end of his term, when the Democratic administration of President Woodrow Wilson was already in office and Williams had submitted his resignation, the *Staats-Zeitung* and other German papers were still attacking him.[45]

Williams defended himself vigorously. He often answered an attack by a metropolitan paper in a forceful interview or in a signed letter to the editor. He usually found, he told the editor of the New York *World* on one such occasion, "that most published accounts of immigrant cases either misstate or omit to state one or more relevant facts. This office will, upon application, cheerfully furnish the current facts in all such cases, except in the few instances in which for a time it may be necessary to treat them as confidential." He fearlessly denounced Congressman Adolph Sabath of Illinois as a liar after this "immigrants' congressman," a member of the House Committee on Immigration and Naturalization, had attacked him in an extension of remarks in the *Congressional Record*. He sometimes sent passes to his more virulent critics, inviting them to come to Ellis Island "on any day" and see what they could find of the "inhuman or cruel" practices that they had complained of. President Taft loyally sustained him. "I want you to know that every day, as I think over the Government, I rejoice that I have a Commissioner like you in the place you fill," he wrote Williams in 1911. He told him to pay no heed to the "barks of the coyotes." The president himself did not hear them: "If I did, I should regard them as only an evidence of the efficiency with which you are discharging your duty to the Government." [46]

While the German language newspapers and German organizations led the attack on Commissioner Williams, they were supported by much of the Jewish press and by many Jewish organizations. German immigration had tapered off, but Jewish immigration, particularly from Russia, where oppression of the Jews was chronic and flared into bloody pogroms from time to time, was still at full tide. The Jews as a group had a more direct and immediate interest in a liberal interpretation of the immigration laws than did the Germans. By the early 1900s the Jewish element, particularly in New York City, was highly organized and highly vocal, with a vigorous intelligentsia and wealthy leaders well established in American life. It furnished much of the leadership in opposition to the national movement for immigration restriction. The older Jewish element was largely German and proud of the fact. It was sometimes dismayed by the crudity, and appalled by the numbers, of its coreligionists arriving from Russia, but it did not repudiate them.[47]

Following the lead of the *Staats-Zeitung*, a number of Hebrew organizations in New York, working with German, Italian, and Hungarian societies, began protesting Williams's administration of the immigration laws at Ellis Island early in 1903. President Roosevelt, as he did with the Germans, at once took note of private communications on the same subject from Jewish friends. While Roosevelt was something of a restrictionist himself, he responded automatically to protest from an important bloc of voters. He wrote to Williams, cautioning him against "the so-called star chamber business in reference to the deported aliens." Roosevelt was, he said, a warm believer in sending an alien back when his presence would tend to the physical or moral deterioration of our people, "but we must remember that so to send him back is often to inflict a punishment upon him only less severe than death itself, and in such cases we must be sure not merely that we are acting aright but that we are able to show others that we are acting aright." The president was evidently not very familiar with the regulations governing the boards of special inquiry that had already been developing for a decade.

Williams replied at length, describing in detail the procedure in board of inquiry and deportation actions and denying the validity of the "star chamber" charges. The terms "star chamber" and "inquisition," he said, referring to Deutschberger of the *Staats-Zeitung*, "were discovered by a disreputable representative of one of the newspapers which publishes daily a column on alleged misdoings of this office." This man was intimately associated with the old ring at the station and naturally viewed with disfavor the changes that had been made. The fact that several Hebrew societies that had attacked Williams used this same paper as their sole mouthpiece, he thought, "casts the greatest suspicion upon their sincerity." Roosevelt had told him to make some arrangements by which reputable representatives of Hebrew, Italian, and other societies might be present at board of inquiry hearings, to avoid any chance of failure to protect the rights of immigrants, or the appearance of such failure. "I beg to state," said Williams, "that this already occurs, and that ever since I have been here representatives of all proper societies have had access to the board room for the purposes stated." The minutes of the board were open for inspection by "all proper persons," and any fact that had been overlooked could be presented before him or in an appeal. He had discussed the president's letter with representatives of the United Hebrew Society and the Italian Society, he said, and read to them his proposed answer. "They are of the opinion, and so am I, that the rights of the immigrants are, and since I took office always have been, scrupulously guarded. Any contrary assertion is either based on ignorance or originates in the desire to embarrass your administration." [48]

When Robert Watchorn replaced Williams as commissioner in 1905, he carried on his administration strictly in the Williams tradition of honesty, integrity, and general competence, but his point of view on admission policy was materially different. He felt that the country could absorb all the immigrants, "new" or "old," that came, as long as they met the established medical and legal standards. He expounded this view in an article for the *Outlook* late in 1907, noting that a million and a quarter immigrants had entered in the previous fiscal year but expressing no alarm over the fact.[49] A poor man and an immigrant himself, he had a broader natural sympathy with all those seeking to pass the gates than did Williams, a man of means and descendant of a line of colonial and Revolutionary ancestors. Williams's "law of kindness" was self-imposed; Watchorn's was spontaneous.

Watchorn's attitude toward the newcomer was also probably influenced by his experience in Romania in 1900. In the summer of that year Romanian Jews began arriving at the Barge Office. The Romanian government, they said, had forbidden Jews to practice crafts and trades. The newcomers were practically all skilled workmen, but they were penniless. They were at first detained, but were allowed to enter after wealthy New York Jews had posted bond for them. It was understood that they were only the vanguard of a large movement. Watchorn was on leave in his native England. He was directed to go to Romania and investigate the causes of the migration, and was told flatly by the assistant secretary that "it is desired that the migration of these people to the United States be discouraged by any proper means that may prove feasible." The *American Hebrew*, learning of his proposed trip, arranged to have David Blaustein, superintendent of the Educational Alliance on New York's East Side, accompany him as interpreter. While Watchorn believed that the migration had been touched off by outside influences, rather than by any new oppressive measures of the government, he found that discrimination against Jews was a settled policy and took many forms. He ventured the opinion "that no hope whatever may be entertained of a change in Roumania's policy in this respect." Conditions surrounding the Jews were, he said, "harsh, unrelentingly harsh." He explained to the Jewish Committee in Bucharest that under the immigration laws of the United States destitute people could not be admitted. He thought that those who did come would be not only self-supporting but also "desirable accessions to our population." He reported what he had seen and done objectively, but the experience probably left a deep impression on him.[50]

In 1906 William Randolph Hearst became the Democratic candidate for governor of New York. He threatened to outbid the Republican progressives in immigrant precincts, where they had been making considerable gains. As reports reached the White House that Hearst would sweep the East Side, President Roosevelt acted promptly. He appointed Oscar S. Straus, former U.S. ambassador to Turkey, as secretary of commerce and labor, thus appointing a Jew to the cabinet for the first time, with control over the department that then administered the immigration laws.[51]

Straus made a number of visits to Ellis Island and took an active interest in its administration. The Immigration Restriction League was convinced that Straus was relaxing the enforcement of the immigration laws, at least as they applied to Jews, and wrote to President Roosevelt on the subject. Roosevelt passed the letters on to Senator Lodge, a member of the recently created Immigration Commission, which was charged with a broad study of the whole immigration problem. Lodge had been the leading champion of immigration restriction in the Senate for years and had worked closely with the league in the past. He assured the president, however, that there was no evidence of lax enforcement under Straus's administration. The commission had found that there had been no increase in reversals of excluding decisions, in which Secretary Straus had the final word on appeals. Although Lodge believed that Straus was "adverse to the laws which affect the entry of poor Jews," he had found no evidence, in unheralded visits to Ellis Island and other immigration stations, substantiating the league's charges. He found Watchorn "an exceptionally capable man" and "in full sympathy with the law."[52]

Nevertheless, there had been a change of policy in interpreting the law at Ellis Island that undoubtedly benefited poor Jews as well as other poor immigrants. Watchorn, on taking office and long before Straus's appointment, had himself rescinded "a rather drastic" order issued by Williams toward the end of his administration, requiring aliens to show at least $10 in addition to tickets to destination. Under this rule, Watchorn explained to the secretary later, refuting stories that he had relaxed the rigidity of inspection, "a very large number of able-bodied men and women, who could not show $10, were deported on the ground that they were likely to become public charges, though they were in every other way eligible to land." The repeal of this rule, which was one of his first acts, Watchorn said, "had the effect of cutting down the number of deportations of that class very noticeably, much to my pleasure." On the other hand, Watchorn had found that aliens certified by the medical department as physically or mentally defective were being admitted as long as they had $10 and railroad tickets. He had put a stop to this and had been able to increase the medical staff and thus tighten medical inspection. Medical deportations had increased accordingly, so that "the very thing that my critics would desire has been done." [53]

It seems to have been this elimination of a fixed monetary requirement for arriving immigrants more than anything else that made Watchorn somewhat more acceptable than Williams had been to Jewish and other foreign-born groups. Philip Cowen, for many years editor of the *American Hebrew*, entered the Immigration Service in 1905 under an executive order of President Roosevelt's, and served on the boards of special inquiry. At a meeting of the order of the Judaeans in the following spring, attended by Commissioner Watchorn and other Ellis Island officials, he described, with the aid of stereopticon slides, the arrival and examination of immigrants. "Money," he told his audience, "plays no part in the admission of persons under the regime of the present Commissioner. Brain and brawn count." He took his own former weekly to task for errors in an article on Jewish immigration statistics. "Your statement that 1,208 Jews were excluded for 'insufficient means' is also delusive," he said in a signed letter to the editor. "They were, nearly all I am sure, excluded because in the judgment of the Board of Inquiry they were persons likely to become a public charge for some physical defect other than a contagious disease," Cowen wrote, "or because they did not seem in the Board's judgment in a position to successfully cope with conditions that would face them in a new land; quite a different story. 'Insufficient means' under the present administration is well nigh an unknown term. Given a good physical condition, and money does not count." [54]

Watchorn's policy on monetary requirements for admission was evidently the chief basis for criticism of his administration by the restrictionists. There is little evidence that he was in any other way less rigid than Williams had been in the examination of immigrants. There were two classes from whom letters came to him regularly every morning, Watchorn told the New York branch of the Council of Jewish Women in 1908, "one complaining that he does not enforce the law vigorously enough; the other call him hard-hearted and callous because he does not allow people to come in who are not legally allowed to land." In the matter of watching for contract laborers he was probably more alert than his predecessor had been, for he had been a coal miner and an important union official himself. In April 1906, 1,000 contract laborers were deported from Ellis Island; in May 1,753 immigrants were sent back from all causes, a record up to that time. This undoubtedly brought the hostility of manufacturers seeking to import craftsmen, but it roused the support of organized labor. When Watchorn was in serious trouble toward the end of his administration, the Central Federated Union of New York, which was always on the watch for contract laborers, was among his defenders.[55]

When Williams returned to office at Ellis Island in 1909, he at once announced a policy of strict enforcement of the immigration laws. "It is necessary that the standard of inspection at Ellis Island be raised," he informed the inspectors. "I am of the opinion that we are receiving too many low-grade immigrants," he told a *New York Times* reporter in explanation of this notice. "I shall do what I can within the law to reduce their number, and it is hoped by giving publicity to the policy to be pursued at Ellis Island that even the embarkation of such immigrants may be prevented." His first notice to the inspectors was soon followed by another, setting a figure of $25, plus railroad tickets, as a desirable minimum in the hands of immigrants. He insisted, however, that this was not a rule for exclusion nor an attempt to create a property test not found in the statutes. It was "merely a humane notice to intending immigrants that upon landing they will require at least some small amount of money with which to meet their wants while looking for employment." "Every day immigrants of the right kind are landed with less than $25," he assured a congressman who had telegraphed an inquiry about the meaning of the new rule. The notice, he said, "has not altered in any particular the methods under which, in my former administration, I interpreted the statute excluding 'paupers' and 'persons likely to become public charges.' "[56]

There was a sensation when the new order was applied at once to cabin passengers. Two hundred and fifteen out of 301 in the second-cabin class of the *Ryndam* were taken to Ellis Island and held because they did not have $25 in cash. "Not all these aliens will be deported," Williams explained to a *Times* reporter, "but the ruling was necessary because certain steamship lines have been careless in accepting passengers, and too many indigent immigrants have been coming in. Many of these people who have not enough money will be met by relatives who can assure us that they will not become public charges."

Most of those detained under the new rule, however, were steerage passengers, and a great many of them were Russian Jews. The Hebrew Immigrant

Aid Society assembled, with the cooperation of other Jewish organizations now coordinated by an American Jewish Committee, a powerful battery of legal talent, and quickly brought a test case before the federal courts in New York. Four immigrants ordered deported as likely to become public charges because they were without funds, but otherwise acceptable, were brought back to Ellis Island from shipboard by writ of habeas corpus. Williams had "altered the law to suit his own views," an officer of the society told the *Times*. "Mr. Williams' enforcement of the immigration laws and especially that section which has to do with the amount of money a person must have to insure their landing is meeting with much antagonism on the east side, where live many who have had arriving relatives held up," it reported. Leon Kamaiky, editor of the *Jewish News* of New York, accompanied by Congressman William S. Bennet, a New York Republican and a member of the Immigration Commission, called at the White House to protest to President Taft against Williams's cash order. "Thousands of able-bodied men and women have been deported in the last month or so because they did not have the amount of cash Mr. Williams has fixed upon," Kamaiky told a reporter in Washington. "In one day 614 were deported. There is no law fixing this amount, and desirable men and women are still needed in this country. This rule seems to me to be entirely too harsh." [57]

The federal courts had been reluctant to take up deportation cases, and Judge Learned Hand, before whom the matter of the four aliens was heard, at first limited the scope of the inquiry sharply. He brushed aside charges that Williams terrorized the boards of inquiry at Ellis Island and stated that the good faith of the immigration officials should not be considered before him. He refused to allow the detained aliens bail. Under persistent argument, however, he finally decided that the case should be adjourned for a week while the plaintiffs prepared a fuller brief, and that the immigrants should meanwhile have a rehearing on Ellis Island. On this rehearing the four aliens, all Russian Jews, were permitted to land, new evidence having been introduced to prove that they would not become public charges. This abated the habeas corpus proceedings and, though the aliens were admitted, the attempt to get a judicial decision on the new order failed. The HIAS counsel made no effort to take the case to a higher court.[58]

But the release of the four Russian Jews did not end the matter. The violence of the protest had made an impression on Williams's superiors in Washington. Secretary Nagel came to Ellis Island and spent several hours in conference with him and with representatives of Jewish societies in New York and Washington. Williams had set up a temporary "court of appeals," which he headed, to give the four Russian Jews their rehearing. This court was briefly revived, apparently for the edification of the visitors, and now reviewed fourteen additional cases in which boards of inquiry had ordered deportations. It reversed the decisions in thirteen of them. Most of the immigrants involved were Jews, and some were practically penniless. The secretary told the press that he was entirely satisfied with the way Williams was running things at Ellis Island, and after his departure Williams declared that "there will be no lowering of the standards at Ellis Island." [59]

Within a day or two, however, the records of six cases in which the appeals of aliens, excluded on "likely to become a public charge" grounds, had been upheld were forwarded to Ellis Island. These records were ordinarily kept in Washington, and the field notified only by telegram or brief form letter of the decisions. Williams was told that "the Bureau transmits herewith for the information of the boards which passed upon the cases, copies of the memorandums upon which the decisions of the Department in ordering them landed were based." The boards of special inquiry were evidently not only to be instructed but also to be reassured of their independence. Williams had already notified the boards to the same effect: "Once and for all times let me say in writing what I have frequently stated orally," he told them, "that it is never my intention to indicate or even intimate my own views as to how any particular case should be decided, or in any manner to influence you in the decision, which must always be your own, rendered according to law." The *American Hebrew* had become critical of the administration at Ellis Island and distressed at the congestion among the detainees there, caused by the enforcement of Williams's new order; much of this, it believed, was no doubt the work of "over zealous" employees who brought about hardships that Williams himself would not approve. It noted that no information other than the press accounts had been given out regarding the conference there, and these accounts "whitewashed" Williams, but it believed that as a result of the meeting "deportation will be a more deliberate proceeding than has been the case recently." [60]

While Williams took down the notice of the twenty-five dollar order that had been posted in the board rooms, he did not rescind the order itself. Two years later, when both men were again under sharp attack, he modified it at Secretary Nagel's request, eliminating any reference to a specific sum but retaining the principle that an immigrant "should have enough to provide for his reasonable wants, and of those of accompanying persons dependent upon him until such time as he is likely to find employment." But the sum of $25 still offered a convenient yardstick for inspectors, and the belief that this sum was required for admittance had spread abroad. As late as the end of 1913, Louis Adamic, emigrating from Slovenia to the United States by way of Ellis Island, had sewed away in the lining of his jacket "twenty-five dollars in American currency," which he believed was "the minimum amount required by law to be in the possession of every immigrant before entering the country." [61] It is a fair speculation that the statistical peak of immigration, which occurred in 1907, might have been in a later year except for the change in admission policy at Ellis Island that came with Williams's return in 1909. He may have accomplished a good bit of what he set out to do.

Williams's twenty-five-dollar order, and the case of the four Russian Jews that followed, brought out considerable comment in the New York metropolitan press, much of it critical. There was no open defense of a strict monetary test for immigrants, but there was sympathy for his position expressed indirectly. If, as was believed, Williams was excluding people who were not likely to become public charges, the *Globe and Commercial Advertiser* noted, "it is needless to point out that the spirit of the immigration laws is being vitiated even though its letter is respected. . . . he is not in office to make new laws but to apply those that congress has enacted." The *Evening Post* was doubtful about the monetary test. It could never be anything but tentative and in incapable hands might become an instrument of injustice. It should certainly not be applied against the victims of pogroms. The existing law provided for the return of immigrants who became public charges; this was an adequate safeguard and "should encourage clemency at Ellis Island, rather than harshness." The immigrant "should be given a chance to show that what this country offers its newcomers is not poverty, but a living." Williams's rule would have stopped most migrations, the *World* thought. "In this country a $25 rule would have kept the great West a wilderness; would have preserved the Great American Desert to this day; would have deprived the Pacific coast of its forty-niners and the railroad builders; would have kept Benjamin Franklin out of Philadelphia. . . . It is always unwise to estimate a man's worth by the amount of his money. This is emphatically true in the case of immigrants."

The *Sun* had been at first critical of the order. However, it announced a little later that it had found that Williams was actually applying the rule flexibly, as he claimed. This it approved. "A strong body, a willingness to work and a clean record; let an immigrant possessing these qualifications enter and it is safe to assert that, to say the least for him, he will not imperil the republic." Support for Williams came surprisingly from the National Liberal Immigration League, a new organization which opposed any further restriction of immigration. "We believe in fair play," the *Times* quoted Nissim Behar, its managing director, as saying, "and Mr. Williams has shown that he is going to use his judgment as to who will be admitted independent of the money test. He has shown that he is inclined to relax the regulations when a desirable immigrant comes to this country, and will administer the law, not in an ironclad manner, but intelligently and justly." The *Tribune*, strongly restrictionist though it had long been, carefully refrained from commenting directly on Williams's order, but applauded his expulsion from Ellis Island of a band of gypsies just at this time. The gypsies had objected violently to being deported. "It would not be surprising if some one should rise in defense of the deported band," said the *Tribune*, "and refer to them as martyrs deprived of their right to become citizens of the land of opportunity, but the whole country is better off without them, even though their wealth per capita was several times greater than the amount commonly required." [62]

Deportees leaving Ellis Island. They are probably the band of gypsies who were deported en masse in July 1909.

—*Courtesy of the National Park Service*

Williams had warm support from other sources. R. M. Easley, director of the National Civic Federation, wrote him, saying, "I am glad someone is undertaking to enforce the law at Ellis Island." He wanted to consult with Williams soon on the reorganization of the federation's committee on immigration. "We want one in entire harmony with the enforcement of the law in shutting out undesirable immigrants." Prescott F. Hall, of the Immigration Restriction League, told him, "I can't help writing you at this time to express my admiration of the way things are going at Ellis Island. Nothing has made me so happy for a long time as feeling that you are there and seeing, as far as I do from the papers, how you are cleaning things up." The superintendent of the Charity Organization Society in New York City wrote to him, saying, "I wish to heartily congratulate you on your determination in the face of opposition to enforce the immigration laws as they now stand." As an employee of the New York State Board of Charities and then in private charity work, he said, "I have had every opportunity to observe the hardships imposed upon this city by the large number of aliens for whom it was compelled to care through both its public and private charity." Madison Grant, an aristocratic New Yorker who some years later was to put the capstone on the nativist ideological structure in his book, *The Passing of the Great Race*, offered his congratulations to Williams on his "effort to secure a proper enforcement of the laws and regulations of immigration." These laws were of "lax character," but their deficiency would be exposed by Williams's efforts.[63]

The controversy subsided, as far as the press was concerned, but Williams and the Jewish community remained at odds. The following January he was invited to address the annual meeting of the Hebrew Immigrant Aid Society. He appeared on the platform with Jacob H. Schiff, a powerful Wall Street banker and one of the most influential leaders of the New York community. Schiff was interested in a wider distribution of immigrants and was at the time trying to promote a Jewish colony in Texas. He seriously warned his hearers against encouraging further Jewish immigration to New York City, which he said could not absorb many more poor Russian, Austrian, and Romanian Jewish immigrants. To this extent, at least, he and Williams were in agreement. At his signal all rose when Williams started to speak. "The Society has long been anxious to get Commissioner Williams to visit a meeting," the *Times* commented, "because he and the Society's agents on Ellis Island are constantly getting into debates as to whether Jewish immigrants detained on Ellis Island for various causes shall go back to Russia or stay here." He was heartily received, nevertheless, and paid compliment to the Jewish immigrants as "promising citizens," admonishing the meeting to remember that "I merely execute the law."[64]

In spite of this fairly friendly meeting, deep suspicion of Williams continued in the Jewish community. A New York Jewish manufacturer wrote to him in pleased surprise at the courtesy extended to his wife at Ellis Island when she went there to meet arriving immigrants, and at the consideration shown to the immigrants themselves. "I take this liberty of writing to you and extending my thanks for the reason that I have heard at various times, that your administration in this office was very severe with immigrants." He also wanted "to offer the highest recommendations for the subordinates in charge." [65]

A year later, at the meeting of the Council of the Union of American Hebrew Congregations, at which Theodore Roosevelt spoke, Max J. Kohler, one of the lawyers who had represented the four Russian Jews before Judge Hand in 1909, vigorously attacked the Ellis Island administration. The percentage of Jewish exclusions had been going up year by year, he said, and "seventy-seven per cent. of all immigrants land at Ellis Island." More than two-thirds of the Jewish exclusions of the past year had been for "likelihood to become a public charge." This number was constantly increasing "because of ever newer misconstructions of the law, furtively forced upon inspectors at Ellis Island day by day, breaking down their judicial attitude and creating an atmosphere of uncertainty and anarchy and cowed timidity." With the advent of "opinionated doctrinaires" into office two years before, he charged, "their own narrow and erroneous opinions and beliefs of what is best for the country have been substituted for law." In reply to this indictment, which by implication included him as well as Williams, Secretary Nagel, speaking extempore, admitted that the boards of inquiry ought to be strengthened but insisted that, if the "likely to become a public charge" clause was strained, it was strained in favor of the alien. "You have no right to come before us with individual cases as typical examples. You should help us in the work." He had heard it said at the meeting "that you are as much interested as anybody in not having the wrong people come in . . . but I never had you call my attention to a wrong person yet. Now that is a fair statement. I am not complaining at all. I am speaking of the service, and we need co-operation and not fault-finding." [66]

In 1912 Henry J. Dannenbaum, a high official of the Jewish order of B'nai B'rith, took up the cudgels in Williams's defense. "In our name," he said, "criticism has been made of the administration of William Williams, the Commissioner of Immigration at Ellis Island, and his removal has been demanded." He was familiar with the operation of the station there and had read all the charges against Williams. It was his deliberate opinion that every charge was "absolutely without support in reason or in truth." He stood ready, he affirmed, "to defend with tongue or pen, at any time and anywhere, the acts of that brave man on Ellis Island, who is humane but firm and who counts duty above popularity." It would become American Jews, he asserted, with evident reference to the German language press, "far more to applaud official service, based upon the law as it is written, than to join in condemnation with editors of foreign tongues, whose columns are filled with the advertisements of foreign steamship companies." [67]

Dannenbaum's speech, made in New Orleans, was printed in the *Houston Daily Post*, and he circulated copies in the East. Williams sent a copy to Theodore Roosevelt, explaining that Dannenbaum had held a position of confidence in the Department of Justice tracking down "white slavers," and that while stationed in New York City he had become familiar with Ellis Island operations. Henry Fairfield Osborn, president of the American Museum of Natural History, sent a copy to Jacob Schiff. Schiff was not impressed. Dannenbaum had already sent him a copy, he wrote Osborn. "I do not know why, for he ought to be ashamed of much he has said." His own opinion of Commissioner Williams, said Schiff, was "that he means to be a conscientious official, but that his actions as Commissioner of Immigration at this Port are largely influenced by his evident restrictionist tendencies, and that instead of tempering justice with mercy, he does the reverse, and seems to apply the law in as extreme a manner as he can stretch it. . . . Much of the opposition which is made to Mr. Williams, not only from Hebrew sources, but also from German and, I believe, Italian, is justified." [68]

Just how much Schiff meant by this last statement it would be hard to say. That deliberate cruelties were inflicted at Ellis Island he must have known to be untrue. That more rigorous standards were often applied to poor or infirm southern Europeans and eastern European Jews than to northern Europeans similarly handicapped, by zealous subordinates seeking to curry favor with the boss, was probably true. That Williams did his best to discourage such immigrants from coming at all was certainly true.

CHAPTER IV

PROBLEMS OF THE FLOOD YEARS

Most of the problems that were to plague Ellis Island administrators throughout the years of high immigration had shown themselves at the old station in the 1890s: corruption, swindling, brutality, and exploitation, on the island and near it; attacks from restrictionists and antirestrictionists alike; misunderstandings with distant superiors who were often subjected to powerful lobby pressure; increasingly complex legislation to be applied at once to exhausted human beings; and enormous numbers of people to be sifted through inadequate facilities as quickly as possible. These problems were intensified as recovery from prolonged depression and a new period of industrial expansion brought a tide of immigrants to the new station that often threatened to overwhelm it. The house cleaning under the Roosevelt administration in 1902 brought more humane treatment of the immigrants, cut corruption to a minimum, and introduced a high standard of efficiency in general. Nevertheless, Commissioner Williams, after a year in office, confessed that though he believed it was possible to keep evil practices well within bounds and give immigrants proper treatment while in the charge of the government, he did not believe "that the millennium can ever exist here." Veteran Immigration Service officer though he was, Watchorn was staggered by the size and complexity of the operation of Ellis Island after he took over in 1905. "To receive, examine, and dispose of 821,169 aliens in one fiscal year," he reported, "is a work so stupendous that none but painstaking students of the immigration service could possibly have any intelligent conception of what arduous duties and unusual considerations it involves." Two years later, when he was under sharp attack, he declared to Secretary Straus that "A saint from heaven actuated by all his saintliness would fail to give satisfaction at this place." [1]

While Williams and Watchorn differed on admission policy, their administrations were in most respects continuous. Both sought to protect the arriving aliens from abuse, larceny, and fraud, on Ellis Island and while approaching and leaving it; both administered the laws strictly but with humanity; both fought battles with powerful interests that profited from the immigrant traffic; both sought to make the physical plant adequate to its desperate needs.

Williams not only made a clean sweep of the old concessionaires for food, money exchange, and baggage service, but also kept a sharp eye on the numerous other agencies represented on the island. One of his early actions was to order off the island an Italian banker who had been allowed to operate there cashing drafts on him drawn by the Bank of Naples. A great many immigrants had been changing their small savings into these drafts and presenting them to the banker on their arrival. He managed the business badly, Williams said. His stand drew a crowd that obstructed operations within the station, and his operation was illegal and unnecessary. The banker brought his case before the Italian ambassador, but Williams stood his ground.[2]

A telegraph boy who had given an immigrant counterfeit coin was promptly sent to jail on Williams's charges. A notice was issued immediately: "Swindling immigrants is contemptible business, and whoever does this, under whatever form, should be despised. It is the duty of all Government officials to go out of their way to protect immigrants against every kind of imposition. Let everyone at Ellis Island clearly understand that all impositions, whenever detected, will be punished as severely as the law permits." Williams's high standards of courtesy as well as honesty were made applicable not only to government employees but also to concession employees. Each official observing any violation on the part of any concession employee, of the order directing that immigrants be treated with kindness and consideration, "will if he fails to report the same be severely dealt with," Williams instructed the supervising inspector. "The Chief of the Deportation Division will direct the officials having charge of detained immigrants pending meal hours, to particularly note the manner in which they are treated while in the dining room, to put an immediate stop to any rough treatment by any waiter and to report any such fact to me, with all details." Similar action was to be taken with reference to employees in the railroad department. "They must," he directed, "maintain the same standard of courtesy that is required of Government officials."[3]

Watchorn kept the lines of discipline tight. On one occasion he suspended a watchman and wrote to the secretary hoping that it could be found practicable to prosecute the man and send him to prison, "for if ever a theft was deliberately and wickedly committed it was by this officer, who, wearing the uniform of the United States Government Service, took advantage of his official connection to rob this confiding immigrant." A case like this, he said, was likely to spread the idea that Ellis Island "is still a den of thieves." When some Jersey City detectives, engaged in an investigation of their own, passed through the island disguised as immigrants and reported to their chief that they had been abused, Watchorn wrote at once for specific data. "I should esteem it a very great favor if they could be sent here to me personally," he requested, "in order that I may have them identify the persons who abused them as well as to learn the exact nature of the abuse complained of. It is just such testimony as they are able to give that I most sorely stand in need of." After Williams returned to duty at Ellis Island he recommended the dismissal from the service of a watchman on the charge "that he had struck an immigrant in order to wake him by striking the canvas of the bed on which he was sleeping." [4]

Tales of a father's or grandfather's sorrows at Ellis Island form part of the legends of millions of American families. As a rule they have not lost drama in the telling. They are likely to be confused, however, with harsh experiences in the steerage or on the barges that brought the immigrants to the island, and with tribulations in the vicinity of the Barge Office after leaving it. The actual time spent at the island by the average immigrant was only a few hours. For the overwhelming majority who were cleared in the primary inspection line and departed the same day, passage through Ellis Island was probably not the most traumatic part of their experience in reaching the new land. For those who were detained briefly or at length in the overcrowded quarters there, caught in the meshes of the law, and for those finally excluded, it was another story. It was chiefly around these unfortunates that the evil legend of Ellis Island grew.

What was it like to go through Ellis Island as an immigrant during that station's busiest period from 1901 to 1914, when immigrant arrivals at the Port of New York rose from just under 400,000 the first year to over 1,000,000 in 1907 and later again approached that figure? Broughton Brandenburg and his wife went to Italy and back in steerage in 1903 to gather material for magazine articles. They saw much brutality in the steerage of a German ship carrying chiefly Italian immigrants, but the examination at Ellis Island, though conducted at the end of a long day when the inspectors were tired, they found no great ordeal. "The more I saw of the inside of the great system at the Island," Brandenburg reported, "the more I was struck with its thoroughness and the kindly, efficient manner in which the law was enforced." Brandenburg was an American and perhaps subconsciously defensive about Ellis Island because it was an American institution. Anyway, he had had a hard time in the steerage, and Ellis Island was, he knew, the last hurdle to home and comfort.[5]

Other observers were not so favorably impressed. Edward Steiner, himself an immigrant of the old Castle Garden days, later professor in an American college, made many trips back and forth in steerage gathering material for books. In 1905 he landed at Ellis Island with a mixed group of immigrants. Steiner did not minimize the real dread with which his fellow travelers approached the island on the crowded barges, their bewilderment at the strange routine, nor the tragedy of separated families and the hopelessness of those destined for probable deportation. "Let no one believe that landing on the shores of 'The land of the free and the home of the brave' is a pleasant experience," he emphasized; "it is a hard, harsh fact, surrounded by the grinding machinery of the law, which sifts, picks, and chooses; admitting the fit and excluding the weak and helpless." Nevertheless, Steiner believed, "The hardships which attend the examination and deportation of immigrants seem unavoidable, and would not be materially reduced if any other method was devised."

Steiner reserved most of his hard words for the steamship companies that brought the immigrants to Ellis Island. Many of them, he declared, "still practice their ancient wrongs upon their most profitable passengers." There should, he said, be an immediate demand for the abolition of the steerage.[6] Unfortunately, the steerage hung on for a long time. When it did finally disappear, it was not for humanitarian reasons but in response to changing economic circumstances.

Paul Knaplund, an intelligent young Norwegian arriving at Ellis Island in 1906, thought that "the newcomers were pushed around a good deal," but concluded that this might be "perhaps an inevitable result of their being so numerous and unfamiliar with the language of the officials." He "had the feeling that he was not being treated as a human being but as a commodity to be processed." Stephen Graham, a British author arriving in steerage from Liverpool in 1913, had the same dehumanized sensation. He thought that the inspection process illustrated "the mechanical obsession of the American people" and commented that "this ranging and guiding and hurrying and sifting was like nothing so much as the screening of coal in a great breaker tower." "It is not good," he observed, "to be like a hurrying, bumping, wandering piece of coal being mechanically guided to the sacks of its type and size, but such is the lot of the immigrant at Ellis Island." [7]

What was it like to work at Ellis Island during this period, examining the immigrants? Fortunately, some thoughtful reminiscences are at hand. Victor Safford, who joined the medical staff at the old station in 1895 and stayed on well into the heyday of the new, compared the medical examination of aliens at Ellis Island to the examination of an automobile for purchase. It was well to see both in motion as well as at rest. Defects, derangements, and symptoms of disease were often recognizable by watching a person twenty-five feet away. The value of this observation, Safford said, was not to see what was wrong, but to see quickly that something was wrong and put proper examination procedure in operation. The "line inspection," which took place at the head of the stairs which the immigrants had just climbed into the great examination hall, was so arranged that the medical officer could scrutinize the immigrant first as he approached, then as he came close at hand. Provision was made for close examination of hands, eyes, and throat. The inspection process might seem to the spectator a rapid, hasty procedure, but no limit was placed on the time taken for the subsequent medical examination of those detained.

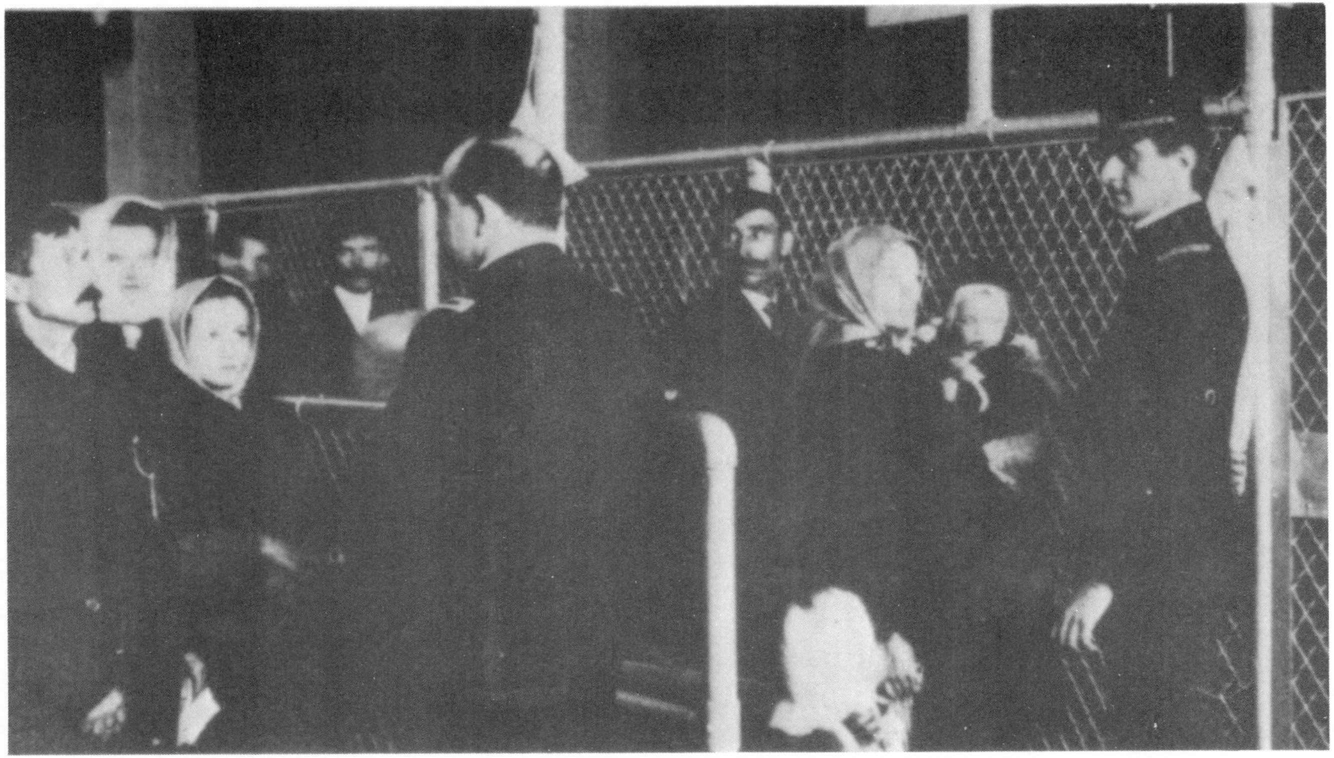

Line medical inspection of immigrants at Ellis Island about 1910. Often they did not realize that they were under inspection until they reached the end of the line.
—*Courtesy of the New York Public Library*

If an immigrant had just carried his baggage upstairs, the condition of his heart could be judged; the carrying of luggage also made lameness more noticeable and revealed deformities and posture defects. By having the immigrant hold an identification card in his hand after it was stamped, defects of eyesight were disclosed, as he always looked at the card to see what had been done. Aliens were also required to make two right-angle turns, thus bringing both sides of the face into view, revealing expressions indicating abnormal mental condition and other defects.[8]

The system that Safford described as in use in the early 1900s was still in use, with only a few variations, toward the close of the period. In 1913 Dr. Alfred C. Reed, of the U.S. Public Health Service staff at Ellis Island, described the work of the medical staff as it then operated. The twenty-five medical officers were divided into three sections: the boarding division, the hospital, and the line. The boarding division, based at the Barge Office in Battery Park, made the inspection of aliens in the first- and second-class cabins as the liners came up the bay from Quarantine. The hospital division operated the two hospitals on Ellis Island, the general hospital on Island No. 2 and the contagious disease hospital on Island No. 3. The line division inspected the steerage passengers as they were brought to the island in barges from the landing piers. While the hospitals were well equipped and now included such specialists as officers "specially trained in the diagnosis and observation of mental disorders," the line inspection was still conducted in much the same manner that Safford recalled.[9]

Once an alien had cleared the medical officers at one end of the examination hall, he was herded into one of the pipe-railed alleyways that led to the desks of the immigration inspectors at the other end. Any inspector on the line had the power to admit him at once if he considered the alien "clearly and beyond a doubt entitled to land." On a busy day the inspector had about two minutes in which to make this vital decision. If he had doubts and marked the alien for detention, he set in motion procedures that sometimes became involved.

When Edward Corsi was commissioner of immigration at Ellis Island many years later, immigration had been reduced to a trickle. He spent much time reading the files on interesting cases and listening to the reminiscences of old-time staff members. One of these was Frank Martocci, an interpreter. Corsi thought that the inspection routine must have been very different in the days of peak immigration. Martocci agreed emphatically. "I can well remember," he told Corsi, "for at that time I was in the registry department, assigned to decide the eligibility of aliens to land. To make things run fairly smoothly in that mixed crowd of poor, bewildered immigrants, we would tag them with numbers corresponding to numbers on their manifests, after they had been landed from the barges and taken into the building. Here in the main building, they were lined up—a motley crowd in colorful costumes, all ill at ease and wondering what was to happen to them." The medical inspection came first, "and whenever a case aroused suspicion, the alien was set aside in a cage apart from the rest, for all the world like a segregated animal, and his coat lapel or shirt marked with colored chalk, the color indicating why he had been isolated. These methods, crude as they seem, had to be used, because of the great numbers and the language difficulties."

All the aliens who had run this gauntlet successfully were grouped according to their manifest numbers and channeled into the inspection lines. While the arrangement of the examination hall was changed more than once, Martocci remembered that at one time there were twenty-two lines of inspection. "Every manifest held thirty names, but one inspector never got all thirty." Some had been detained by the doctors, and others had been held back for other reasons. The inspector sat at the end of the line with his manifest before him and proceeded to cross-question the alien. Before a barrage of questions such as sex? married status? occupation? where born? where last resided? where going? by whom was the passage paid? is that person in the United States or not? if so, how long? to whom is the alien going? the immigrant would do his best, wondering what it was all about and when and how it would end. The rush periods, chiefly spring and early summer, stood out in Martocci's memory. "Three or four times a week," he told Corsi, "from nine o'clock in the morning to nine in the evening, we were continuously examining aliens. I thought it was a stream that would never end. Every twenty-four hours from three to five thousand people came before us, and I myself examined from four to five hundred a day. We were simply swamped by that human tide." [10]

Immigrants who were passed by both the medical officers and the immigration inspectors—usually 80 percent or more of the total—passed downstairs. There they met their friends and took the ferryboat to New York or went to the railroad waiting room–ticket office to await the barges that would take them to the railroad terminals on the New Jersey shore for passage inland. The detainees who had been screened from the inspection line were of many types and were held for varying periods. Those held on medical grounds were either physically ill, in which case they were hospitalized, or had easily detectable physical or mental deficiencies making their legal admission doubtful. In either case, they were under the care of the medical division until preliminary determination was made by the medical staff of their right to land. A board of inquiry, taking the medical findings into consideration, made the final determination of their admissibility, but after the passage of the immigration law of 1903 medical certificates excluding immigrants because of disease were held to be binding on the boards of inquiry.[11]

Many aliens without funds of their own, but claiming to have relatives or friends who would care for them until they found work, were held briefly until funds came by letter or telegram, or a responsible person arrived to meet them. Mostly women and children, these aliens were "temporary detainees." Separate quarters were assigned to them as far as was possible. If no money

"The World's Greatest Clearing-House for Immigrants." Inspection of immigrants in the great registry room in 1905. The medical inspection is taking place near the head of the stairs; the final interrogation goes on at the far end of the room.
—*Courtesy of the New York Public Library*

came and no one called for them within five days, it was the general practice to turn them over to a missionary society or deport them, at their own choice.[12]

Aliens were held for immediate action by boards of inquiry for a wide variety of reasons. A foreign government might have sent the word that a man was a wanted criminal; a labor union might have passed the tip that a group of aliens were contract laborers; or a deserted wife might have reported a runaway husband. They might, from 1903 on, be suspected anarchists, panderers, polygamists, or prostitutes. The great bulk of them, however, were held because, on first inspection, they were suspected of being contract laborers, paupers whose passage had been paid by some foreign jurisdiction anxious to get rid of them, or—the most numerous class of all—they were believed "likely to become a public charge" for one or more of a variety of reasons. If their cases were passed on at once and they were ordered deported, they were sent out, sometimes on the same ship they had arrived on, but usually on the next ship of the line that had brought them, within one or two weeks. If they appealed an adverse decision their stay might be longer, but protracted detentions, except for hospital treatment, were uncommon in this period of Ellis Island's history.

Statistics now available on the various types of detentions are fragmentary, but the evidence is clear that temporary detentions were by far the most numerous, followed by detentions for special inquiry and, far down the scale, detentions for hospitalization. Detentions in all categories might run as high as 20 percent of all aliens received, but those awaiting funds, the temporary detainees, usually made up far more than half the total. Hospitalization detainees rarely ran over 1 percent of total alien admissions, and board of inquiry detentions rarely more than 10 percent. For instance, in 1907 there were 195,540 detentions and a total of 1,004,756 admissions at the Port of New York. Of the detentions, 121,737 were temporary, 64,510 were for special inquiry, and 9,293 were for hospitalization. Exclusions following board-of-inquiry action never ran much over 15 or 20 percent of the cases heard. In 1914, against a total of 878,052 admissions, there were 175,580 detentions of all classes; of these, approximately 70,000 were held for special inquiry and 16,588 were finally excluded. Maximum exclusions on a percentage basis occurred in 1911: approximately 13,000 against 637,000 admissions, or just over 2 percent. Ellis Island was also the point of deportation for aliens who had entered the United States illegally or had become public charges since their legal admission, and who had been picked up in New York, New Jersey, or at more distant points. Such deportations were not always listed in the annual reports as distinct from exclusions, but they formed a relatively small proportion of the total during this period.[13]

Among those who preyed on trusting immigrants were shyster lawyers; they had been a pest at Ellis Island ever since the law of 1893 had brought more formal and detailed examination procedures, boards of special inquiry, and

Hearing of a detained alien before a board of special inquiry. Improved board rooms such as this were provided in 1911.

—Courtesy of the New York Public Library

increased detentions and deportations. Both Senner and Fitchie had tried to cope with them. Williams was ruthless with them. They were usually foreign born themselves, and preyed upon their own nationals, but occasionally an American law firm with a good front and a good professional address would go into the business. Such a firm reported to him by the Society for the Protection of Italian Immigrants as having charged an Italian immigrant $30 for alleged services in securing the release of his son, "an alien who had already been deported," was disbarred from practice at any immigration station in the United States. By the rules of the department, lawyers were permitted to charge only $10 for appearing in behalf of a detained alien, and this firm had done nothing for its excessive fee.

When Watchorn had his attention called to a crooked lawyer's advertisement in the foreign language press, he wrote sharply to the man. It had come to his notice, he said, that in this advertisement "it is stated that you are acquainted with the authorities at Ellis Island and guarantee to procure the admission of Bulgarians and Macedonians, by reason by such acquaintance." Such a statement, as the lawyer was well aware, was without foundation, "and the knowledge this office has obtained of you and your transactions in the past would not be conducive to the result which you claim to be able to accomplish. Unless such misleading statements are eliminated from your advertisements, I shall be compelled to take the necessary action to abate this evil." [14]

In spite of their best efforts, aided by the better immigrant aid societies, Williams and Watchorn could never eradicate this evil. As the North American Civic League for Immigrants reported in 1911, many nationalities had no organized legal assistance "and are preyed upon by shyster lawyers." Immigration regulations provided for expulsion from Ellis Island of lawyers overcharging aliens, "and from August 1904 to October 1908 there were some 25 attorneys disbarred from the Island." But these actions came up only on complaints by immigrants. Of course, many never complained or even knew that they were being overcharged.[15]

Nor was it possible to get rid of the swindlers that mingled with the immigrants in the crowded conditions that prevailed at Ellis Island during rush periods. Conditions were worse at the Barge Office, but it was comparatively easy to get a pass to the island from a steamship company when one of its ships was coming in. Friends, relatives, and petty racketeers mingled on the ferryboat. The island swarmed with visitors, in spite of efforts to discourage them. A young Polish immigrant, who had just been admitted and was about to leave the main building for the ferryboat, was approached by a man in uniform who demanded to see his money. The immigrant had a new fifty-dollar bill that he had just received in exchange for his Russian money. He displayed it, and the man in uniform took it and told him it was no good. He gave the young Pole an Argentine nickel coin worth about four cents. On the alien's complaint a search was made for the swindler, but the man had disappeared.

When a reporter asked officials in the commissioner's office "how it was that a swindler could dress up in a uniform and walk about in the immigration office to rob the ignorant immigrants," he was told that "men come from New York to the island with caps and uniform jackets in their pockets, and that it was hard to keep them out." [16]

Detained immigrants probably never had a very happy time, and often there was very real suffering in the crowded dormitories into which they were locked. There were those that recounted their experiences in lurid and highly exaggerated terms to the press. The Rev. Sydney H. Bass, a British subject, complained at great length to the Washington office about his treatment at Ellis Island, and afterward gave his story to the *New York Journal* when it was collecting ammunition to fire at Williams. The commissioner-general forwarded his letter to the island, and Williams answered it in full. The reverend gentleman had been held in a room that reminded him of "The Black Hole of Calcutta," he said, and he had been very badly treated generally. Williams had gone into the case thoroughly and found that most of his complaints were either gross exaggerations or downright lies. "It would seem," Williams concluded, "that Mr. Bass found solace in only two things while he was at Ellis Island–his reading of the Scriptures and a 'fig' given him during the night by a fellow immigrant. . . . I do not know what part of the Scriptures he read; but he either failed to read, or reading it he failed to heed, the ninth commandment–'Thou shalt not bear false witness against thy neighbor.' " [17]

Immigrants themselves, in fact, caused a great deal of trouble to the officials at Ellis Island by giving false information. The addresses on the manifests, to which the immigrants said they were going, often proved to be inaccurate. On one ship in 1904, it was found that of 105 immigrants who said they were going to New York City, 46 gave faulty addresses, "some of them relating to places which were empty lots." It was hard to say why this was done or who had done it. If it could be shown that the steamship line was responsible, Williams noted to the commissioner-general, of course fines could be imposed. He asked for suggestions for dealing with this vicious practice, which vitiated the government statistics on immigration and was likely to lead immigrants astray. The Washington office was not very helpful, suggesting only that fire insurance maps showing street numbers and buildings be checked. Sometimes the manifests showed a group of immigrants going to the address of an immigrant banker in New York, when actually they were headed for California or elsewhere inland. Often they did not have tickets or enough money to buy tickets. This left them at the mercy of the banker. There was no way of knowing whether the immigrant would leave New York with funds or not. "It is left," Williams explained in one case during his first administration, "to the banker to decide whether or not he is to become a public charge." He thought the practice of immigrant bankers and ticket brokers advertising abroad should be prohibited. There was protection as well as ticket service at Ellis Island.[18]

Later on, Williams would deport in such cases, unless the banker came promptly to Ellis Island with cash and tickets in his hand.

Manifest sheets almost invariably showed the immigrants as having paid for their own tickets, although it was well known that most of them were assisted in one way or another. On questioning, the alien usually insisted that he had paid for his ticket, and there was no way of disproving it. If an arriving alien had been properly coached, as he usually was, he knew how to steer between the Scylla and Charybdis of deportation as a contract laborer and deportation as likely to become a public charge. Fiorello La Guardia, later mayor of New York City, was an interpreter at Ellis Island for several years during its busiest period. "Common sense," he said in his memoirs many years later, "suggested that any immigrant who came into the United States in those days to settle here permanently surely came here to work. However, under the law, he could not have any more than a vague hope of a job." In answering the inspectors' questions, immigrants had to be very careful, La Guardia explained, because "if their expectations were too enthusiastic, they might be held as coming in violation of the contract labor provision. Yet, if they were too indefinite, if they knew nobody, had no idea where they were going to get jobs, they might be excluded as likely to become public charges." Many were tripped up and deported on the one charge or the other; most performed the intellectual balancing act successfully. La Guardia thought that most of the inspectors were fair as well as conscientious. They were not infallible, and there were a good many deportations in what seemed to him to be borderline cases.[19]

Sometimes an alien, to establish that he was not likely to become a public charge, would claim a skill that he did not possess. If it were feasible, the board of inquiry would give him a chance to demonstrate. Williams reported to the commissioner-general on the appeal of a man and his wife who had $3.20 between them. He claimed to be a carpenter, and he had been sent to the Ellis Island carpenter shop. The shop foreman reported that "He doesn't know how to use the ordinary carpenter's tools and cannot recommend him as such a mechanic." In addition, it had been impossible to locate an aunt to whom the couple wished to go. Williams thought that the board of inquiry was right in excluding the couple.

Philip Cowen, after he entered the Immigration Service at Ellis Island, served for some time on boards of inquiry. He thought that as a general thing the immigrant told the truth. "Not so the witnesses that appear in his behalf," said Cowen. "They want to make an impression of importance before the Board and so overstate their earnings and savings." It was a common thing for them to show false bank books on the immigrant banks that then existed in great numbers, or money that they had borrowed for the occasion. Many people made a business of loaning money for this purpose. In later times, after the federal income tax had been established, this practice was curbed by having Internal Revenue Service men sit with the boards of inquiry and demand proof from the witnesses of having paid income tax based on the earnings they claimed to impress the boards and their greenhorn friends. The false testimony presented by friends at board hearings early became a serious problem. On Williams's suggestion, the secretary of commerce and labor in 1903 presented to the attorney general a dossier of documents on the subject. "The said papers," he said, "have relation to the admissions of certain aliens at Ellis Island in consequence of statements made by friends appearing in their behalf before the Board of Special Inquiry, which statements afterwards proved to be utterly false." He wanted the case placed in the hands of the U.S. attorney at New York with a view to having the persons mentioned prosecuted.[20]

Resident aliens eager to have their relatives passed and admitted by the boards of inquiry would often make lavish promises of aid. Sometimes they repented and became delinquent in fulfilling their obligations. "Your son," Williams wrote to a man in New York, "is a public charge, as you doubtless know. You also know that you were instrumental in inducing the Government to allow him to land on the ground that you, his father, were here to look after him although it felt that he was clearly a proper subject for deportation at the time when he arrived. What have you to say? Please reply by return mail."

Occasionally immigrants with trachoma or some other disease making them subject to deportation would be accepted for treatment in the Ellis Island hospital on the promise of relatives to pay the costs. Watchorn reported a case of this sort in which a husband and father was delinquent in the amount of $62 for medical treatment for his wife and little daughter, both suffering from trachoma. Trachoma was a stubborn disease, and they had been in the hospital more than six months. In reply the Washington office told Watchorn that the man had asked to be relieved from paying the expenses of treatment, "in response to which he was apprised that this could not be done and instructed to deposit the required amount for the month of March." As the man continued delinquent, and as the government could pay no part of the expenses in such a case, the wife and daughter were ordered deported on the next ship of the line that had brought them.[21]

Missionary activity, actually or professedly in the interests of the immigrants, had been a prominent feature of the operation of Castle Garden. It continued so at Ellis Island. *Leslie's Weekly*, viewing the new administration of Commissioner Williams in 1902 and giving it enthusiastic approval, also had words of praise for the missionaries. "One of the notable features of the care taken of the immigrants," it reported, "is the attention paid to them by missionaries of several religious denominations and the agents of benevolent societies." These people were continually on the watch for cases of need and distress, and had been the means of preventing injustice and affording succor in countless instances. "The work they are doing," said *Leslie's*, "is of the kind that merits unstinted praise." [22]

Williams's own view of the missionaries, as he became familiar with the intricacies of the vast beehive of the immigration station, was more reserved. One of his early actions was to exclude missionaries from the examination floor while examinations were going on. There were protests, and the *New York Tribune* sent a reporter over to inquire into the matter. "I have taken this step," Williams said, "because the upper room is crowded and I desire to have the work done as quickly as possible. The representatives of the societies are at liberty to meet the immigrants anywhere else." In fact, he cooperated fully with legitimate missionary societies, but he came to see that there were some that differed little from the old-style immigrant boardinghouses. He was severe with those that he believed to be primarily commercial in character, and from time to time ejected their representatives from the island. In informing the head of the Lutheran Immigrant Home that neither he nor anyone representing him would be allowed to come to Ellis Island or the Barge Office any longer, he said, "I propose to draw a line between the true missionaries (of which there are a number on Ellis Island) and the boarding-house runners who, parading under false colors, are for that reason the most dangerous people to whom an immigrant may be turned over." Commissioner-General Sargent congratulated him, saying, "This scoundrel ought to be treated to a coat of tar and feathers and cast off the island, without any regard to his means of transportation to the mainland." Representatives of a Polish immigrants' home, a home for Scandinavian immigrants, and an Austro-Hungarian home were also expelled from Ellis Island during Williams's first term.[23]

Under Watchorn's regime immigrant aid societies seeking to place agents at Ellis Island were carefully investigated as to their standing and the purposes for which they desired representation. On the commissioner's recommendation, the Bureau of Immigration gave them authority to visit the detention rooms to interview aliens of their nationality. These agents were not to try to secure the landing of an alien by misrepresentation to the inspectors or boards of inquiry, nor were they permitted to exact any fee for their services. If any agent abused the privileges accorded, the commissioner-general informed an inquiring official in Buffalo, "the society was requested to withdraw him." Watchorn required a monthly report from every society, giving full data on all aliens turned over to it. When it came to his attention that the agent of the Hungarian Relief Society had requested Hungarians in West Virginia to telegraph money to relatives at Ellis Island, though the arriving aliens were actually already provided for, he wrote sharply to the society. In one case, he pointed out, "the Board of Special Inquiry admitted the alien before receipt of the remittance in question, indicating clearly that no additional amount of money was deemed essential. I shall be pleased to receive your explanation of the occurrence."[24]

Watchorn also sought to curb excessive religious zeal at Ellis Island. In a speech delivered at an annual meeting of the American Tract Society, he told the members frankly to keep their hands off Jews arriving at the station, to whom they had been distributing Christian tracts in Yiddish and Hebrew. There was no little consternation when he told them: "A great many of our immigrants are Hebrews, who are on their way from persecution by one style of Christians, and when they have Christian tracts—printed in Hebrew—put in their hands, apparently with the approval of the United States Government, they wonder what is going to happen to them there." There would be over a million immigrants come to our shores that year, he said, of whom more than 800,000, perhaps, would be strangers who were not Jews. "It seems to me that ought to afford a pretty large field for the society." Later, after he had issued an order forbidding the practice, he was interrupted in speaking before the John D. Rockefeller, Jr., Bible class, by a woman who asked him if it were true that on Ellis Island he refused to permit the use of the words "Jesus Christ." He did not forbid the use of those words, he replied, but he did "refuse to allow missionaries to go among the Jewish immigrants, many of whom are fresh from persecutions abroad. I insist that the missionaries wait until the immigrants have rested from the effects of the hardships to which they have been subjected in countries in which their persecutors said they did their work for Christianity's sake."

An official of the American Tract Society wrote to the White House complaining about the order, charging that it was a result of Secretary Straus's sympathy with the Hebrew people. This gave President Roosevelt a chance such as he loved to deliver a moral lecture. He dictated a reply pointing out that Secretary Straus had not been aware of the existence of the order and reminding the clergyman that Straus had been of considerable assistance to his society in Turkey when he was the American ambassador there. "The President feels," the reply concluded, "that while the immigrants are in the Government's care missionaries, whether Protestant, Catholic, or Jewish, should work among their coreligionists so as to avoid any appearance of proselyting. Mr. Watchorn is a Presbyterian and a brother of a Presbyterian minister, and it is nonsense to suppose that he is inimical to the interests that you represent." [25]

By the time that Williams returned to Ellis Island, both the U.S. Immigration Commission and the New York State Immigration Commission had made extensive investigations into the operations of immigrant homes and aid societies. Among other abuses that they found, they had come up with the unpleasant information "that many women agents for disorderly houses had been in the habit of obtaining women to work in such houses from some of the so-called immigrant homes." In all cases, Congressman Bennet, a member of the federal commission, told a *New York Times* reporter, "the girls had no idea of the character of the places to which they were to go."

The official reports were not so charitable. The state commission found that most of the immigrant homes, though supported by charity, charged for board and lodging; that almost all of them acted as employment agencies and usually charged for their services; that in some of the homes the sanitary conditions were not good; and that "the protection afforded women, in every case but one, was found to be inadequate." The references they obtained from employers were not always satisfactory, and even when they were the woman might leave on the very next day and her whereabouts be unknown. Procurers who imported women sometimes utilized immigrant homes for their purposes, instructing the women to appear helpless in order to be sent to a home, where they notified their employers. The commission found one home "willing to send a girl to work in a disorderly house for five dollars." Pertinent information was turned over to Williams, he made further investigations of his own, and a new flurry of expulsions from Ellis Island followed. For a time, he stopped the long-standing practice of discharging to homes certain classes of aliens, especially young women, who had no money. Thereafter, he announced, they must stay on the island until their friends called for them. By the end of his second term, he believed that the false missionaries had been pretty well routed from the island.[26]

The principal concession contracts at Ellis Island, awarded to reputable firms in 1902, came up for renewal three years later. Congressman Herbert Parsons, shortly to become county leader and President Roosevelt's lieutenant in the New York County Republican organization, wrote to the commissioner-general in behalf of Bernard Biglin, expressing the hope that he would be awarded the baggage contract. Parsons had been eager to help turn the rascals out of Ellis Island three years before, but he had tasted power since then, and accepted the burden of keeping the minority Republican party in New York City supplied with all the patronage available. Federal agencies, including the custom house and the immigration station at Ellis Island, were among the best sources of patronage for the party that controlled the national administration but not the local one. Parsons privately deplored the fact that Ellis Island was heavily staffed with Cleveland Democrats who had been protected since 1896 by classified civil service status, and sought to place good Republican party workers there. He did not always get what he wanted, but his recommendations were received with great respect.[27]

The juiciest plums at Ellis Island, however, were not jobs but concession contracts. Barney Biglin was a Republican with considerable influence, and had had the baggage contract at Castle Garden. His office, by overcharging immigrants and dilatory delivery of their baggage, had caused the New York State commissioners of emigration much grief and brought them a great deal of criticism. He held on through the first period at the Barge Office and transferred his business to Ellis Island. In 1893 he was found charging more than the contract rate for delivering baggage, and Commissioner Weber threatened to have his contract terminated. He evidently lost out to a Democrat during the next administration, but bobbed up again at the Barge Office after the fire at the island and held the baggage contract until 1902. Biglin did not get the principal baggage contract back in 1905, in spite of Parson's influential sponsorship, but he did obtain subsidiary contracts for taking immigrants and baggage to the Grand Central Station for the New Haven Railroad, and to the boats of the Fall River and Norwich lines, a work he had been engaged in almost continuously since Castle Garden days.

Commissioner Watchorn considered Biglin and his associate, Peter McDonnell, the baggage contractor for the Old Dominion Line, a couple of "importunate and contentious leeches," who had "risen from the position of porter, or runner, to the rank of several times millionaire,—out of immigrants." They would, he said, "destroy me utterly if they could, for having dared to question the methods they have, until recently pursued." He had withstood for eighteen months, he wrote the secretary confidentially, "an army of politicians" who had pressured him in their behalf, and he had forced Biglin and McDonnell to take passengers and baggage by direct boat passage from Ellis Island to the piers of the steamship lines, instead of routing them through the city. But Biglin, whose contract also called for taking immigrants from the Barge Office to Grand Central Station in covered wagons fully provided with seats, at 50 cents a head, took them instead by subway and pocketed "the poor immigrant's 45 cents—several hundred per diem—to swell his similarly acquired millions." Watchorn wanted a regulation to put an end to this. He could not stand the strain much longer without it, he said.[28]

Watchorn later wanted to abolish Biglin's contract and to have railroad and steamship tickets from Ellis Island to all distant points cover the passage from the island to railroad stations or steamship piers. He finally got authority to void Biglin's contract and bar him from Ellis Island, in spite of the latter's political backing, "until a contract is made between the Department of Commerce and Labor and the transportation lines for which he has acted as agent for many years." The New Haven Railroad objected strenuously to making such a contract and, on its definite refusal to do so, Watchorn ordered Biglin, "after thirty years at the immigration station as baggage transfer agent," to move his belongings from the island.

But this was only a temporary victory for Watchorn, won at the evident cost of alienating the New York County Republican organization. When the concession contracts came up for renewal in 1908, Biglin's bid for the baggage contract was accepted and he returned in triumph to Ellis Island. Watchorn apparently gave up the fight against him, but Williams on his return renewed it, after an interval, with the support of the Taft administration. "My written complaints against him," he told Secretary Nagel in 1911, "do not in any way convey an adequate idea of the just causes of complaint which the Government has against him." Williams was "satisfied that immigrants have been through his bad methods overcharged to the extent of thousands and thousands of dollars." Barney Biglin's contract was finally terminated under a face-saving mutual rescission agreement, and Williams tried to make sure that a bid was never accepted from him again.[29]

Even more lucrative than the baggage contract was the food concession. Detained immigrants were no longer fed on prunes and bread, as they had sometimes been in the past; food was plentiful, if plain, and officials of the commissioner's office checked the menu daily to see that it stayed that way. On complaint, special foods were served to both individual and group detainees. But although the detainees no longer went hungry, the profits of the contract seem to have been considerable, and there was always keen competition for it at renewal time.

Hudgins & Dumas, the contractors whom Williams had installed in 1902, confidently expected to win a renewal three years later, but they were disappointed. Commissioner-General Sargent came to Ellis Island and conferred at length with Watchorn before awarding the contracts. When the awards were announced, the *New York Tribune* said: "There were reports that Sargent, in line with Watchorn's demand, had recommended that Hudgins & Dumas, the present restaurant contract holders, have the contract for three years, but that Secretary Metcalf had turned him down. Sargent denied this and so did Metcalf." Evidently Watchorn had been satisfied with the service rendered by Hudgins & Dumas, for he told a *Tribune* reporter in Washington before the awards were made that "The present holders of the restaurant privilege are giving first class meals, nicely served, and cooked in a kitchen as clean as mine at home." [30]

In 1908 the bidding at Ellis Island was again spirited. There was most interest in the food contract. Harry Balfe, the current contractor, had won three years before from Hudgins & Dumas, who had improved the service of the old days "when food was doled out by helpers regardless of sanitation, and when immigrants were impressed into the service of serving food." Balfe had further improved the service, the *Times* said; he had "opened new and improved eating rooms for immigrants and maintained a first-class restaurant for employees." It was generally believed on Ellis Island that his contract would be renewed. This time, though Balfe placed a low bid and Hudgins & Dumas bid even lower, the award was held up for months. A report had been sent to the president recommending that the contract be awarded to Balfe, and he had approved it. But attorneys for Hudgins & Dumas "got very busy," and the matter was reopened to permit some new facts to be presented. Hudgins & Dumas, it was reported, "are backed by Congressman Bennet, while Harry Balfe, a personal friend of the President, is backed by Timothy L. Woodruff," another Republican politician, at the time New York State chairman of the party. That the contract was a political football seems certain. The award was not made until October, and then went to one Fritz Brodt, both the leading bidders losing out.

Commissioner Watchorn evidently had limited control, at most, over the award, but later he was attacked venomously in connection with it. Balfe told the press that he was going to law in the matter, and Hudgins & Dumas became active. Letters denouncing the award began reaching the White House and were forwarded to Secretary Straus. As the letters "reflect upon the character, competency, and honesty of the Commissioner at Ellis Island," Straus said in returning them, he had referred them to Watchorn and he enclosed Watchorn's reply to the "insinuations and charges." Fritz Brodt's bid, he pointed out, was the lowest, $1,077,750, while Hudgins & Dumas had bid, on the same basis of estimate, $1,271,300. The lawyer making the charges for the latter firm, he noted, "seems to carefully avoid making any reflections upon me personally," but "I regard it no less an effort to cast reflections upon me in his endeavor to besmirch the character of the Assistant Secretary of this Department and the Commissioner at Ellis Island, in both of whom I have the fullest confidence." [31]

That winter, as the end of his second term approached, President Roosevelt nominated Watchorn for reappointment to a four-year term as commissioner of immigration at Ellis Island. Opposition developed in the Senate, and Watchorn's name was withdrawn pending an investigation. "Ever since Mr. Watchorn took charge of Ellis Island charges have been lodged with more or less frequency against him," the *New York Times* noted. "Many of these charges have been thoroughly investigated and were found to be absolutely without foundation in fact." For this reason the president would have the present charges investigated and be ready to present all the evidence to the Senate when Watchorn's name went in again. "It is declared that the strict interpretation of the immigration laws have won for Mr. Watchorn many powerful and insistent critics," said the *Times*, but the "particular accusation which is likely to bring forth an investigation was concerned with the last food contract for immigrants." At the White House, this journal noted, he was regarded as "somewhat in a class with" Dr. Harvey W. Wiley, father and administrator of the recent Pure Food and Drug Act.

Watchorn, accompanied by Secretary Straus, had a long conference with the president at the White House, and it was reported that his reappointment was practically certain. Secretary Straus said that the case had been turned over to him for disposition. "Secretary Straus has looked into these charges before and has supported Watchorn in all of them," said the *Times*. If no better evidence came up, Watchorn's name would go again to the Senate for confirmation. Straus designated Commissioner of Corporations Herbert Knox Smith to go to Ellis Island, look into the charges, and report. After what seems to have been a painstaking investigation, the charges were dismissed and Roosevelt sent Watchorn's name back to the Senate. By this time, however, the president's term was nearly over, it was the end of a crowded session, and no action could be had.[32]

When Williams got back to Ellis Island, he promptly found the food service unsatisfactory. Fritz Brodt was ousted, and Hudgins & Dumas got their old contract back again. After Williams's departure from the island, they in turn came under heavy attack. A prolonged investigation sponsored by the Bureau of Municipal Research and conducted under President Woodrow Wilson's new commissioner-general of immigration, Anthony Caminetti, took evidence for weeks. Accounts of the hearings seemed to indicate no great failure on the part of the food contractors, and the special commission that had conducted them dismissed all serious charges, while recommending some improvements in the restaurant service. The Bureau of Municipal Research, quite naturally, charged the commission with a whitewashing job. Just why an incoming Democratic administration should whitewash a holdover Republican contractor was not made clear.[33]

The small steamers and barges that brought the steerage passengers to Ellis Island from the landing piers, where the cabin passengers were discharged, were operated by a contractor for the steamship lines. The same vessels, under contract with the railroad lines, took inland-bound immigrants from Ellis Island to the railroad docks on the Jersey shore. They were old and slow vessels, and they were often badly overcrowded. Immigrants were hurried onto them and packed tightly, with their baggage, on open decks or in stifling cabins with inadequate toilet facilities and limited drinking water, regardless of weather. At the end of the trip to the island they sometimes had to wait for hours, on busy days, until their turn came to disembark for examination. Williams was troubled by this situation, over which he had little control, and in 1903 sought to do something about it. Finding that the Steamboat Inspection Service disclaimed any authority to remedy the evils that he had pointed out, he took the matter up with the secretary of the treasury. He asked permission to confer with the steamship companies and the owners of the barges, "with a view to obtaining some immediate relief for the immigrants from the conditions complained of. That you have the power to compel the granting of such relief seems to me beyond question."

The steamship lobby was a powerful one and nothing much seems to have happened, for Williams wrote again nearly two years later, complaining of the same evils to the commissioner-general. "The government has spent thousands of dollars in preparing for the reception of immigrants a station at which they are decently protected, housed, treated and fed," he pointed out. "It is altogether inappropriate that transportation companies should be allowed immediately before and afterwards to subject them to gross discomfort and even danger." Again no really constructive action followed, but Williams did get one measure of relief for immigrants detained for hours on the barges. The steamship companies were ordered to feed them when their landing at the island was unduly delayed.[34]

Watchorn took up the problem during his term at Ellis Island and tried to get authority to place watchmen on the steamboats and barges to prevent their overcrowding. This authority was first granted and then withdrawn, but he was advised to make an occasional count on days when immigration was heaviest, "to ascertain definitely whether overcrowding takes place." As the

Immigrants in barges in front of the main building. Sometimes they had to wait for hours in these crowded, seatless craft until their turn came for examination.
—*Courtesy of the New York Public Library*

crowding was notorious, this was a clear case of bureaucratic stalling. No record has been found that any material improvement took place in this unhappy situation during the period of heavy immigration ending with the outbreak of World War I. Immigrant accounts as late as 1913 bear witness to the seatless, crowded barges and the tedious wait in them.[35]

In 1903 twelve railroads and three coastal steamship lines were represented at Ellis Island. They operated as a pool, sharing the immigrant traffic to inland points. After an immigrant had been passed in the inspection line, he was turned over to the railroad pool to be forwarded. This was an arrangement of long standing, dating from Castle Garden days. Williams found that some immigrants destined to Chicago were sent by the Old Dominion Line to Norfolk, thence to Newport News, and thence to Chicago, the journey requiring from fifty-two to seventy-eight hours. This routing required them to pass through New York City. The fare was a little lower than by direct rail, but the time involved was much longer and the immigrant was exposed to more incidental expenses and hazards. Williams accordingly issued an office order to the effect that all immigrants should thereafter proceed directly to Chicago without passing through New York City unless they already held tickets or orders purchased in Europe requiring them to take another route. "The general policy of this office," he announced, "will be to prevent immigrants destined to western points from unnecessarily spending a night in or even passing through New York City, where they fall into the hands of unscrupulous people. Anyone, whether an official, privilege holder, or any other person at this station violating the terms of the foregoing, will be severely dealt with."

Commissioner-General Sargent, who knew from long experience the power of the railroad lobby, warned Williams that this order was well calculated to "stir up the animals." It seems to have had little effect. During his second administration, Williams tried again to control the routing of immigrants to the interior. The procedure was handled by the railroad pool, or Railroad Clearing House, on the principle of sharing the traffic without much consideration for the convenience of the immigrant. In his attempt to control the operations of the railroad pool, Williams, for once, had the backing of the steamship companies, which often sold through tickets to inland destinations only to have the routing changed by the pool. But the move threatened the breakup of the pool, with resulting chaotic conditions at Ellis Island, and was soon abandoned.[36]

Williams also investigated the treatment of immigrants on trains and sent inspectors by various routes to inland cities to check on conditions. The reports gathered evidently contained some rather grim material, but nothing much seems to have come of them, though Williams declared that any railroad maltreating its passengers should "be requested to show cause why it should not improve its methods, or be relieved of its privileges at Ellis Island."[37]

Watchorn proposed to build on Ellis Island a railroad terminal connected with the Jersey shore by trestle, so that immigrants going inland could avoid a second barge trip and the swarms of thieves and confidence men that preyed upon them in the railroad stations. He won approval from the Washington office, but the big railroad lines objected and offered instead to build their own immigrant terminals, separate from their regular passenger facilities. This was accepted, and Watchorn had the satisfaction of having the railroads come to him for help in designing the new facilities. Watchorn also tried, after investigation, to improve the treatment of immigrants on the trains. He brought the matter before the Interstate Commerce Commission, and hearings were held before a special examiner in New York. Watchorn's principal charge was that immigrants paid first-class rates but by no means received first-class accommodations. The railroads admitted the essential truth of the evidence presented. "The Government," the *New York Times* reported, "was not endeavoring to show that immigrants ought to have first-class service. The point aimed at was that the foreigners, ignorant, poor, and unable to speak English, should not be obliged to pay for something they failed to get."

The railroads seemed to want to settle, and asked for an adjournment to this end. Commissioner Watchorn would "have the support of public opinion in holding the railroads to the expected reform," the *Times* affirmed editorially. The evidence presented at the hearings "was something of a revelation to the prominent railroad people present," said the *American Hebrew,* "for before the testimony was half in they asked the privilege of a conference and agreed with Commissioner Watchorn to take up the matter outside of the Interstate Commission and adjust the prices." [38]

Just how much price reform actually took place is doubtful. The New York State Immigration Commission, which made its investigations in 1908, noted Watchorn's efforts of the previous year and tried to find out what had followed. His investigators had found that there was discrimination against immigrants in service, first-class rates being charged for the use of inferior cars and the tickets being limited while other first-class tickets were not; that proper food was unobtainable on immigrant cars and the immigrants themselves were not allowed to leave them; that the cars were unclean and not equipped with adequate toilet facilities or wash stands; that there was undue delay in the forwarding of aliens on longer journeys, which often started on so-called through trains, from which the aliens were required to transfer their children and baggage to other trains. "So far as the Commission has been able to learn," it was reported, "nothing has been done to remedy these abuses and railways have not, so far as the tariff shows, made any changes in their rates, or practices." The reduced immigration following the panic of 1907 had temporarily lessened the evils, but "any increase in the volume will again make them serious." The immigration did, indeed, increase in volume thereafter, and immigrant trains remained primitive throughout the period. In his last annual report, Williams recommended funds to permit inspection of immigrant trains "to considerable distances." [39]

Immigrants going to New York or its vicinity were taken on a government ferryboat from Ellis Island, with their baggage, to the Barge Office. On leaving its shelter they were fastened upon by a horde of leeches of all descriptions. Battery Park, in which Castle Garden stood, had been the haunt of unlicensed boardinghouse runners and other vultures for generations. With the revival of heavy immigration, they swarmed to the Barge Office, where the ferryboat from the island landed at regular intervals. With them were mingled often hundreds of friends of the immigrants eager to receive them. This mixed crowd sometimes threatened to storm the gates before the arriving aliens could be landed, and was beaten back by the police, who used their nightsticks freely. The situation became so bad in the spring of 1902 that Commissioner Fitchie received orders to investigate stories of police brutality to immigrants. Fitchie told newspaper reporters that the police were not beating immigrants, but the crowd seeking to get at them. The police on duty at the Barge Office told the same story: "The only way we can handle the crowd on a busy day is to make them stay on the opposite side of the street until the immigrants are landed and sent away. To do this, nothing short of absolute violence will avail. We drive them over the way, and before we are back at our posts they are on our heels again."

Collier's ran an article at this time, describing the sufferings of the mass of immigrants then coming in. Conditions were bad enough at Ellis Island, it said, where much sickness and even broken limbs from the steerage trip were encountered, but much worse at the Battery. "Many of the old schemes of the hawks who prey upon the simple immigrants, the schemes which were used in the old days of Castle Garden, have been revived." A combination had been formed between the drivers of express wagons and the proprietors of cheap lodginghouses for immigrants. When a boatload of immigrants landed at the Battery, they were confronted by a score of wagons backed to the edge of the sidewalk. The drivers would snatch the immigrants before their waiting friends knew they had landed and tumble them, almost forcibly, into the wagons. They would be driven out of their way, overcharged, hauled to boardinghouses where they were further fleeced, and sometimes had trouble getting away, even when they had the addresses of friends in the city. *Collier's* thought that the police, instead of protecting the immigrants, had "actually been aiding the sharpers . . . often beating the inoffensive foreigners and forcing them to take refuge in the first opportunity offered, and this refuge is the arms and the wagon of the eager 'runner.' " [40]

Such complaints brought a minimum of action, and there was a police ruling that express wagons had to stay on the other side of the street. "This practically broke up the expressmen's business," for the moment at least, "and most of the

Admitted immigrants landing from the ferryboat at the Barge Office. A mixed crowd just outside the gate is ready to pounce on them.

–Courtesy of the New York Public Library

immigrants got away without being molested." It was in 1902, and in large part due to the situation at the Battery, that the Society for the Protection of Italian Immigrants, with a governing board largely composed of prominent Americans, was formed. Commissioner Williams gave the society his active support, and Italian immigrants, at least, thereafter had some protection. But the evils were not eradicated and were not confined to the immediate vicinity of the Barge Office. In 1904 Williams sought help from Commissioner of Police William A. McAdoo. "If you were to find it possible to detail one or more men to make an investigation during a stated period of one or two weeks," he said, "and note the persons who follow the immigrants onto the elevated trains, and in other directions in which immigrants go in large numbers, I believe that it could be shown that many thieves make a practice to accost immigrants and take money from them, often times under threat." [41]

McAdoo assigned five experienced detective sergeants to the problem, and some improvement followed. Several arrests were made, and a number of licenses were revoked. Unlicensed persons were no longer permitted to station themselves at the Barge Office, and no licensed person was permitted to molest an immigrant or compel him to accept any service. To replace the "unlicensed boarding-house runners, 'sharks,' etc.," Williams reported, a number of immigrant aid societies had provided responsible guides who, at a very reasonable charge, conducted immigrants to their destinations. As the tide of immigration mounted, the rackets revived. When the New York State Immigration Commission was preparing its report, Commissioner Watchorn sent it an appeal for help: "I hope you will look carefully into the situation at the Barge Office. This is outside of my jurisdiction, but it has given me a great deal of concern." He supposed that as long as water ran downhill they would be receiving gullible people at Ellis Island, and there would be sharpers to prey on them. "More of that kind of work has been done between the Barge Office gate and the elevated station at South Ferry than in any other like area in the whole country." Largely as a result of the commission's report, a local committee of the North American Civic League for Immigrants, a Boston group, was formed, and by the end of the period this organization had established "an excellent guide and transfer system at Ellis Island," which took a great part of the immigrants safely past the Barge Office and its environs.[42]

Guerrilla warfare constituted the normal relations between the commissioner of immigration and the steamship companies. It had developed during Dr. Senner's regime, died down somewhat while Fitchie was in office, but broke out again as soon as Williams took over and did not cease thereafter. While the law of 1893 called for the detailed manifesting before embarkation of all aliens, the tradition of the immunity of cabin passengers from the immigration laws was strong. It was considered a great annoyance to bother cabin passengers with the highly personal questions needed to fill out and later check the detailed manifests, and this part of the law was not at first enforced.

"For the saloon passenger our doors still swing wide open," said *Harper's Weekly* in describing the workings of the new law. "He may come and go freely, save for the inquisitive customhouse examiner and the boisterous and importunate cabman." For some years the cabin passengers appeared only on the customary passenger lists, or were accommodatingly entered on the new manifest forms by the ship's purser after the ship had sailed. Steerage manifests, also, were often very imperfectly prepared. Cabin passengers were not examined at all, as a rule, although Senner recommended it.

When Powderly was commissioner-general, he found that many contract laborers and diseased aliens were coming in second class to avoid examination. In 1898 he issued an order calling for all aliens to appear on the detailed manifests and be subjected to examination, as the law required. There was vociferous protest on the part of the steamship companies and influential travelers, and enforcement of the order was limited at best. There was a great outcry when a British businessman, long resident in Philadelphia, was held up because he had a false arm. The steamship officials called the proceeding outrageous, and as showing the immigration laws to be unjust, autocratic, and inhuman. They contended that the laws were never intended to apply to anything but "immigrants," by which they meant, of course, steerage aliens. The immigration authorities now held that they applied to all aliens. "In October, 1898, this new order of things was established by a circular of the Commissioner of Immigration, approved by the Acting Secretary of the Treasury." Since then representatives of the Immigration Service and the Marine Hospital Service had boarded steamships at Quarantine, "whose duty it is to make a rather careful examination of the aliens in the second cabin, and a cursory examination of the aliens in the first cabin, but not heretofore has it been supposed that they would interfere with the liberty of an alien in the first cabin." [43]

When Williams began demanding complete ships' manifests as soon as he took office in 1902, and insisted that the law applied to first-cabin passengers as well as steerage, there was protest. The Washington office at first backed him up, piously declaring that "This bureau has always held that it is as necessary for cabin passengers to satisfy the immigration officer of their right to land as it is to comply with the customs laws." If there had been any distinction in the past, "it has been permitted in contravention of the views of the Department as officially expressed to your predecessors in office on a number of occasions." This stand was soon modified, however. Pressure on the commissioner-general mounted, and Williams was instructed that "A literal compliance with the law as relating to steerage passengers and a *reasonable* compliance so far as concerns cabin passengers" was to be the rule.

There was a widespread feeling in Washington circles—not confined to the steamship lobby, the *Tribune* noted—that there was no excuse for "badgering the better class of incoming passengers with the insulting questions prescribed by the law," if the steamship company had furnished the required information on the manifests. Williams finally told the press that when he was satisfied that "every proper effort" had been made to obtain the information, he would "not be disposed to enforce the penalty provided by law for an erroneous statement on the ship's manifest as to a first cabin alien." Evidently, if the companies would only prepare the manifests, he would have his inspectors refrain from cross-questioning such passengers.[44]

While most of the steamship lines, under the pain or the threat of fines, soon fell into line concerning the preparation of reasonably complete manifests, the bickering continued on other matters. "If your foreign agents will observe the physical and other characteristics of those we have been deporting," Williams lectured the Anchor Line, "they will receive much assistance in reaching a conclusion as to what kind of people it is desirable to book." They should watch out for trachoma, favus, tuberculosis, and other loathsome or dangerous contagious diseases. They should have the final destination and address correctly stated on the manifest. They should make sure that aliens were not so lacking in funds that they could not reach their destination with adequate means for temporary support. All these things were likely to cause deportation or at least detention at the expense of the company. When the French Line asked that a number of excluded aliens be held at Ellis Island a week longer because their next ship was fully booked for the return voyage, he refused. The deportees were a poor lot, he said, and no further hearings would alter their case; the detention quarters were crowded because ineligible aliens were persistently brought in; it was no concern of the government that the *Lorraine* was fully booked. "Deportation cases naturally take precedence over all others."[45]

Word of Williams's tough new policy reached Berlin, and it was reported in the following winter that the directors general of both the Hamburg-American Line and the North German Lloyd Line had "directed their agents in Middle and Southern Europe to take no one who is unable to fulfill the requirements of the authorities at New York. . . . It was pointed out to Herr Ballin that the deportation of one out of every five immigrants would wholly absorb the profits of the Hamburg-American Line's emigration business." This was precisely what Williams was hoping for, and the *New York Tribune* welcomed the story. "In many thousands of instances," it asserted, "the solicitors, 'touts' and 'cappers' of the steamship lines from Sicily to Scandinavia have been indefatigable in persuading the refuse of the Old World to take the chances of travelling over the Atlantic and seeking new homes on this side of the ocean." This country welcomed good material, but "does not desire scum and offal from any part of the globe," the *Tribune* proclaimed, "and it will insist upon the thorough enforcement of well considered statutes for the regulation of immigration."

The impact of the Berlin action, assuming that the German lines actually carried it out, was scarcely noticeable. The tide of immigration rose to new heights within the next few months. A confidential agent of the Bureau of Immigration, sent overseas to examine into the causes of the unwelcome phenomenon, reported to Commissioner-General Sargent after three months in Europe that "it is the desire for business on the part of the great transatlantic steamship lines that is causing the present alarming increase in immigration to this country." [46]

In his annual report for 1903, Williams said that there had been unceasing effort to enforce the laws "with the utmost rigidity." Of 631,885 aliens brought to Ellis Island for inspection during the year, 6,839 had been excluded and deported at the expense of the steamship companies. There had been many protests to the president, to members of Congress, and to the immigration authorities. The new immigration law permitted the imposition of a fine of $100 on steamship companies bringing in detectable cases of loathsome or dangerous contagious diseases. It had been used effectively, and over $7,500 in fines had been imposed. He believed that the companies would now obey the law.

He proved to be overoptimistic. Medical inspection by the steamship lines continued to be extremely careless. The Washington office, writing to Williams in November 1904, said that it was satisfied from his recent letter that three aliens arriving on the *Majestic* were afflicted with trachoma at the time of embarkation and that "the existence of said disease might have been detected at such time." The assistant secretary therefore directed "that the White Star Line, owners of said vessel, pay to the Collector of Customs of the District of New York, at which such vessel arrived, the sum of $300.00, in conformity with Section 9 of the Act approved March 3, 1903, and that you certify this sum to said Collector for collection." This language had become practically a form letter. Over $31,000 in fines was collected from the steamship companies in 1904 alone, chiefly for bringing in diseased immigrants.[47]

Williams found that the steamship lines failed to report crew members who deserted while in the Port of New York. Occasionally these were apprehended and brought to Ellis Island. He thought that the failure of the ships' officers to bring to his attention "the fact that aliens had left their vessels and entered the country without inspection" amounted to a violation of law. He asked permission to seek indictments. Stories that ships' officers were allowing deported aliens to escape brought an effort to tighten the deportation procedure. There were then about twenty inspectors in the Deporting Division at Ellis Island. They usually put deported aliens aboard ships the night before sailing. They were not always able to see them all personally the next morning, but had to take the steward's or purser's word that they were still aboard. Captain Passow of the American Line was arrested just as his ship, the *St. Paul,* was about to sail. "This was the first time that the commander of an Atlantic liner had ever been dragged into such a transaction," the *Times* noted. Usually stewards, stevedores, or even cooks were blamed as accepting bribes when escapes of deportees were reported. This was only the beginning of a campaign that Williams and his legal staff had planned, it was understood. Steamship lines found the return of deportees expensive and "The temptation to connive at escapes, especially if the person ordered deported has money and friends to go to in this city, is very great." That it had been frequently done was well known.[48]

Watchorn had been in office only a few months when he gave a *Tribune* reporter an interview on operations at Ellis Island. He had "come down rather hard on some of the steamship companies for turning in false manifests," he said. He had fined one company $500 for this kind of offense. They had made a pitiful protest and asked that two-thirds of the fine be remitted. He had told them that when he took his oath of office he had not promised to enforce but one-third of the law. It was all right or all wrong. If they thought he was wrong, all they had to do was to make an appeal and prove it. "They did not do so. I guess they agreed with me that I was doing my duty." A little later Watchorn spoke at a meeting of the National Civic Federation on immigration, at which varied views were presented. He noted that a steamship representative at the meeting had said that "we are obeying the laws." Watchorn believed that they were obeying the laws because they were compelled to do so, and for no other reason. "Now, I have no fault to find with the steamship companies as such. I think that they obey the law not because they have been scrupulous about violating it, but because they do not like the punishment meted out to them if they do not."[49]

When a man who had been deported as having trachoma returned in first class, and came over to Ellis Island to meet his family, who had come in steerage in the same ship, he was recognized and detained. Watchorn took a hand in the examination and decided to deport the whole family. He also announced that there would be a thorough investigation of the line that had brought the man after he was once deported. Plots to get trachoma victims into the country were suspected. A day or two later he issued orders to the medical boarding inspectors for "thorough examinations of all first cabin passengers, on incoming steamships." They need not be made as minutely as in the case of steerage passengers, he said, but he desired "that the inspectors be sufficiently careful to allow no first cabin aliens suffering from disease to get into this port."[50]

Neither Williams nor Watchorn won all his battles with the steamship lines. The spring and early summer of 1906 had been a grueling season for the Ellis Island staff, and when the tide slackened in midsummer Watchorn issued a rule that there would be no Sunday inspections of immigrants for the time being. This rule required the immigrants to be kept aboard ship over Sunday, and the steamship companies did not like the additional expense of providing for them an extra day. "Ellis Island employes have always worked on Sundays," the *Times* explained, "and until the order was issued by Commissioner

Watchorn they hardly knew what a holiday was." It so happened that five liners with 3,000 steerage passengers came in on the Sunday when the inspectors were taking their first holiday. The steamship companies made the most of the suffering of the immigrants held over in the hot steerage and took the matter to President Roosevelt, who immediately revoked the Sunday closing order. Steamship agents were delighted with the decision, but employees on Ellis Island thought it "the hardest kind of luck and did not hesitate to say so." [51]

Watchorn was pleased with the immigration law passed early in 1907. He was no restrictionist, no nativist, as Williams was. The immigration question "is not one of quantity—as the law of supply and demand will regulate that—but one of quality," he told a reporter for the *American Hebrew*. "The new bill will go a long way towards determining that, and the American people are to be congratulated on its passage." One of the things that he liked best was the increase in the number of those classified as defective immigrants, for the transporting of which the steamship companies could be fined. "Hereafter, we can impose a fine of $100 for every epileptic, idiot, imbecile, or victim of tuberculosis brought here as an immigrant," he pointed out. "Now all these defectives cannot only be kept out absolutely, but the steamship companies can be fined for even trying to get them in. They are sent back, of course, at the expense of the offending companies." [52]

But Watchorn knew that the sending back of deported immigrants "at the expense of the offending companies" was often largely a matter of form. A few months later he wrote in strict confidence to Secretary Straus on a number of matters involving the many means "resorted to by the opulent & powerful, and by petty grafters to squeeze the last dollar out of the immigrant in quest of work & wages." Straus had visited Ellis Island several times and had expressed great concern at sending back home deported aliens who were without funds. A wealthy man and a philanthropist, he had suggested to Watchorn that he might set up a fund to help them on their way. The money was to be placed in Watchorn's hands, to be dispensed as he saw fit, except that it should be "without regard to creed, country or race," and the name of the donor should not be disclosed.

Watchorn advised against such a fund, telling Straus that "your offer is characteristic, & does great credit to your large heart," but "you would more likely be contributing to the bursting coffers of the S.S. companies than to the relief of a poor fellow mortal." It was a felony to commit highway robbery, he said, but robbery on the high seas seemed to be quite permissible. The companies felt they were entitled to return passage if they could get it. "Impotent observation of iniquity is one of the most painful experiences to which an honest man can be subjected." If a man was unfortunate enough to be deported, he explained, "he is made, by forced search, to pay for his return voyage. They —the companies—will deny any such charge, but I *know* it is an awful fact." If Straus wanted proof, he should write to Senator Dillingham (head of the

Immigration Commission then beginning its detailed study of the whole immigration problem) and let him investigate this point. "This practice should be reversed, the Company should be compelled to return all passage money to deported aliens, at the discretion of the Sec'y." [53]

How long Watchorn's staff continued the medical examination of aliens in the first cabin is not clear, but under the tremendous pressure on the whole Ellis Island organization during 1906 and 1907 it seems to have been abandoned and not resumed. The examination of second-cabin passengers had been more or less systematic, though comparatively superficial, since 1898. As it was common for aliens who were likely to be held up at Ellis Island to take second cabin if they, or whoever wanted to get them into the United States, could afford it, second-cabin examinations usually resulted in a good number of detentions. But the percentage of detainees resulting from first-cabin examinations was likely to be minimal. Moreover, the brief detention on Ellis Island of a first-cabin passenger was likely to produce an indignant front-page story in the *Times*. Thus it was easy for the immigration authorities when under heavy pressure, as they very often were, to let the first cabin go entirely.

When Williams got back to the island in 1909, he found that fewer inspectors were working in the Boarding Division than had been during his first term. Yet the ships were getting bigger and more numerous. As he wrote to the commissioner-general, "many second cabin passengers arrive in no better condition than do steerage passengers," so the work was of immense importance and the staff should be increased. He seems to have gotten at least some action, and in 1910 he recommended that "we should begin to go into the first cabin more regularly." Every time he sent an inspector there, he noticed, the government collected some head tax money, since, "on almost every first cabin manifest there are listed as citizens some persons, usually servants or attendants, who are in fact aliens." It was another two years, however, before enough inspectors were available to make first-cabin examinations standard procedure. "For years the immigration law has been more or less a dead letter as regards aliens traveling first class," Williams said in his 1912 annual report. "Only a few years ago some transportation agents even took it amiss that they should be required to fill out the manifest sheets as to such passengers. But this is no longer so, and in addition they are now regularly inspected except only on occasions when arrivals are so heavy that there are not enough officials for the performance of this work." [54]

Early in 1908, New York City Commissioner of Police Theodore A. Bingham launched an attack on Watchorn for not deporting alien criminals. Bingham, a former army general and a martinet, was trying to cope not only with deep-seated and pervasive corruption in his own force but also with spreading crime in immigrant neighborhoods. Ellis Island offered a convenient scapegoat, and tact was not one of Bingham's virtues. There had been a long series of crimes involving blackmail, dynamiting, and murder, attributed to

Italian secret criminal societies, usually referred to as the Black Hand, sometimes as the Mafia or the Camorra. Facts sufficient to warrant the deportation of fifty alien criminals had been placed before the immigration officials at the Port of New York, Bingham told the press, and only six had been deported. He declared also that the immigration authorities refused proper cooperation in preventing the incoming of vicious foreigners. Roused by a recent spectacular Italian murder in Brooklyn, he announced renewal of warfare on the so-called Black Hand and "expressed the opinion that murders similar to that of Marchione will continue in this country until a Commissioner of Immigration is appointed who will keep the bars up against the criminal class."

Assuming that Bingham's remarks had been correctly reported, Watchorn told a *Herald* reporter, "he never did a person, official or unofficial, a grosser injustice." Watchorn did not know what Bingham meant when he referred to fifty criminals being reported by the police to Ellis Island, with deportation being ordered in only six cases. Certainly no felon had been permitted to go free at that station against whom there was any case. Bingham, he said, sent meager information to Ellis Island, not even including the port of entry. "We are obliged to forward to Washington absolute evidence before any decision can be given legally under which an alien can be deported." Perhaps the law needed strengthening, but during his term the existing law had been enforced with severity. Many criminal aliens now avoided New York on this account, he declared, coming by way of Quebec or remote ports in the South.[55]

Watchorn was deeply concerned about this attack, which was not an isolated one, and wrote to the secretary on the subject of "the growing impression among many officials—both state, county and municipal—that your administration is not disposed to execute the expulsion features of the immigration laws. This has been said so frequently to me, and I have resented it just as frequently." He had hesitated writing before, he said, "because I know that you are disposed to enforce the law, quite irrespective of the views of those who would commend and of those who would censure." Straus replied at once, calling Watchorn's attention to the fact that during the past fiscal year, when he had been in office, deportations under warrant had increased 47½ percent over those of the previous year. If the criticism were made that his administration had been more severe than the preceding one, that would be the real truth. But "some little humane discretion should be exercised by the Department, and I am proud to say such humane consideration is exercised, and will be as long as you are at Ellis Island and I am here, and I don't care who knows it."

Watchorn admitted that Straus's position was sound and invulnerable, "but the state and municipal officials who have to do with the indigent poor and the helpless and afflicted, have so many foreign people of these classes thrust upon them, that they are disposed to look at the whole matter from another point of view than that which presents itself to you and me." This was a depression year, the burden of charity had grown, and Watchorn may have been having second thoughts about his policy of not requiring a financial test for immigrants. If so, he did not admit it. The criticisms, he continued, were not confined to this class, "for Police Commissioner Bingham, with great want of tact and consideration, publicly and demonstratively proclaims his belief that there is no intention to enforce the law, and no evidence that it is being enforced, as it pertains to criminals." [56]

Straus had already taken action in an effort to clear the department of Bingham's charges. There had been a recent revival of the recurring fear of anarchism, along with the Black Hand outrages. An order was issued, with considerable publicity, directing immigration authorities to take steps necessary to "securing the co-operation of the police and detective forces in an effort to rid the country of alien Anarchists and criminals falling within the law relating to deportation." Along with this activity, the *Times* noted, "there will be taken precautions against admitting to the country any more of the same class." The order, it was said, had "the hearty indorsement of President Roosevelt." Its wording carefully avoided any reference to alleged Italian criminal secret societies, and had the fine Rooseveltian political touch about it.[57]

Bingham continued his attack, nevertheless, blasting both Commissioner Watchorn and Secretary Straus. He sent them both copies of "a list of alleged Italian aliens who have criminal records, and who are now in New York, and who he claims are subject to deportation under the law." Straus was upset and wanted to know what Watchorn was going to do about it. He did not want to start any controversy with Bingham, but he did want to show him and all police authorities "that the Department is not only ready to cooperate in ridding the country of the class that can be deported under the laws, but in securing the cooperation of the municipal authorities in enabling us to fully carry out the law, for it all depends upon discovering the crime and the criminal." [58]

Not long after, William F. Hazen, former chief of the Secret Service, arrived in New York from Washington, "armed with several warrants for the arrest of aliens," with the intent of deporting them. "With the arrival of Mr. Hazen," said the *Herald*, "it is presumed that a concerted move will be made to round up alien criminals, many of whom are known to the police and have been kept under surveillance since their appearance in this country."

Watchorn, in whom Straus had great confidence, had meanwhile been sent to Europe on a fact-finding mission, perhaps to get him out of the line of fire. In company with William B. Howland of the *Outlook*, one of the founders of the Society for the Protection of Italian Immigrants, he was received by the king of Italy. The king minimized the role of criminal societies in both countries, holding them to be "for the most part mythical." He advised them to study the statistics on crime in Italy while they were in Rome. These data showed a wonderful diminution of crime over the last twenty years, he said. When Watchorn got back, he gave the Italian government high marks in crime control. "The Italians have the finest system in the world for keeping track of their people," the *Times* quoted him as saying. "Every citizen that goes out or comes into the country is registered."

But "Somebody Is Being Fooled," the *Herald* declared editorially. Black Hand murders, Black Hand bombs, and Black Hand threatening letters were reported from several places in New York City at the same time that "the King of Italy was assuring New York's Immigration Commissioner that no such thing as Black Hand crime exists in that country or America. Lines must be crossed somewhere." The *Times*, on the other hand, held the Black Hand to be a myth. There was never such a society in Italy, it said, and neither the Mafia nor the Camorra was domesticated here. "Among the millions of industrious Italian citizens of this country there are some thousands of criminals, a pest to their neighbors, who have escaped to our shores through the lax enforcement of the immigration laws." They did not come through the usual ports of entry, since they could not get passports. "There is no regular organization of these criminals outside the columns of the yellow press." [59]

Watchorn, at Straus's direction, conferred with New York City police authorities shortly after he got back from Italy. Thereafter, cooperation between Ellis Island and the "Italian Squad" of the city detective force was close. When Lieutenant Joseph Petrosino, head of the squad, was assassinated in Sicily in 1909, he had been trying to set up with local police authorities centers of information "to detect every man with a criminal record who sought to come to this country." Funds were supplied by the Italian community of New York, and he was working with Commissioner Watchorn on this project. It was believed that his assassins had followed him from New York.

Watchorn deplored Petrosino's death. "I was frequently in consultation with him," he told a *New York Tribune* reporter, "and we worked together very advantageously." It was his firm opinion that not one criminal in a hundred came to this country as a passenger. The criminals of Italy could not get passports, and therefore left the country unlawfully. "They go to France, Belgium and German ports, obtain employment as coal passers and ordinary seamen on freight steamers, and on reaching an American port take advantage of their shore leave and elude the authorities of Italy and America." It was in an effort to get to the bottom of this problem that Petrosino had gone to Sicily. "These men are hard to find," Watchorn declared, "and I think the law should be amended so that any alien who is suspected of being a criminal should be deported at once." [60] This statement, evidently made in grief and shock, may not have represented Watchorn's considered opinion. But however the Italian criminal element arrived in the United States—whether through Ellis Island as Watchorn stoutly denied, or by devious routes as he affirmed and most of them probably did—considerable numbers of them unquestionably came in before, during, and after Watchorn's time.

One of the many reform movements that took shape in the first decade of the twentieth century, generally summed up under the head of Progressivism, was the effort to stamp out international prostitution, the "white slave" traffic, as it was called. Authorities at Ellis Island, of course, became deeply involved in this effort. Immigration officials knew that prostitutes were brought into the country, contrary to a law that had been on the books since 1875, and there had long been matrons at the island to keep special watch for them. It was also known that they often came via cabin class to avoid inspection, but it was doubted that the traffic was highly organized. Investigations in Philadelphia in 1902 tended to show that the traffic was, in fact, organized and widespread, funneling through the Port of New York. The National Woman's Christian Temperance Union took the evidence to Secretary of the Treasury Shaw early in 1903 and persuaded him to appoint women immigrant inspectors at Ellis Island. They were to "board all incoming steamers and make investigation into suspicious cases in the first and second cabins and to give needful information and advice to those who may be ignorant of the real character of the houses in which they may have been promised honest employment." [61]

The use of women boarding inspectors was to be an experiment, and Mrs. Margaret Dye Ellis, in charge of legislative matters for the WCTU, persuaded President Roosevelt to suspend the civil service regulations regarding appointments. She had already selected five young women engaged in social settlement work in New York City, and had designed a uniform for them, with bloomers and long skirts. Williams was highly skeptical of the whole affair; he insisted that one of the number should be an experienced matron from Ellis Island, and he rejected two of Mrs. Ellis's list, choosing other applicants, of whom there were a great many. His male boarding inspectors also showed masculine resentment and doubted the ability of the young ladies to cope with the job.

Newspaper reporters and photographers turned out in numbers to watch the girls climb the swaying ladders up the sides of the moving ships when they first went into action. Sure enough, trouble developed almost at once. On one of the first liners that they boarded at Quarantine, a woman traveling alone in first cabin showed them an address they believed to be fictitious. She became indignant and then hysterical at the highly personal questions they asked her, and lodged a complaint.

The project got off to a very bad start in general. While it was later admitted that the women inspectors had sent to Ellis Island a number of young and unprotected girls, they had found "no indication of organized illicit traffic." At the end of thirty days Williams sent to Commissioner-General Sargent a report declaring the experiment a failure. The women were not adding much to the inspection service; they could not detect real prostitutes, and found few girls in cabin class needing help, he said. The chief of the Boarding Division said that second-cabin female passengers readily submitted to general inspection by the male inspectors, but resented being singled out for special investigation by female inspectors.[62]

How much of this was due to male chauvinism it would be hard to say. Williams and his staff looked for the failure of the experiment and found it. The commissioner-general relayed Williams's negative report to the secretary, and he, in turn, notified the Civil Service Commission that no eligible lists would be needed for permanent appointments. The American Institute of Social Service held a meeting and presented the president with a set of resolutions protesting the removal of the women inspectors, but they were formally dismissed at the end of the three-month trial period. The WCTU, however, did not give up, and presently there was set up under civil service regulations a class of "boarding matrons," who were to board the liners and assist the male inspectors. Williams was carefully instructed to select from the eligible lists "those who are found to be kind-hearted, who have tact and good judgment, and who will appreciate the position they occupy and not presume upon the authority vested in them." They were to act in an advisory capacity only, "leaving the final determination of all doubtful matters to the judgment of the boarding inspectors." [63]

The immigration law of 1903, in the drafting of which both Williams and Sargent had helped, added a number of new categories of excludable aliens, including prostitutes as such, whether imported by agents or not, and also procurers, who had not before been excluded. Nevertheless, the traffic increased noticeably, and in 1905 Watchorn admitted that his office was unable to stop it. "Men coming over here earn a living in that way," he told a *Times* reporter. "The women, when they get here, know enough to say that the men who meet them are relatives. The only remedy for this infraction of the law is to increase the penalty." The immigration law of 1907 did increase the penalty. The importation of women for purposes of prostitution was already a felony, and the penalty of five years' imprisonment was reaffirmed. In addition, any woman alien practicing prostitution within three years of her arrival, as well as the procurer who had brought her in, was made subject to deportation.[64]

Later in that year it was announced in Washington that "A systematic effort will be made by the Bureau of Immigration to put an end to the white slave traffic, which, it is asserted, has been conducted especially in cities on the Atlantic seaboard for a long time." On Watchorn's recommendation, a special woman immigration inspector was appointed at Ellis Island "for the particular purpose of developing information regarding this traffic." Under the new law, it was announced, there was to be a careful inquiry in all the large cities, "and alien women who have not been in the country three years and are found to have been brought here illegally will be deported." They were to be required to furnish evidence against those who had brought them here, and those responsible for the traffic were to be prosecuted. The crusade against white slavery, stimulated by muckraking periodicals, was gathering momentum, and several agencies were at work in New York, Chicago, and elsewhere, in the effort to stamp it out. There were persistent raids in the New York Tenderloin district, in which immigration officers assisted. Prostitutes were also more frequently spotted on the incoming liners by inspectors from Ellis Island. As they were usually cabin passengers, they were detained in the limited quarters set aside for other cabin class detainees, including other women with children. As Watchorn pointed out, this created "a deplorable state of affairs." [65]

Naturally, under the new three-year deportation law, alien prostitutes rounded up in New York and elsewhere tried to establish that they had been in the country longer than three years. If they could do this, they were immune from deportation. Watchorn sought the help of the president of the Board of Magistrates in New York City in getting complete and accurate data from such women under oath, instead of merely accepting the statement of the arresting officer. It soon developed that there was a racket in the Tenderloin, in which data were sold to prostitutes and procurers showing that they had landed more than three years before their arrest. Watchorn was warned by the Washington office that an operation of this sort could hardly be carried on "without the connivance of some one having access to the statistical records at Ellis Island." His investigation must be made as quietly as possible "in order that those implicated may not be put on their guard." Boards of inquiry sitting in all warrant cases of this nature were to be directed "to pay particular attention to" claims of landing which took them out of the operation of the law, and all such claims were to be fully investigated before being accepted and were to be rejected if "not conclusively and satisfactorily established." [66] This was a stricter rule than had been applied to suspected alien criminals in the past.

The Immigration Commission, which had been collecting all sorts of data on immigration since 1907, prepared a special section on "Importation and Harboring of Women for Immoral Purposes" for its voluminous report. Although the multivolumed report was not published until 1911, most of the data on this topic had been gathered two or three years before, and a preliminary report on the subject had been presented to Congress late in 1909. The traffic, which it said was carried on principally by Frenchmen, Jews, and Italians, was described in detail, and Ellis Island came under criticism. Authorities there had been careless in the past. The examination of manifests there by agents of the commission showed that formerly "many women who gave as addresses well-known disorderly houses in the city of New York had been admitted without serious difficulty, as were several women who were booked for Seattle and San Francisco, and gave addresses in the districts where prostitutes lived." The Ellis Island officials were now taking "much greater care . . . in this regard." [67]

The crusade continued, rising eventually to the point of national hysteria. In 1910 legislation designed to curb not only the international but also the interstate traffic in prostitutes was passed. The 1907 immigration law was first amended to remove all time limitations on the deportation of alien prostitutes and on the prosecution of those engaged in the traffic. Penalties for procurers were stepped up to ten years' imprisonment plus fine; house madames who employed alien girls were made subject to the same penalties. A few months later the White-slave Traffic Act, better known in later years as the Mann Act, was passed, providing severe penalties for the transportation of females for immoral purposes in both interstate and foreign commerce. The commissioner-general of immigration was designated as the authority of the United States to collect information on the international traffic and examine those apprehended, in accordance with an international agreement looking to the suppression of the traffic, made in Paris some years before and adhered to by the United States in 1908.[68]

After the time limit on deportation of prostitutes had been lifted, "the Immigration Inspectors, aided by the civil authorities," the *Times* noted, began "gathering up undesirable women all over this country and ordering them deported." This not only put an additional strain on Ellis Island but also made the steamship companies unhappy, since they were responsible for the free transportation of "persons deported after they have lived here more than three years fixed as a limit by the old statute." Commissioner Williams admitted that he had another fight on his hands, but thought that the companies would have to give in.

It was in 1910 also that Fiorello La Guardia, who had been working at Ellis Island, was transferred to duty as interpreter in the New York City night court. (This assignment, he said later, enabled him to attend law school in the daytime and saved him from going back and forth to the island.) The court at that time dealt almost exclusively with commercial vice, and the Immigration Service was interested in all aliens engaged in the business. Before this time the efforts of the special woman inspector based on Ellis Island had been aggressively supplemented by those of a male inspector named Andrew Tedesco. While the Department of Justice had its own agents at work, La Guardia gave Tedesco "most of the credit for preventing importation of white slaves from foreign countries on a systematized basis." In face of the opposition of hotels, resorts, and politicians, "Tedesco cleaned up the red light district along Sixth Avenue, which was part of the notorious Tenderloin."[69]

Although La Guardia believed that the international traffic had been pretty well broken up, the rounding up of foreign prostitutes continued year after year. In the spring of 1914 the *Times* noticed the passage through Buffalo of two cars filled with men and women ordered deported by the government. "Among the forty-five women are hardened residents of the underworld of a dozen great cities, as well as many young girls from Russia, Spain, and Italy." They were to be "taken to Ellis Island and at once sent out of the country." The train had started from San Francisco and picked up undesirables in a number of cities along the way. There were both federal marshals and Chicago city detectives on guard.[70] This policy, continued in the months that followed, was to make trouble for Ellis Island when war broke out in Europe and deportees could not be sent home.

Of all the difficulties that beset the administration of Ellis Island, none was more hampering or more persistent, and none gave rise to more criticism, than the lack of adequate space. From the beginning the physical plant bulged at the seams, as the great American industrial expansion of the early 1900s brought a mounting tide of immigrants. In spite of improvisation, some long-range planning, and extensive new construction, the island's facilities were never quite equal to the demands placed upon them.

The new station was put into operation before the hospital had been completed. Surgeon George W. Stoner, in charge of the Medical Division, warned that it would not be big enough when it should be completed. He insisted that another pavilion be constructed, in addition to the one being built, and warned that even then the hospital would be crowded. The Ellis Island hospital was opened for the reception of patients on March 1, 1902, but the ward space, as Stoner had predicted, was barely sufficient for half the immigrants needing care and treatment. The contract that had been in effect for some time with the Long Island College Hospital was therefore continued. As there were no contagious disease facilities in the new hospital, cases of this nature were sent, as they had been during operations at the Barge Office, to the New York City Health Department. Stoner again urged duplication of the ward space and construction of a separate pavilion for isolation and observation wards.[71]

There was a special appropriation in 1903 to enlarge Ellis Island for the construction of additional hospital quarters. The proposed contagious disease hospital was to be on a new connecting island, "located a sufficient distance from Ellis Island to eliminate all danger of infection." But during the year ejectment proceedings had been brought in the New Jersey courts to divest the government of its title to Ellis Island, the case being later transferred to the New York courts. Although Commissioner Williams strongly protested the delay, no steps were taken toward spending the money for enlargement while the title to the whole island was in question.

Late in 1904 the question of title to Ellis Island was settled. The United States formally filed with the New Jersey Riparian Commission an application for permission to enlarge Ellis Island, thereby acknowledging New Jersey's title to the submerged lands, the claim that had been the basis of the suit. The Riparian Commission shortly conveyed to the United States by deed approximately forty-eight acres surrounding and including the original island and the area already filled in. This meant that work could go ahead on the building of the new connecting island. It was finished by the middle of 1906, and "gratifying progress" had been made in the construction of the hospital itself. But Commissioner Watchorn argued strongly that another $250,000 would be necessary to complete the contagious disease hospital on a scale adequate to the mounting needs, in addition to the like sum already appropriated. It would be a mistake, he pointed out, to build that hospital on too small a scale, as had been done with the other buildings.[72]

It was apparent that the hospital could not be completed for another two or three years, and he urged that temporary quarters for the purpose be provided. "At the present time," he stated, "we are compelled to send all cases of measles, diphtheria, or scarlet fever to outside hospitals. . . . This involves a long, tedious haul, and the exposure incident thereto produces a rate of mortality that is well nigh appalling." During the past fiscal year 2,551 cases had been sent to outside hospitals; among them the number of deaths was 278. These cases were, of course, mostly children. Some temporary wooden wards were erected shortly afterward, close to the existing hospital because there was no other place for them.

The general hospital on Island No. 2 was being doubled in capacity, as Stoner had long urged, by 1908, and the larger appropriation for the contagious disease hospital had been obtained. The completion of the program then under way, Watchorn believed, would "meet every situation incident to the care of the sick and disabled." In the following year the extensive group of buildings constituting the contagious disease hospital on Island No. 3 was completed, but their use was delayed for two years for lack of furnishings and lighting facilities. The second immigration station on Ellis Island had been in operation for ten years before it was able to give adequate care to all the sick immigrants that it received.[73]

In his first annual report Williams declared that the main building, "the handsome structure" which had been expected to meet the needs of the Immigration Service at the Port of New York, had in many respects failed to come up to expectations. He renewed his complaints about the main building in 1903, declaring that "no amount of repairing, unless the building is remodeled, will ever render it suitable for an immigration station." To cite one of its main defects, he pointed out that "every alien, be it man or woman, encumbered with heavy and unwieldy baggage and often surrounded with clinging children, has first to mount stairs and then to descend, in undergoing the process of examination"; this, too, at a time when few of them were in a condition to undergo fatigue.

To meet the need of additional accommodations for detainees, Williams had already erected temporary barracks, so that sleeping quarters for 1,800 people were available. Quarters for 3,000 were needed, he declared. He pointed out other specific needs, for which space was "shockingly inadequate." To remedy these conditions, he recommended that the main building be extended to the rear about 70 feet, in accordance with plans already prepared by the supervising architect. Although he was able to obtain funds for many minor improvements, he did not get the money for a general enlargement of the main building, though he renewed his request in the following year.[74]

When Watchorn entered on duty, he reported that though some improvements had been made by rearrangements in the existing structures, they were still "totally inadequate" for the proper inspection of immigrants. "There is not a single feature connected with the reception, examination and detention of aliens that is not susceptible of very great improvement," he said. The matter of handling baggage, for example, was a very serious problem. Baggage was placed in the main building and then trucked "almost the entire length of the Island." The station had been handling 5,000 immigrants a day. It "could not have handled more and given due and lawful care to each and every examination." Even if more persons could have been examined lawfully, it was doubtful whether the baggage could have been handled for a greater number. "This has caused thousands of people to be kept on board of ships from one to four days," he admitted, "and a great many complaints have been made by those who strongly sympathize with passengers who are subjected to such delay and embarrassment as was necessary in this instance."

Sleeping space was in such demand on Ellis Island, Watchorn pointed out, that a temporary barrack had been erected by his predecessor. "This is a wooden structure, one story in height, in which 700 aliens may sleep, and in order to prevent their escape all the doors and windows are necessarily barred, and I need only to leave it to the imagination of the Bureau as to what would occur if the place should ever unfortunately take fire." It had been built "to tide over what was then thought to be an extraordinary emergency, but which has proved itself to be rather the normal condition." The original plant had been "constructed on the presumption that half a million would be a maximum year," but immigrant arrivals were now approaching 1,000,000. Late in 1906 Watchorn seriously considered hiring barges as supplementary detention quarters.[75]

Watchorn finally got an appropriation of $400,000, ostensibly for alterations in the main building, but he spent the money chiefly on a new attached building to handle baggage and add dormitory space—stretching the language of the appropriation to the limit in the process. He privately justified to his superior the heavy expenditure of funds for his new building. More space was desperately needed, and alterations in the main building would not meet the situation. "An acknowledged disgraceful condition has prevailed at Ellis Island for the past five years," he told the commissioner-general in 1908, "and owing to the severe pressure to which the detention quarters were subjected last year, an intolerable situation was reached—a condition which no private corporation would have permitted to continue for a single day if the laws relating to health and decent comfort in any city of the United States had been applied to it."

When Williams returned to Ellis Island in 1909, he noted with approval the physical improvements that Watchorn had made. The "fine new dormitory building, recently built," would greatly facilitate operations, although it was "already taxed to its utmost." While the number of immigrants had fallen off sharply in 1908, he observed that it was already rising again. As it was his intention to execute the immigration law "with the thoroughness which its importance requires," he believed that facilities should be made available to permit more thorough examinations than had been possible in the past.[76]

"About 11% of arriving immigrants," he told the commissioner-general, "are detained for special inquiry and, even now, with relatively low immigration, the available space is utterly inadequate." The limited available detention space was reduced by furniture and hand baggage piled upon the floor. "When there are from 800 to 1,000 persons packed into these quarters, as has frequently occurred during the past few months, the conditions are indescribably bad. The toilet facilities, too, are inadequate and the ventilating system is incapable of carrying off the foul air." There were not enough rooms for the boards of inquiry. The existing witness room was too small. "These persons come from New York to wait for periods ranging from an hour to five and six hours. It has been estimated that at times 300 persons were endeavoring to get into this room, it and the stairway leading thereto being packed to suffocation. It contains no toilet facilities." [77]

As immigration moved upward again sharply in the following year and detentions increased, Williams asked for funds for a new building corresponding with the baggage and dormitory building. He did not get the new building, but he did get enough money to make many improvements. These included a third story on the north wing of the main building, added in 1911. This eased the special inquiry operations considerably and made possible many other long-desired changes. The medical offices were moved from the second floor to larger space on the lower floor of the main building. The removal of the medical offices, in turn, left the whole of the second floor available for the legal examination of immigrants. The capacity of the floor for such inspection had been doubled. The iron pipes dividing the floor into passageways were removed, and simple but comfortable benches were installed in their place. Williams was also able to get rid of the dangerous and unsightly temporary wooden barracks erected some years before.[78]

The most urgent remaining need, he believed, was for more adequate and better space for detainees. There were not over 1,800 beds on Ellis Island, almost all of the three-tiered bunk type. Frequently more than 1,800 persons had to be accommodated overnight in crowded dormitories which also had to serve as day rooms. In the largest men's dormitory the passageways between the tiers of bunks were only two feet wide. "When all of the beds are occupied, as frequently they are," Williams observed, "the congestion in this room is very great, and since it has only an easterly exposure the temperature on summer nights may be 100°. In addition, the ventilation is very imperfect." The former Siberian convict who spent eight days in this dormitory may not have exaggerated when he declared that it was "very much worse than a Russian prison," except that he wasn't beaten and the food was a little better.

Williams asked for another $525,000 to add improved dormitory space and housing for the voluminous records piling up at the station.[79]

An appropriation for a third story on the baggage and dormitory building was forthcoming, and work on it began before Williams's second term ended. Funds for an additional story on the south wing of the main building, as well as for a number of other improvements, followed. "Two important additions for which Congress still declines to grant appropriations," he noted in his last annual report, were "(a) the creation of quarters in which cabin passengers may be detained so that they need not be confined with what are commonly known as immigrants—(many of them persons of filthy habits); and (b) an additional ferryboat."

During fiscal year 1914, the last full year of operations before World War I cut off the major flow of immigrants, a number of physical improvements were completed or under way at Ellis Island. Projects for which Congress had made no provision, in spite of repeated requests, included a covered way between the two hospital islands; an additional ferryboat to relieve the overworked *Ellis Island*, built in 1904; and suitable accommodations for detained cabin passengers. As for the covered way, it was considered "not creditable to this Government to have sick children exposed to the elements and the spray from the bay while being transported across the present open walk." As for the detention quarters for cabin passengers, it was noted that during periods of normal immigration such detainees now averaged more than 100 a day. "There can be no wonder that such passengers complain when placed in the present detention rooms, though they be the best Congress has given us." [80]

There had been many and frequent special allotments of funds to meet the unforeseen demands on the immigration station, though never enough to meet the needs as the island's administrators saw them. "No one has preached as hard or as persistently as I have about the inadequacy of the quarters at Ellis Island," Commissioner Williams declared in testifying before the House Rules Committee in 1911. "I have repeatedly asked for more money, and Congress usually has given me only from one-third to one-half of what I asked." Nowhere in the country, he wrote the *Times*, was "false economy more out of place than at Ellis Island," for that was the place where the immigrants got their first impressions of the country. The one appeal that seems to have found Congress always with a deaf ear, aside from that for a second ferryboat, was the request for "class" detention quarters. Their almost total absence had brought many complaints to the island in the past. Even Lord Bryce, the British ambassador, had filed a polite protest on the subject, following it up with a personal visit to the island.[81] Such quarters were to be sorely missed when the postwar rush of immigrants began.

CHAPTER V

WARTIME INTERLUDE

With the outbreak of general war in Europe at the beginning of August 1914, the great tide of immigration slackened. The leading emigration ports of Hamburg and Bremen, in Germany, came under British blockade, and the German liners sought shelter wherever they happened to be. The flow from Liverpool, another important emigration port, was reduced. Immigration continued for a time from some of the Mediterranean ports, but became increasingly hazardous as submarine warfare developed and was reduced to a trickle after Italy entered the war in 1915. The heavy migration from the Austro-Hungarian and Russian empires was cut sharply at once and soon ceased almost completely.

The impact of the war was felt at Ellis Island almost immediately, and was reflected statistically in the years that followed. In the fiscal year 1914, the last full year of migration, 1,218,480 immigrant aliens were admitted to the United States, 878,052 of them through the Port of New York. During the fiscal year 1915 there were only 326,700 admissions, 178,416 of them through New York. Immigration had been reduced by approximately 75 percent in a single year, and a larger percentage of what there was came across the borders rather than through New York. As the war went on the numbers diminished, the low point being reached in 1918, when only 28,867 immigrant aliens entered the Port of New York.[1]

One natural consequence of the lessened traffic through Ellis Island was a reduction in the working force. The Department of Labor ordered many furloughs and transfers from the veteran staff that had been carefully built up under Williams and Watchorn. This process went so far in the first year of the war that it impaired the efficiency of the station and made it "difficult to perform properly and promptly the duties incumbent upon it," even though immigration had "so greatly diminished." After the United States entered the war the old staff was further dispersed. It is probable that the organization never again attained its prewar efficiency while Ellis Island remained a major point of reception for immigrants. Some of the odium heaped on the island during the immigration revival of the early 1920s is undoubtedly attributable to wartime administrative and personnel dislocation.

Another and more constructive result of the falling off of immigration was the opportunity given to improve the medical examination. Much more thorough inspection was made of those immigrants who did arrive. "The results attained," it was reported, "show conclusively that the medical inspection heretofore accorded aliens has been totally inadequate to the conditions existing." As it was assumed that after the close of the war there would be a considerable influx of diseased and mentally deficient aliens, this seemed the time to introduce a system of inspection that would reduce admissions of such undesirables to a minimum. It was recommended that the more intensive individual examination be permanently established in place of the old line inspection.

There was more opportunity, also, to look into the activities of the missionary and immigrant aid societies that maintained representatives at Ellis Island. These organizations had always been a part of the scene, and their work as a whole was undoubtedly very helpful. Commissioner Williams had gone far toward eliminating the commercial and vicious among them. Now it was possible to make a systematic check of missionary operations. At this time forty such organizations were represented at Ellis Island, and fifteen of them maintained immigrant homes in New York City, where arriving and departing aliens could obtain board and lodging. Many immigrants needing help, particularly females, were discharged to their custody. Periodic inspection of these homes by the commissioner's office, it was reported in 1915, "has tended to raise the standard of service and help extended to the immigrants." Apparently the more sinister operations of some of these homes had been greatly curtailed within recent years, but some of them, it was found, were acting as ticket agents of the steamship companies. This practice was believed "incompatible with the purposes for which they are granted the privilege of representation at Ellis Island," and it was recommended that it be discontinued.[2]

The slackening tide of immigration also made possible a policy of "humanizing" Ellis Island. This policy was inaugurated by the new commissioner, Frederic C. Howe, a well-known municipal reformer, a former graduate student of President Woodrow Wilson's, and recently director of the People's Institute at Cooper Union in New York City. Howe entered on duty about one month after the beginning of the war. At Cooper Union he had heard Ellis Island referred to as the "Island of Tears." It was, he recalled later, "a storehouse of sob stories for the press; deportations, dismembered families, unnecessary cruelties made it one of the tragic places of the world." With great zeal he set out to change it.[3]

The New York metropolitan press greeted Howe's appointment warmly. The *Times* noted with approval that Howe was not a local machine Democrat, while the *Globe and Commercial Advertiser* viewed his selection with "peculiar satisfaction." It declared that much of the administration of Ellis Island for the past year, since Williams's departure, had been "scandalously inefficient, a fact of which the Department of Labor at Washington has shown only slight appreciation." Sweeping reforms were expected under President Wilson's new man. "Dr. Howe can be relied on not only to turn the rascals down but also to turn them out. Insisting on efficiency in others, he demands it of himself." The *Sun* thought that "the country may congratulate itself on what it has escaped in the way of possible successors to the highly competent Commissioner William Williams." [4]

Howe's early activities as commissioner of immigration were described with enthusiasm in an issue of the *Survey*, spokesman of the social service profession, a few weeks after his appointment. "Commissioner Howe has two advantages over previous commissioners at Ellis Island," it noted. "In the first place, the great falling off of immigration since the war began, has given him time for experiments and a small group with which to experiment. All former commissioners have been so buried under the administrative detail of dealing with a million immigrants a year that they had no imagination for additional work."

Howe had determined to change some of the old tradition at Ellis Island, which undoubtedly stressed efficiency at some cost in human warmth, and "to make of it a comfortable waiting room for those newcomers whose start in America must be safeguarded by certain precautionary measures." In other words, he sought to make life a little less grim for detainees. This process began with the simple steps of taking benches out of storage, placing them on the lawn, and letting people out of detention quarters to sit on them. Next followed an outdoor playground for the children, and a teacher to direct it. Inside the detention quarters he broke a doorway through the wall separating husbands and wives, created a common social hall, and made it possible for families to see each other at other than mealtimes. Cheap sewing materials were provided for the women, there were toys for the children, and illustrated foreign newspapers were distributed. Swings were set up on the piazza. On Sunday afternoons there were band concerts, to which the public was invited. Commissioner Howe talked of adding folk dancing. By arrangement with the Board of Education in New York City, he planned to set up a school for detained children and English classes for adults.

He found the sleeping and boarding arrangements fairly adequate. The food was good, he thought, but he stationed inspectors in the dining hall to take complaints. The bunks in the sleeping quarters he thought not bad, and space for 1,000 detainees had just been provided. "In fact," said the *Survey*, "the commissioner regards the regimen of the plant at Ellis Island as pretty well managed;—it is the fact that human beings are inside it, not digits in an annual report, which he believes has been forgotten." [5]

High praise for Howe's administration came also from the *Outlook* at almost the same time. Howe was formerly the head of the People's Institute in New York City, this periodical noted, and his training there was of service now in enabling him to attack the problem of what could be done to turn an alien into a good citizen. "The only thing that is lacking over here is imagination," he told the *Outlook*'s writer. "No one ever seemed to try to imagine what a detained immigrant must be feeling." The authorities had concentrated on eliminating the 2 percent of undesirables and had lost sight of the other 98 percent. Ellis Island had been, with great difficulty and labor, developed into an efficient sieve for separating the fit from the unfit. "Now, under its new Commissioner," the *Outlook* concluded, "Ellis Island gives promise of developing a new function—that of a beginner's class in American citizenship." A few months later Howe was a guest speaker at the annual meeting of the Hebrew Immigrant Aid Society. Judge Leon Henderson, president of the society, introducing him, said: "Dr. Howe belongs to that young, inspired band of lovers of humanity who are devoting themselves to the improvement of society in concrete practical work." [6]

This picture of growing sweetness and light was only a little dimmed at first by the natural resistance to change on the part of the staff, by lack of harmony between Howe and his immediate superior in Washington, and by the gradual accumulation on Ellis Island of deportees who could not be sent home because the ships were no longer sailing to their home ports. After a German submarine sank the *Lusitania* in the spring of 1915, President Wilson forbade the sending of immigrants back to England and France, and the scheduled return of sixty Russian deportees on a munitions ship to Archangel was canceled.[7]

Nearly a year after Howe had taken office, the innovations that he had made on the island were again described admiringly. "These changes," said the *Immigrants in America Review*, "have been due to the humanizing personality of Dr. Frederic C. Howe, the present Commissioner, who was appointed last fall by President Wilson for this very purpose." Howe had tried to make the main examination hall attractive by placing plants in the windows, hanging historical pictures on the pillars, and draping large American flags from the balcony. He trusted that these would "express in some measure ideals of patriotism, beauty and service to the new arrivals." He wanted to have the immigrants well started on their way to becoming good American citizens before they left the island. As it had been and still was, "they arrive, we see that they are qualified to enter, tag them and then pass them on to shift for themselves." Ellis Island, he thought, ought to be a concrete expression of the best of America.

Visitors to the island at this time noticed their courteous treatment from all employees. "It is evident," said the *Review*, "to one familiar with the Old Ellis Island, that a new spirit of service is permeating the entire official force there." Detainees were no longer cooped up in the cheerless detention rooms. There were handball courts and other recreational facilities. There were work rooms for those who wanted them. Complaint and suggestion boxes were placed in various parts of the station. The staff had been organized on a "democratic basis," each division sending a delegation to a weekly staff meeting to discuss suggestions. Prominent government officials and immigration experts attended and spoke at these meetings. Howe was not clear about the need for further restriction of immigration, but he was sure that "The thing for us to do is to look after these immigrants when they get here. We do not do it now, but we must begin at once." He thought that the government should set up internal bureaus to protect immigrants after their entry and prepare them for citizenship. Howe was obviously in the forefront of the growing movement, led by social workers, to "Americanize" the immigrant.[8]

The winter of 1914–15 had been one of serious unemployment in New York and elsewhere, in part due to the war. Commissioner Howe, finding himself with empty sleeping quarters on his hands, had opened two buildings to the local unemployed, chiefly immigrants. Some 750 men, rounded up by Howe's staff along the waterfront, were given shelter there during the winter months. The Ellis Island ferry took them to the Battery every day so that they could look for work, and a charitable organization set up a soup kitchen for them there. "The expense to the Government," Howe said later, "was practically nothing."[9]

Perhaps inevitably, Howe's reforms gradually created enemies for him and his administration. As there was plenty of room at Ellis Island, he proposed to the Washington office to have second-cabin as well as steerage passengers landed there. The staff had been so reduced that it was difficult to handle examinations on shipboard. A more thorough examination would be possible on the island than the hurried one usually given to cabin passengers on the way up the bay in the midst of preparations for landing and often in poor light. Many smaller ships now charged little more for second-cabin than for steerage passage, and immigrants were urged to come second-cabin on the ground that inspection was not so severe. (This was, of course, a device of long standing, but Howe discovered it all over again.) Many prostitutes and other immoral characters were alleged to be coming to the United States at this time. They usually traveled cabin class and could be more easily detected on the island. Second-cabin passengers often bought prepaid railroad transportation as steerage passengers did, and their orders could be honored only at Ellis Island. This meant that after landing at the piers they had to pay baggage transfer and other charges and were often delayed in hotels overnight. By the time that they reached the island they had been put to a good bit of unnecessary expense and delay. Howe asked his superior for an order to be issued for the examination of all second-cabin passengers at Ellis Island.[10]

An order requiring the steamship lines to land these passengers there was approved by the secretary of labor, but the lines immediately protested, claiming that they had not been consulted. The order was suspended almost at once, pending a hearing in Washington. By the time the hearing took place, the secretary had been deluged with telegrams and letters protesting the order from New York, Hoboken, and Jersey City. At the hearing, the secretary revoked the order for the time being and appointed a commission to look into the matter further. Howe, in a letter to the editor of the *New York Times*, tried to counteract the impression accepted by much of the press that "Ellis Island is a place of terrors and inquisitions" and that the proposed landing of second-cabin immigrants there would be an experience of fear and horror. This had not been true of Ellis Island for many years, he said.

The commission, headed by Solicitor J. B. Densmore of the Department of Labor, met at Ellis Island in January 1916 and listened to further argument on the subject. Members of the Ellis Island staff defended the proposed order. Two congressmen from New Jersey, a representative of the mayor of Hoboken, a number of individual hotelmen and representatives of the Hotelmen's Association of New York, the New York Produce Exchange, the Maritime Exchange of New York, the Merchants' Association of New York, the Hoboken Board of Trade, the New York Board of Trade and Transportation, the Chamber of Commerce of the State of New York, the Cunard Steamship Company, the Trunk Line Association, the Pennsylvania Railroad, the American Line, the Lloyd Italian Line, the Scandinavian American Line, and others protested it. The entire business community, it appeared, regarded the second-cabin passengers as their legitimate prey. The steamship companies promised to provide better lighting and other improved facilities for shipboard examinations, and the order was permanently revoked.[11]

Howe had already found that the rate paid by steamship companies for the care of aliens detained in hospital was a purely nominal figure based on a calculation made many years before. He had the actual cost of the hospitals worked out by accountants on a per diem basis and obtained an order from the department fixing the charges on the basis of cost. This brought in thousands of dollars in revenue, but "organized the hostility of the steamship companies," as Howe recalled it later. He also crossed swords with the railroad companies. He found, as Williams had found long before, that the railroad pool at Ellis Island, which divided up the business of transporting immigrants to inland points, often sent passengers to the West by the most circuitous routes. "They lost days of time," according to Howe, in the process, and "often reached their destination late in the night without friends to meet them. They were open to all sorts of graft on their unprotected arrival." He tried to get an order to correct this practice, which was based on what the railroads considered fair sharing of the traffic, but could not get action.[12]

Ellis Island had been the major point of deportation for alien prostitutes and procurers since 1907, and the size of the operation had increased greatly since 1910. Deportations of this nature were in general handled like other deportations, which usually involved incarceration in local jails before transportation to the port. A few months before the outbreak of war, Mrs. Kate Waller Barrett, president of the National Council of Women, had attended the meeting of the International Council of Women in Rome as a special agent of the Immigration Service. At this conference an international committee was formed, looking toward cooperation with the American immigration authorities in the care of women returned to their homelands. On her return, Mrs. Barrett had conferences with representatives of the Immigration Service in Washington and at Ellis Island, and assisted in working out improved procedures for handling the cases of women deportees. The new procedures looked to "more kindly and considerate handling of the cases than had been practicable by a system under which such cases were handled in the main like other deportations." In particular, every effort was to be made to avoid incarcerating women in jails; where suitable quarters were not available, they were to be held in the homes of philanthropic and religious societies pending deportation. On their deportation, they were to be placed as far as possible under the care and surveillance of proper women's societies abroad. Selected women employees were designated to care for women deportees at Ellis Island and other immigration stations.

By the time these new regulations were promulgated, the European war had been raging for many months, and, as far as international cooperation was concerned, they were already canceled. Deportations, in the main, became impossible, and Ellis Island began to fill up with alien men and women rounded up from all over the country on immorality and other charges. The war itself brought a new hue and cry against the white slave traffic, which was assumed to be "an alien vice." There were many arrests of aliens throughout the country, and hundreds of them were sent to Ellis Island for custody pending deportation. Most of them, from southern and eastern Europe, could not be deported because of the war. Howe, who could not reconcile himself to the fact that deportation proceedings were conducted largely outside the Bill of Rights, found that many of them had been arrested and marked for deportation without much in the way of due process of law, and that many of the women were not real professionals. He invited a group of prominent New York women to the island to listen to the evidence of some of the arrested women. On the basis of this committee's report, he proposed to the secretary that casual offenders in the group be paroled. This action was approved, and many were released. This, too, made enemies.[13]

The food contract at Ellis Island expired at the end of fiscal year 1916. Howe believed that the government could do better for the immigrant by operating the restaurant itself, and the secretary approved his plan. A favorable opinion as to its legality was obtained from the attorney general's office. At this point, Congressman Bennet of New York, who had been the attorney for the food contractors, introduced and secured approval of an amendment to the pertinent appropriation bill forbidding the use of the appropriation for this purpose. Howe injudiciously criticized the action, and Bennet denounced him as "a half-baked radical with free-love ideas," demanding an investigation of his administration.

Howe had, Bennet charged, failed to separate the sexes on the recreation ground, had admitted prostitutes to the United States contrary to law, and "by proposing to have the government sell food to the immigrants on the island in place of granting a restaurant concession to contractors he was committing the government to a socialistic practice." Howe defended himself ably and was supported by the secretary of labor. He was able to fend off this attack after hearings before the House Immigration Committee, but some of the mud clung to him. He was marked as a radical and a dangerous innovator.

One of Howe's defenders at this time was the *New York Times*. The immigration laws, it asserted editorially, were "barbarous and cruel." Howe had been appointed to the "petty Czarship created by the law" at Ellis Island. While his utterances were "often of the half-baked kind," he had "devoted himself to mitigating the savagery of the hard laws" and had tried to prevent immigrants from being robbed and from "all the terrible inflictions which our laws encourage and almost demand." In doing this he had run up against a commercial interest. Bennet came to its rescue "with a farrago of charges" that were "preposterous." These charges should be pigeonholed and Howe "encouraged to go on with the beneficent work he is doing at Ellis Island" and stay off the lecture platform. At a later date, the *Times* was to join the chorus demanding Howe's resignation.[14]

Just when the Howe-Bennet controversy was at its height, Ellis Island suffered its worst disaster since the burning of the first immigration station. Early on the morning of July 30, 1916, there began a series of tremendous explosions at Black Tom Wharf, just behind Bedloe's Island and less than a mile from Ellis. The wharf and a number of moored barges were piled with munitions on the way to Russia. It was afterward determined that the explosions were the work of German saboteurs. Plate glass was shattered all the way to Times Square, and there was panic all over New York City.

A rising tide and a west wind carried some of the flaming barges over to Ellis Island, where they set fire to the cribbing of the seawall. Heroic tugboat crews towed them away before they exploded, and the station escaped complete destruction. The immigrants in the detention quarters became panicky but were finally loaded on the ferryboat and taken to the Barge Office. The hospital patients, including a number of insane, were taken outdoors to the tennis courts on the sheltered side of the island. Flaming debris fell in showers, and New York City fire fighters arrived to help put out the fires. Although there were more than 600 people on the island, not a single life was lost and there were no serious injuries.

"Visiting the little islands of the immigration station group a day after the explosion," a reporter for the *Survey* declared, "one feels that he is treading ground where a miracle has been wrought." Shrapnel and bullets had rained down upon buildings and grounds; windows were blown out; locks and hinges were wrenched away; tiles were loosened in patches on the roofs; window panes and transoms were either pulverized, bitten into, or jarred into patterns of lace. With all this destruction, the lack of casualties did seem little less than miraculous.

It was officially estimated that replacements and repairs would cost over $400,000, but the fabric of some of the buildings had also been shaken. It was feared that injuries difficult to correct would show up later. Congress granted an appropriation of $150,000 to begin restoration, and there was a later supplement of $247,000. While repair work was going on, other improvements for which funds had been provided were delayed.[15]

When the United States entered the war, in April 1917, the crews of the German ships in the harbors of New York and New London were picked up and transferred to Ellis Island for internment. The move had been prepared in advance, and the operation proceeded smoothly. There were about 1,150 officers and crewmen involved. "The burden put upon the station through this emergency called for a complete rearrangement of quarters, the shifting of detained aliens to other rooms, and the reorganization of the administration," it was reported later. The entire detention and dormitory quarters in the baggage and dormitory building were assigned to the German crews, over which a stricter supervision than usual for detained immigrants had to be maintained. According to the *New York Times*, they were quite comfortable and suffered from nothing but boredom and the lack of beer. A detachment of soldiers was detailed by the War Department as a military guard for the island, and the ground floor of the same building was used as barracks for them. A stockade was built around the power plant, and floodlights were installed on the various buildings.[16]

In addition to the interned sailors, Ellis Island became host to a considerable number of enemy aliens arrested on warrant by the Department of Justice throughout the country and brought there for custody. Other arrests were made less formally by other government agencies, including the army and the Immigration Service itself. These people, suspected of being spies and saboteurs, required even closer supervision than the other Germans and were kept under strict surveillance at all times. At the same time, the staff of the station was depleted by the detail of interpreters and inspectors to other stations and to other government agencies. A new immigration law, requiring more rigorous inspection of arriving aliens, had gone into effect in the spring of 1917, and called for more inspectors on the station itself just when the ranks were being thinned.

The immigration law of 1917, passed over the veto of President Wilson, was a detailed general act repealing all prior immigration legislation inconsistent with it. It codified previous provisions for exclusion and added new categories. There were now thirty-three different classes of aliens to be excluded from the United States, the most important new category being the illiterate. This law remained a basic piece of immigration legislation until 1952. In addition to adding a literacy test to the accustomed routine of immigrant examination, the law called for the medical examination of all alien members of arriving ships' crews. This meant that every arriving merchant vessel had to be boarded, whether it carried any passengers or not. This put a great strain on the Boarding Division of the Ellis Island medical staff.[17]

Both the War and Navy departments had their eyes on Ellis Island from the time the United States entered the war. After the interned German seamen and many of the other interned enemy aliens were removed to a new internment station at Hot Springs, North Carolina, to Fort Oglethorpe, Georgia, and to other stations, and the sick immigrants and internees were turned over to private institutions, the Ellis Island hospital was taken over by the Medical Department of the army early in 1918, for the remainder of the war. At the same time, the navy took over the baggage and dormitory building and considerable space in the main building. Several thousand navy enlisted personnel were quartered there in succession, pending assignment to ships. The army's Medical Department, in addition to using the regular Ellis Island hospital group of twenty-one buildings fully equipped to receive patients, was also granted hospital space in the main building. The Immigration Service retained physical control over the whole station, supplying heat, light, power, refrigeration, telephone service, and building maintenance, retaining minimum quarters for its own reduced operations.

One piece of major repair work after the Black Tom explosion had been the restoration of the damaged ceiling over the great registry room on the second floor of the main building. The new ceiling was in the form of a "Gustavino arch," a self-supporting terra-cotta construction, and its installation added greatly to the general appearance of the large hall. A new red-tiled floor was also laid in the room, in a pattern to correspond with that of the ceiling, in place of the worn old asphalt floor. This sanitary and easily cleaned surface made the room suitable for hospital use and it was so employed by the army.[18]

After the army and the navy took over most of Ellis Island, the regular inspection of arriving aliens had to be conducted on board ship or at the steamship piers. This added greatly to the difficulties of the work, involving as it did a wide dispersal of activities. The commissioner-general, in his 1918 annual report, asked for additional medical officers and inspectors, even though the head count of arriving immigrants was the lowest in the island's history.

The use of the island by the War and Navy departments came to a close in 1919, the navy relinquishing its quarters at the end of March and the army releasing the hospitals at the close of the fiscal year. The commissioner-general took occasion to observe, in suitably patriotic language, that "it is pleasant to record that the Immigration Service was in position to furnish housing accommodations at our greatest port of embarkation to thousands of American sailors who were required to man vessels carrying troops and supplies overseas." He also noted that "hospital facilities were available for thousands of returned heroes whose illness and wounds demanded hospital care when they were removed from the transports at New York." [19]

Even while the army and navy were using most of Ellis Island, the Immigration Service had granted space to the Department of Justice as detention quarters for alien enemy suspects pending examination and internment or other disposition. Toward the end of the war the national fear of the "Hun," which had been for a time at the point of hysteria, subsided, only to be replaced by a new fear, that of the "Red." An act passed just a few weeks before the Armistice (October 16, 1918), drafted and backed by the Department of Justice and the Bureau of Immigration, had made the deportation of alien anarchists and other radicals much easier. It had, in fact, introduced the principle of guilt by association and authorized the deportation of any alien simply on grounds of belonging to an organization that advocated revolt or sabotage. Soon Ellis Island became the principal point of concentration for this class of undesirables, as it had been for suspected wartime enemies.

As Commissioner Howe saw it later, in his bitter book, *The Confessions of a Reformer*, "The administration of Ellis Island was confused by by-products of the war." The Department of Justice and hastily organized espionage agencies made the island "a dumping-ground of aliens under suspicion, while the Bureau of Immigration launched a crusade against one type of immigrant after another, and brought them to Ellis Island for deportation." He tried to see that as little injustice as possible was done. "Within a short time I was branded as pro-German. I had to war with the local staff to secure decent treatment for the aliens, and with the army of secret service agents to prevent the island from being filled with persons against whom some one or other had filed a suspicious inquiry." He became a jailer instead of a commissioner of immigration, "a jailer not of convicted offenders but of suspected persons who had been arrested and railroaded to Ellis Island as the most available dumping-ground under the successive waves of hysteria which swept the country." The final outbreak of hysteria was directed against the Reds. "For two years we were in a panic of fear over the Red revolutionists, anarchists, and enemies of the Republic who were said to be ready to overthrow the government.

For a third time I had to stand against the current," as alleged Reds were herded into Ellis Island.[20]

The first such group, mostly members of the Industrial Workers of the World (the IWW, or "Wobblies"), arrived from Seattle in February 1919, aboard a train popularly dubbed the "Red Special." It had been generally expected that these aliens would be deported at once, and the progress of the train eastward was "welcomed by one daily newspaper after another," which united "in commendation of such a skimming of the great American melting-pot." Commissioner Howe was in Europe when they arrived. Acting Commissioner Byron Uhl held the men incommunicado, saying that he acted under orders, and refused permission to Caroline A. Lowe, an IWW lawyer, to interview them. He and his assistant, Superintendent P. J. Baker, contended that their cases were closed, but suggested that application for a writ of habeas corpus might be tried. A federal judge in New York was applied to, but he denied the writ on the ground that Miss Lowe could not produce evidence that the men in custody had asked her to represent them. Back at Ellis Island, Uhl suggested that she take the case to the secretary of labor, as the records of the individuals involved were in his office. This she did, and a few days later, at a conference in Washington with Commissioner-General Caminetti, IWW lawyers were given access to the records and permission to see the aliens.[21]

On Howe's return to Ellis Island in March, although he had been "advised by the commissioner-general to mind my own business and carry out orders," he did what he could to assist in getting the men a further hearing, refusing to rush them into deportation. Secretary Wilson supported him. While he recognized that it was the duty of the department to enforce the new deportation law, he instructed the commissioner-general that "every alien taken into custody under this Act shall have his case considered on its own merits before it is finally disposed of." A number of the Seattle group were released after their cases were reviewed in Washington; others had a hearing on a mass writ of habeas corpus before Judge Augustus N. Hand in the federal court in New York. All but a few of them were eventually released.[22]

In March, also, the New York City police bomb squad raided the headquarters of the Union of Russian Peasant Workers of America and arrested about 200 men and women. The immigration officials were called in to help determine the status of these people, who had congregated in "the building that was suspected of being a rendezvous for undesirable elements that came here recently from Russia." Most of them were soon released, but three of them declared that "they believed absolutely in force and violence." The assistant district attorney sent them to Ellis Island and sought Howe's help in getting them deported. Howe, this official declared later, "told him he was too busy with other matters just then and let the men go on surety of $1,000 each, furnished by their attorney." While Howe pointed out that the bail had been authorized on orders from Washington after the men had had extensive hearings on the island, this action tended to confirm local suspicions that he was himself a Red.[23]

During the summer and fall of 1919, marked by large-scale strikes and mysterious bombings, the fear of Red revolution mounted, though no further mass deportations were attempted for some time. In the press and in Congress, Howe, along with Secretary Wilson and a number of other government officials, came under attack for alleged radical sympathies. In the House, Fiorello La Guardia, then a freshman congressman from New York, offered an amendment to the appropriation for the enforcement of the immigration laws. He would cut the salary of the commissioner of immigration at Ellis Island from $6,500 to $2,500. The commissioner, he charged, "is very rarely at his station, unless he goes there for the purpose of defending a detained anarchist." Howe was sworn to enforce the immigration laws, including the provisions on anarchists. "We are able to take care of the anarchists in New York City by our municipal police," La Guardia asserted, "but after we get these anarchists and turn them over to the immigration office at Ellis Island we find that the immigration commissioner, instead of deporting them according to law, acts as their counsel." Congressman Isaac Siegel of New York, a member of the committee on immigration, supported La Guardia, suggesting Howe's possible impeachment.

In the Senate, William King of Utah noted that Howe had presided at a pro-Russian meeting in New York. This meeting, he said, "was a meeting ostensibly to present the truth respecting Russia, but it was a meeting in the interest of radicalism, in the interest of the Russian Soviet, in the interest of class government, in the interest of those who are seeking the overthrow of organized government, including the republic of the United States." Howe, he concluded, "ought to be removed from office by the President of the United States or whoever has the authority to remove him." [24]

Senator King had already demanded Howe's removal, but Commissioner-General Caminetti had told him that Howe was a presidential appointee. King had said that he would ask for a resolution and an investigation on the subject. The meeting which had roused King's wrath was held in May at Madison Square Garden. It was organized to protest the intervention of Allied troops in Russia and the maintenance of the food blockade against that country. A number of eminent men had attended and Howe had presided. As the *New York Times* reported it, the meeting was orderly and was interrupted only by cheering. The only untoward event, apparently, was a little booing at the name of President Wilson. The *Times,* though restrained in its criticism of Howe, nevertheless supported King's proposed investigation, declaring that "a bolshevist sympathizer as a Commissioner of Immigration is impossible." [25]

Howe had spent several months in Paris, at the request of President Wilson, as a member of the American delegation to the peace conference. When he returned to his station at Ellis Island, he found himself in constant and increasing conflict with the commissioner-general, who was cooperating closely with the Department of Justice in a policy of swift and wholesale deportation of radical aliens, and with members of his own staff over the handling of the radical aliens and over deportations in general. One morning on his return to the island after an absence he found that he had lost control entirely. Aliens who, he had been promised, were not to be deported were being sent home to what he believed was certain death. "I had an understanding with the department that aliens should enjoy the right of counsel," he recalled later. "I had protested against deporting aliens to devastated areas or countries in revolution. But orders of the Secretary of Labor and agreements I had with him were ignored by bureau officials."

He went at once to Washington, where he had a stormy interview with the commissioner-general. He found that "even the Secretary was being carried along by the hysteria" and that there was a powerful demand for his resignation. He soon complied. After burning his personal papers relating to Ellis Island, intended for a book, he wrote his resignation to the president.[62]

A short time later there was an investigation of his administration by the House Committee on Immigration and Naturalization. Figures were produced showing that of over 600 aliens arrested and sent to Ellis Island for deportation since early 1917, only 60 had actually been deported. Howe bore most of the blame for this, and many other charges were brought against him: he had received friendly letters from the famous anarchist Emma Goldman and other "notorious agitators"; during his administration immorality and gambling had existed; the island had tended to become "a forum for the preaching of Bolshevism"; he had permitted Red literature to circulate there; women held for morals deportation had been allowed unwarranted freedom; he "had interceded for the I.W.W. members and others" and had directed Superintendent Baker not to deport them; he and Commissioner-General Caminetti had "frequently disagreed," Howe dealing directly with the secretary. Acting Commissioner Uhl testified that employees on the island did not approve conditions under Howe's administration. "So far as I received their individual opinions," Uhl told the committee, "they were all of opinion that the conduct at that time was utterly improper."

There seemed to be a widespread agreement that "many sins of both omission and commission had been uncovered," and the editor of the Republican *Cleveland News*, in the light of the committee hearings, luridly described Ellis Island under Howe's administration as

> a government institution turned into a Socialist hall, a spouting-ground for Red revolutionists, a Monte Carlo for foreigners only, a club where Europe's offscourings are entertained at American expense and given the impression that government officials are subject to their impudent orders, a place where the inspection of immi-

grants required by law is made a mere pretense even when immigration is lightest, a place of deceit and sham to which foreign mischief-makers are sent temporarily to make the public think the Government is courageously deporting them.

When Howe demanded the right to present testimony in his own defense to the committee, and to cross-examine witnesses, he was ejected from the hearing room.[27]

The New York *World*, in spite of its tradition of friendliness to the alien, had become ardent in demanding the expulsion of the "Bolsheviki." But during the committee hearings it sent a reporter to interview Howe and get his side of the story. He had never released an alien from Ellis Island except on orders from Washington, he said. He had no authority to do so. "The only discretionary power I had with regard to alien Anarchists," he told the reporter, "was in the privileges they were given on the island. The thing I insisted on was that every man or woman brought there for deportation should have opportunity to confer with his counsel, to appeal for a rehearing of his case, and to sue out a writ of habeas corpus–rights which are guaranteed to him under the Constitution of the United States." He had been instructed by the department to see that this policy was carried out. It was not approved by "other officials on Ellis Island," and he encountered opposition in carrying it out, but he said that his conscience would not permit him to "become merely a rubber stamp." There had been only about 100 such cases sent to Ellis Island during his term. "The reasons why only a few were deported were that the evidence did not warrant it, that there were no facilities for deportation and that there were no funds available to pay for deportation." "Until last June," Howe concluded, "the navy was using most of the island and we had to confine all aliens in one room. Conditions were so congested that the bureau in Washington decided it was better to release many rather than hold them for deportation when they couldn't be deported." While the *World* continued to advocate the expulsion of Reds, it evidently respected Howe's explanation and did not attack him personally.[28]

More mass arrests of alien radicals began in November 1919, under the leadership of Attorney General A. Mitchell Palmer, and Ellis Island was soon filled with them. For the next several months it was primarily a detention and deportation center, though immigration also was beginning to revive. With Howe's departure, Acting Commissioner Uhl cooperated with the commissioner-general and his allies in the Department of Justice in speeding deportations. On December 21 the army transport *Buford*, popularly known as the "Soviet Ark," sailed from New York, to great public applause, carrying 249 deportees, anarchists and others, to Russia (by way of Finland since Russia was still under British blockade). Many wives and children were left behind. The island soon filled up again. On January 2 there were raids in many principal cities on the headquarters and affiliated activities of the newly organized

Communist and Communist Labor parties. More than 4,000 people were arrested, many with warrants, many without. After rough handling and a preliminary screening, about 600 of the aliens arrested in New York and nearby cities were taken to Ellis Island.[29]

The *New York Times* found that deportation hearings before a board of special inquiry were under way at Ellis Island a few days later. Acting Commissioner Uhl was faced with serious overcrowding, and many more radicals were scheduled to arrive from all parts of the country. Each prisoner was allowed counsel if he wanted it, Uhl affirmed, and pending the arrival of counsel his case was put over. Many of the radicals, however, waived a hearing and declared themselves ready to go back to Soviet Russia at once. Their quarters were equipped with three-tier steel lattice bunks, but they had plenty of army blankets. The quarters were spotless, and there were so many windows that artificial light was unnecessary. Uhl declared that he had had no complaints, and the men were allowed to smoke.

The left-wing press, on the other hand, depicted the conditions under which the radical aliens were held in highly inflammatory language. "Three More Radicals Die in Ellis Island Pen," said the *New York Call* on January 21, 1920, asserting that two of the men had died on the previous Sunday after being seized with convulsions and denied medical attention. All were coughing and suffering from nausea "due to the execrable food and stuffy air." They refused to go to the hospital, the *Call* declared, because conditions there were "even worse than in the cells." Secretary Wilson at once directed an investigation of the matter, including the whole physical arrangement for the care of the detainees.

The acting secretary and the commissioner-general went immediately to Ellis Island. They found that three of the radical aliens had died since reaching the island, all of pneumonia and none on the previous Sunday. One of the men who had supposedly died of convulsions on the floor of the detention room without medical care was found in the hospital recovering from tonsilitis. The detention rooms were reported as commodious, well ventilated, and as clean as circumstances would permit. The food was good in quality and ample in quantity. The hospital was excellent, and medical officers were always on duty to receive calls. All detention quarters were visited by doctors and nurses several times a day.[30] The physical needs of the detained Reds were probably met fairly well, all things considered, once they had reached the shelter of the island.

This time the public clamor for wholesale deportations was tremendous. The Red agitators, the *World's Work* noted, "must themselves have been surprised to find that, while the Government's former commissioner of Ellis Island might lead one of their meetings, the American Legion was likely to break up the next, and that the public, suddenly awakening to them, turned hostile and the Government followed suit so that on all sides their members were on the way to jail and deportation." But liberal protest also made itself heard, conservative lawyers and church groups joining in, and the Department of Labor was at last aroused to curb the highly irregular activities of its Bureau of Immigration and the Department of Justice. Secretary Wilson, in a sharp memorandum to the commissioner-general, insisted on the early right to counsel in deportation proceedings and directed a liberal bail policy. Within a few weeks the Red colony at Ellis Island had been reduced to about 100, hundreds having been released on $1,000 bail each, "the Washington authorities having modified their rules." As the mass raids had not been continued, the *Times* commented, "it was likely that the colony would soon become only a memory." [31]

Secretary Wilson and Assistant Secretary Louis F. Post, a lifelong liberal, also began a meticulous examination of all the radical cases, after canceling many arrest warrants already issued. Wilson decided, against the bitter opposition of the Department of Justice, that the Communist Labor party did not advocate illegal doctrines, thereby freeing the members of that group that had been arrested. Wilson was in ill health much of the time, but Post, as acting secretary, insisted on reviewing on its merits each individual case among the Communist party members. He finally ordered about 700 deported and canceled 2,700 other warrants. He was charged with "coddling the Reds," and the House Committee on Rules investigated his administration. He defended himself with a great deal of spirit, and the hearings were dropped. Thereafter the Red hysteria began to abate, and many newspapers commended Post for simply doing his duty.[32]

The Department of Justice did not give up its hold on Ellis Island easily. As late as May 1920, the *Times* reported, "representatives of the Department of Justice visited Ellis Island . . . and reopened the cases of about ninety alleged Reds which had been closed and forwarded to Washington for decision." As deportation proceedings were by law not under the Department of Justice but under the Department of Labor, such a proceeding was clearly illegal. During the war, the Department of Justice had censored the mail of enemy aliens, who were under its jurisdiction, at Ellis Island. This practice was continued in connection with the alien radicals held there, who were not under its jurisdiction at all. After this practice was brought to Post's attention, he took steps to stop it. What particularly infuriated him was that a special delivery letter addressed to him from Ellis Island had been opened and censored. Even after it had been determined that there were no longer any aliens at the island under any other custody than that of the Department of Labor, it took a formal interdepartmental request to get the practice discontinued.[33]

Post, while he was still fuming over the situation at Ellis Island, also instructed the commissioner-general, in a long letter bristling with legal citations, on the limits of his authority in warrant and appeals cases. Post was evidently in the mood to put a stop to Caminetti's freewheeling methods. The commissioner-general had for some time been acting much like a Chinese warlord, largely ignoring his legal superiors, exercising extralegal authority, and making outside alliances of his own. Nowhere in the immigration law, Post told him, was there "any authority, other than such as is purely ministerial, in any other official than the Secretary of Labor with reference to warrant cases. His authority in these cases being exclusive and quasi-judicial, no such power resides in the Commissioner General of Immigration." Caminetti was also to keep his hands off appeals, "in which the Commissioner General has only ministerial functions." Neither he nor the commissioner at the port had any other. "Every particle of quasi-judicial authority, every phase of administrative judgment in deciding appeal cases, is manifestly vested by the law in the Secretary of Labor." His authority was "primary as well as final." [34]

CHAPTER VI

REVIVAL AND RESTRICTION OF IMMIGRATION

As the Red scare subsided, the normal business of Ellis Island revived. There was only a moderate rise in immigration in 1919. The lines of European continental and maritime transportation had been badly disrupted by the war, and were not restored all at once. Political and economic conditions in many lands were at first chaotic. For a time, the outward movement through the Port of New York exceeded the inward, as many new Americans returned to Europe to see how their relatives had fared during the great conflict.[1]

In the following fiscal year there was a noticeable upturn, with 225,206 immigrant aliens being admitted at New York. The departure of the army and navy had made Ellis Island available to the Immigration Service once more. Inspection of steerage passengers was resumed there, and the maintenance and guard staff were recruited up to prewar strength. By the end of the fiscal year pressure on the station, increased per immigrant by the more detailed examination procedures now in vogue—which included the literacy test and a check of passports as well as an individual medical examination, with a resulting higher percentage of detentions—was beginning to mount. With the increase in immigration "already noticeable" and the assurance that unless it was restrained by the action of foreign governments or by new U.S. legislation, it would continue to increase for many years, it was seen that the available space would become inadequate, "notwithstanding the immensity of the structures at Ellis Island." The commissioner-general, reporting for the year, foresaw the need of a large new dormitory as well as suitable accommodations for detained cabin passengers.

The island's function as a deportation center had by no means ceased, though deportation was no longer attempted on a mass basis nor in a mood of hysteria. A special deportation and transportation section was organized by the bureau, and parties of aliens subject to deportation on a variety of grounds were collected over the country and shipped periodically to Ellis Island or, increasingly, to the Mexican border, for embarkation or ejection. This system remained in use for many years, and it continued to demand a share of the available dormitory space at the island and a portion of the staff services. Ultimately it became the major operation.

Another function that had resulted from wartime legislation was the examination of all alien members of ships' crews. While this examination continued to be held on shipboard, or sometimes at the Barge Office, seamen held on medical grounds, usually venereal disease, were brought to the island for treatment. They proved to be a difficult class of patients. With sick immigrants, sick deportees, and diseased alien seamen, the hospitals that had only recently been returned to the Public Health Service were busy. Nearly 6,000 cases were handled in the first year.[2]

The literacy test embodied in the 1917 immigration law had been long agitated, and was intended by its sponsors to cut down appreciably the number of those admitted. As the postwar movement developed, it did not serve the purpose very well. The literacy rate had risen even in the backward nations of Europe since the device had first been proposed. By the latter part of 1920, the rate of immigration was approaching that of the prewar years and Ellis Island was in serious trouble. It occasionally became necessary to compel steamships once more to lie idle with their steerage passengers while the island cleared itself. Naturally, this brought a scolding from the newspapers. "Ever since 1914 it has been obvious that the end of the war would bring a tide of immigrants, yet not one effective step has been taken to cope with it," said the *New York Times,* declaring that conditions at Ellis Island "are actually worse than during the record immigration before the war." The *Newark Evening News* was less critical of the immigration authorities. Ellis Island had always been understaffed, it said. During the war, with immigration reduced to a minimum, it had been possible to make proper examinations and to weed out undesirables. "The Commissioner-General reported this in detail and urged that due preparation be made against the time when the rush would be on again." But his pleas had gone unheeded. "The island station is blocked. Ships are held idle at great expense. Incoming aliens are delayed and inconvenienced. No proper examinations can be made of the newcomers, and undesirables are bound to filter through with the desirables." [3]

Reporters for the *Survey* prepared a group of articles on the revival of immigration. They were generally sympathetic to the problems of the administration at Ellis Island, "the Plymouth Rock for the new Pilgrims who are leaving war-stricken Europe to reach the land of milk and plenty, America." One of them recalled that the inadequacies of the plant had often been pointed out and wondered that "after the great machine has extracted patience, starch and intelligence from both the clientele and the practitioners, there is still such a remainder of personal interest and kindliness left in the attendants." The special-inquiry detention room, built to accommodate 400 people at the most, had a "quota of sitters-upon benches" of "frequently above a thousand." Their stay was anywhere from one day to much over two weeks. Cases for special inquiry were sometimes at the island for as many months. "The sleeping quarters, adequate for fifteen hundred, have been at times in demand for more than three thousand immigrants who sometimes sleep standing up before being put to bed on the floor." The dining rooms, with facilities for 800, often had to feed 3,000 at one meal. "When the crowd is too great to be taken care of, the people are not even taken off the barges, but are fed coffee and sandwiches there. The antediluvian toilet rooms, the missing laundry facilities (the women wash their babies' clothes in a wash basin with sample sizes of government soap and then hang them on their beds to dry), the stinted, cramping detention quarters are things that God in His mercy and an appropriating Congress will have to care for." [4]

With the more detailed examination procedures, the staff could handle only 2,000 aliens a day, instead of the 5,000 often admitted in prewar times. Some examinations of steerage passengers had been made aboard ship, but the Public Health Service had stopped this. The *Times*, noting these facts, commented of Ellis Island that "the facilities there for detaining, examining and distributing the arriving immigrants are inadequate to a degree that is a disgrace as well as a danger to the country." [5]

Frederick A. Wallis had entered on duty as commissioner of immigration at Ellis Island on June 1, 1920, replacing Byron Uhl, who had served a second time as acting commissioner after Howe's resignation. Wallis had been a deputy police commissioner in New York City, was an active Democrat, an elder in the Fifth Avenue Presbyterian Church, and had shown interest in the problems of the immigrant. His working background was chiefly in the insurance business. He had been an active candidate for the position at the time of Williams's resignation in 1913, but President Wilson had then passed him by. He entered his new office full of noble plans for the betterment of the service at Ellis Island, which he considered "the most important and interesting spot in the world today." These plans, after a promising start, were largely swept away by the new rush of immigration, and Wallis was soon on the defensive, desperately trying to cope with a situation that would have tried even such a veteran administrator as Williams.

While Wallis was able to get his staff increased, and even to obtain modest pay raises for some of them, he had difficulty in recruiting first-grade personnel for the more responsible positions. Postwar prices were high and government salaries were low. He went to Washington with a plan for a $5 million construction program for Ellis Island. The secretary presented it to Congress, but that body was seriously considering bills to halt immigration altogether and was in no mood for enlarging the station's facilities or even repairing the existing structures. The new rush of immigration, at first widely welcomed

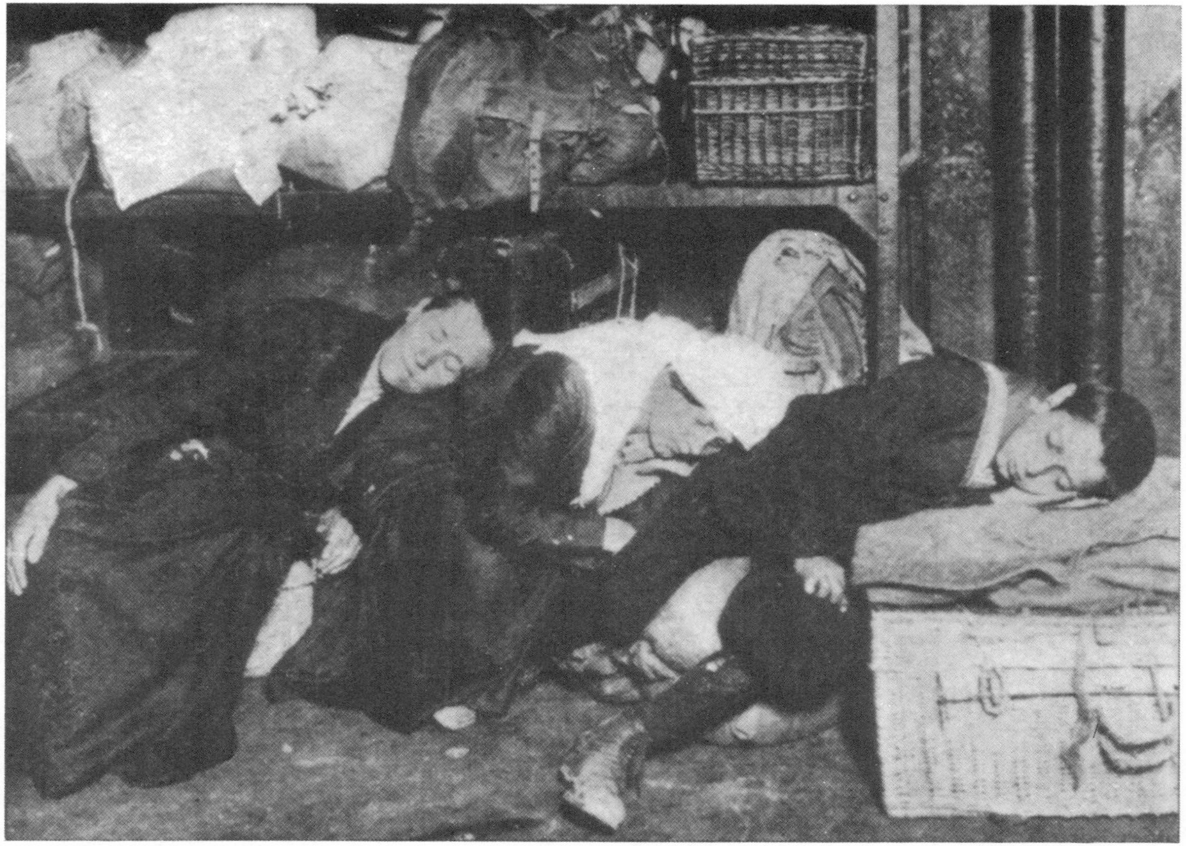

Immigrants sleeping on the floor at Ellis Island in 1921. The postwar rush from Europe is on. The station is not equipped to handle it.
—*Courtesy of the New York Public Library*

by manufacturers as relieving a labor shortage, was soon viewed with alarm as a brief depression set in late in 1920. The restrictionists were led by Chairman Albert Johnson of the House Immigration Committee, who visited Ellis Island and pronounced the revelations "staggering." He made the most of the situation and was actively supported by organized labor.[6]

One byproduct of the war had been the outbreak of typhus and other epidemics in Europe. Some of these were still raging or endemic in parts of the continent. Body lice, carriers of typhus, common enough among some classes of prewar immigrants, were now regarded as a national health hazard. Sometimes the discovery of lice among them held up whole bargeloads of immigrants for hours at Ellis Island. The U.S. Public Health Service, the New York City Health Department, and New York State medical officers at Quarantine agreed to cooperate to prevent any landing of an immigrant until he and his baggage had been put through a delousing plant. Superintendent Baker of Ellis Island notified shipping companies that "the immigration authorities would receive no more aliens not in presentable condition." Shipping companies and health agencies scoured the neighborhood for delousing facilities.

Dr. Royal S. Copeland, New York City commissioner of health, who had a flair for personal publicity that was soon to carry him to the United States Senate, started an antityphus campaign in the city. He claimed that the immigration authorities were not properly delousing the immigrants, and set up a delousing station at the Battery, sending thirty policemen to the Barge Office to wait for arrivals from Ellis Island. Commissioner Wallis was notified by the secretary that he should "permit no interference by municipal officers with present examinations," but he, on the other hand, could not interfere with activities beyond the Barge Office gates. Copeland's policemen were ordered out of the Barge Office itself, but they stood outside and tried to pick up immigrants as they mingled in the crowds coming off the Ellis Island ferry. With considerable fanfare they seized 200, marched them off to the delousing station, and found lice on a few of them.

Copeland visited the island and declared conditions there "a menace to the country." There were not enough medical inspectors; 40 men, he said, had to examine 4,000 immigrants a day, or 100 each. They should not have to examine more than 20. He saw filthy blankets piled in a corner. Commissioner Wallis told him that 1,000 immigrants had slept on these blankets on the floor the night before. The sleeping facilities on Ellis Island were inadequate, Copeland discovered, and there were vermin everywhere. One day there were 15,000 immigrants waiting in ships in New York Harbor, he said. He went to Washington and extracted a promise from the commissioner-general for more medical personnel and examinations on ships or piers, if necessary, to clear the congestion. On his return to New York, Copeland announced that "we may hope to have normal conditions soon. Then when the crowds are dispersed Ellis

Island can be cleaned and fumigated, and the entire country will be safer because of improved methods." [7]

As Wallis's frustrations grew and the barrage of criticism to which he was subjected increased in intensity, he became querulous. Soon he was agreeing with his critics publicly, describing conditions on the island as "deplorable." There was, he proclaimed in talks to various organizations throughout the East and in newspaper interviews, "filth, inefficiency, and red tape." These difficulties and the misery that resulted, he said, were all the harder to bear "because we have managed to pass laws bearing no relationship to our needs, such as the literacy test, and then, to make matters still worse, their application is made as inhumane and cruel as it is possible to imagine." The literacy test kept out sturdy workers but not educated criminals; moreover, it often separated families. Immigrants were regarded as a mass and not as individuals. "Our present immigration system," Wallis declared, "is simply criminal."

This breast beating was hardly calculated to inspire confidence in Wallis's administration, but whatever his personal contribution to the situation may have been, conditions at Ellis Island were certainly deplorable. Some of the buildings, never adequate to the needs of the station, were no longer new, and all had received hard treatment during the war. Little had been done toward rehabilitation afterward. Now they were inundated with a new wave of immigrants. The administrative staff was evidently not as efficient as it had once been. It was composed chiefly of new men, and Wallis either did not remain on the island enough, or else lacked the personal force, to bring them under effective discipline. Detentions averaged higher than they had before the war, partly because of new legal restrictions, partly because many of the postwar immigrants were practically refugees and arrived penniless. It was necessary to hold them until relatives or friends could be notified and money could be sent to them. The dilapidated detainees' quarters were as crowded as they had ever been when the buildings were new.

"Go down to Ellis Island!" challenged a widely circulated Newspaper Enterprise Association report. "You will find":

> Immigrants herded like cattle in the ill-ventilated, fetid detention-room.
>
> No separate quarters provided for mothers with babes in arms.
>
> Vermin on the walls and floors of detention-room and in dormitories.
>
> Immigrants forced to sleep indiscriminately two in a bed or on the floors.
>
> Only 1,100 beds, tho the overnight population averages from 2,000 to 3,000 and often is as high as 4,500.
>
> No mattresses for beds—only blankets spread over strips of steel; bunks built in tiers, three high.
>
> Only six bath-tubs for use of all the women and small children.
>
> No bath-tubs for men; thousands forced to use sixteen shower-baths.
>
> Lavatories so inadequate that they are a menace to health.
>
> Many wash-basins on upper floors without a water-supply.

Only two pumps, with low water-pressure, inadequate against fire.

Many immigrants forced to wait weeks because affidavits and even money sent by relatives had been lost.[8]

Describing in detail the intolerable conditions under which women and children detainees were kept on the island, the *Delineator* urged its subscribers to "Read this story of what women and children endure at Ellis Island, where many immigrants get their first taste of America. Then, while you are still boiling with the sense of injustice and outraged decency, write your congressman that conditions must be changed." Although some of the criticism was deliberately sensational, much of it was factual. It was through an Ellis Island older, shabbier, and less well run than that seen by the prewar arrivals that a new tide of 560,971 immigrant aliens passed in the fiscal year 1921. The national total for the year was 805,228, edging up toward the record figures of the 1900s.[9]

The crisis at Ellis Island furnished the immediate impetus for a revision of the immigration laws. Johnson's bill suspending immigration for one year was passed in the House early in the session of 1920–21, to meet the existing situation and give Congress time to work out a permanent policy. The movement to bring about an absolute reduction in immigration had been strong ever since the 1890s. After the war, which had brought about a general revulsion against all things European, it became for all practical purposes a national consensus, the only measurable opposition coming from industrial areas where manufacturers were concerned about their labor supply and where the foreign-born voters were most numerous. In the Senate, where the Immigration Committee was dominated by eastern Republicans from manufacturing states, lengthy hearings were held at which such opposition was given its day in court. But the demand for a real curtailment of immigration was too strong to be stopped. Such influential periodicals as the *Saturday Evening Post* gave it added impetus in sensational articles stressing what had long been alleged to be the deteriorating quality of the immigrants. There was the mess at Ellis Island to be cleared up; there was the lingering fear of Bolshevism; there was more than a touch of anti-Semitism, as many Jewish refugees were coming in; most of all, there was the fear of hungry Europeans inundating a jobless America.

The method of reducing numbers by the literacy test had failed. Now another means was to be tried. The Senate substituted for the House bill a measure limiting immigration by basing it on percentages of national representation in the 1910 census. This passed both houses and was repassed early in the administration of President Warren G. Harding, after President Wilson had vetoed it. This law, since known as the First Quota Act, was adopted as a temporary measure pending further study of the problem of immigration, but it proved to be the most important turning point in American immigration policy to date. It imposed the first absolute numerical limits on European immigration and established a nationality quota system based on the preexisting composition of the American population. The principle remained basic in immigration law until 1965. It insured, as it was intended to do, that the new immigration from southern and eastern Europe could not reach more than a small fraction of its prewar level, while not affecting what had long been the normal migration from northern Europe.

The act provided that the number of any European nationality entering the United States in any given year could not exceed 3 percent of foreign-born persons of that nationality who lived here in 1910. Nationality was to be determined by country of birth. Not more than 20 percent of the annual quota of any nationality could be received in any given month. The total of immigrants admissible under the system was set at 358,000, but there were numerous classes exempted from the quota system.[10]

This act, passed and approved by President Harding on May 19, went into effect on fifteen days' notice, on June 3, 1921. Since not more than one-fifth of a national quota could be used in any single month, steamship companies rushed to land their immigrants as early as possible in June. The result was the exhaustion of many national quotas within the first few days. Surplus immigrants were held on board while the immigration authorities wrestled with the problem.

Immigrants brought in before June 3 were, of course, exempt from the quota. "The final week before the new law became effective," Edward Corsi, combing the old files at Ellis Island, noted years later, "saw a mad dash of thousands to American shores. Imagine the ships, bulging with human cargo, racing through the Narrows and into New York harbor, actually colliding with one another in their hurry to be at Ellis Island before the last minute of grace." One of the last of the immigrant ships to get under the wire was the Cunard liner *Saxonia*. Her immigrants were admissible outside the quota, but there was no room at Ellis Island. "Guarded by Customs officials and Cunard Line detectives, her eight hundred human souls were landed on Pier 53, North River, at the foot of West Thirteenth Street, where they camped on the floor for four days." A storm of press criticism was the natural result. "Once more fuel was thrown on the flames of opinion, which for nearly thirty years had raged at the mention of Ellis Island."

During the month of June more than 10,000 aliens of various nationalities in excess of the quotas for the month were brought to the United States, most of them to New York. As the immigration authorities saw it, these aliens were "the helpless victims of the transportation companies" and were "entitled to a full examination under the immigration law and also to an appeal to the Secretary of Labor." Yet, under the new law, they were barred from entering. The situation was "an utterly impossible one." After due deliberation, the secretary directed that these aliens be admitted temporarily on bond, the admissions to be charged to succeeding monthly quotas. The decision was believed to be "necessary in the interests of humanity." [11]

The steamship companies continued their mad race, month after month, in the keen competition for the reduced immigrant traffic, and the policy of general admission under bond could not be continued indefinitely. Whole shiploads were turned back. The results were tragic, and the blame fell largely on the island's administration. A woman physician on the Ellis Island staff later described a scene produced by such an adverse ruling:

> A greatly magnified tragedy was a shipload of 500 immigrants from southeastern Europe who had disposed of their homes and all their possessions to start life anew on American shores, only to find that they were above the quota and were forced to return. The ensuing demonstration of these excitable people is one of my most painful reminiscences of service at the Island. They screamed and bawled and beat about like wild animals, breaking the waiting room furniture and attacking the attendants, several of whom were severely hurt. It was a pitiful spectacle, but officials were helpless to aid. Again it may be asked why they were permitted to leave their native port without a determination of the quota. Again, however, the Island was culpable in the eyes of those who were blind to facts. Still the officials were forced to do their duty.[12]

Commissioner Wallis, who was probably miscast as an administrator but was a real humanitarian, was as unhappy about the quota law as he had been about the literacy test. The combination was too much for him. "I do believe," he wrote to Secretary of Labor James J. Davis, as he was about to leave his post, "that our nation is committing a gross injustice for which some day it must render an account, in allowing these hundreds of thousands of people to sell all they have, sever all connections, come four thousand miles out of the heart of Europe and other countries, only to find after passing the Statue of Liberty that they must go back to the country whence they came." Inspection and examination should be conducted on the other side, he urged, thus saving thousands of people "the suffering we see at the Island daily which is indescribable and that would melt a heart of granite." [13]

Quite aside from the problems of administering the new quota law, which itself was freely belabored in the press, Ellis Island continued under vigorous attack. The *Chicago Tribune* sent Genevieve Forbes, a member of its feature staff, to Ireland and back as an immigrant. She gave the editors the grisly account no doubt expected of her. Her articles in the *Tribune* were widely syndicated. While her unhappy experiences had to do chiefly with the steerage and with the barge trip to Ellis Island, she did complain of the treatment that immigrants received there. W. W. Husband, the new commissioner-general of immigration, was sharply questioned on the subject by the House Committee on Immigration and Naturalization:

Aerial view of Ellis Island about 1921. Immigrants are landing from barges in front of the main building. Others, who have been admitted, are gathering at the ferryhouse. The slip between the two hospital islands has been partially filled.

—*Courtesy of the National Park Service*

Mr. Raker. . . . You have been at Ellis Island during the last four or five months?

Mr. Husband. I have been there a very considerable number of times.

Mr. Raker. It is being circulated throughout California—and clippings have been sent to me—that horrible treatment has been imposed on these immigrants at Ellis Island by the officials themselves, the men insulting women and such things like that. The article is by Genevieve Forbes, and she has gotten it in most of the California papers, and I suppose all over the United States, but for what purpose I cannot say. Is there anything in the idea that the officers of the Government there under your direction are maltreating these people?

Mr. Husband. Well, Judge Raker, I have said, in commenting on the statements made by Miss Forbes, so far as they relate to Ellis Island, and so far as they relate to rough treatment, loud talking and so on, on the part of employees at Ellis Island, that they are perhaps 10 per cent true, that is 10 per cent too much, 10 per cent more than there ought to be at Ellis Island.

The officials at the Island tell me that I am wrong in that, that it is not 10 per cent as bad as Miss Forbes says it is, but I would stand on the statement that 10 per cent of her charges, so far as the treatment of the immigrants by employees at Ellis Island is concerned, are true or were true at the time she wrote the articles.

Mr. Free. What does that mean? Does that mean rough or abusive treatment?

Mr. Husband. No; it means yelling at them, "Here, here, here, go this way," and taking hold of them, if it is necessary, and directing them not too gently. . . .

Mr. Siegel. . . . Miss Forbes has told more truth as to general conditions at the Island than has been disclosed in a long time. . . . but you will never be able to get at the Island 100 per cent politeness and courtesy when you bear in mind the salaries the men are getting; there is no getting away from it. Furthermore, the physical condition of the buildings is such that you can not get the perfection you desire.[14]

Commissioner Wallis, a Democratic appointee, had submitted his resignation not long after the beginning of the Harding administration. The secretary of labor, in reply, had asked him to stay on until October. The administration had already chosen his successor. He was Robert E. Tod, a New York banker, yachtsman, and philanthropist of Scottish birth, a successful administrator and man of affairs. He had served as public works officer at the American naval base in Brest, France, during the war, and had been cited by General Pershing and decorated by the French government.

Tod, however, had been planning a European trip and was reluctant to take on the responsibilities of Ellis Island. Secretary Davis persuaded him to convert his journey abroad into a fact-finding trip on the problems of emigration from Europe and immigration into the United States, as a special commissioner of the Bureau of Immigration. He was particularly to look into the feasibility of arrangements for the examination of aliens by American consuls or other officers of the United States stationed overseas, and to report his findings on his return.

Tod returned early in October, reporting a general reluctance on the part of American consular officials to take on the new responsibilities and recommending that Immigration Service officers be appointed as vice-consuls. Meanwhile, he urged strict limitation of the visaing of emigrant passports to the quota allowed for each country. "You will find," he noted, "that many persons who have been warned by the Consuls that the quota has been filled for that month persist in getting a visé and coming to the United States in the belief that by some means they may be able to enter. I believe that many emigrants think that, having landed at Ellis Island . . . they can appeal to the Courts here and with the powerful assistance of different organizations will succeed in landing." [15] Tod had put his finger on a problem that was soon to haunt him.

Wallis at once asked to be relieved, and Tod accepted the appointment at Ellis Island, entering on duty late in October 1921. The next issue of the *Outlook* indicated its belief that the change in administration was long overdue. It pointed out the inconsistency of the current enthusiasm for "Americanization" of the immigrant at the same time that most new arrivals had to pass through Ellis Island, "one of the most efficient factories in the world for the production of hatred for America and American institutions." The writer referred to three documents that lay before him describing conditions there, one of them a "calm and dispassionate" report by a committee of the Merchants Association of New York. "The foul sanitary conditions and the inefficiency of administration at Ellis Island" were "frankly pointed out in this report."

Two of these reports, including that of the Merchants Association, by a "curious coincidence," said the writer, "refer with approval to the successful administration of Ellis Island by Commissioner William Williams in 1909." It was clear that while the organic law was responsible for some of the defects and injustices of our treatment of immigrants, "much depends upon the character and ability of the Commissioner, who has great power." The *Outlook*, an influential liberal Republican periodical of which Theodore Roosevelt had been a contributing editor, had been hoping for a reorganization of Ellis Island under the Harding administration. "That hope is justified," it proclaimed, "by the announcement of the appointment by President Harding of Robert E. Tod to succeed the present Commissioner, Frederick W. Wallis, who was appointed by President Wilson." Tod was competent, the *Outlook* declared, "to deal successfully with the complicated and perplexing problem which faces him at Ellis Island." [16]

"I can never forget," the secretary told Tod in assuring him of backing to the limit in making the island what it should be, "that your predecessor spent most of his time out lecturing and telling stories about the deplorable conditions at Ellis Island, yet no one in his audiences ever seemed to have intelligence enough to ask him why, as the administrator of affairs at Ellis Island, he did not correct these conditions rather than going around telling sob stories designed to discredit the immigration laws." Tod thanked Davis for his letter and the enclosed clippings on Ellis Island conditions, which he said they both knew were not as bad as depicted. "There is certainly an endeavor by the steamship companies and others to have articles published which will cause public indignation," Tod asserted. The steamship lines were actively trying to defeat the quota law.[17]

The secretary and the commissioner-general had not waited for Tod to assume office before trying to improve conditions at the immigration station. As part of the economy program of the Harding administration, the staff at the island had been reduced from 780 to 520 people. Beginning in July, "a committee of the Department and Bureau was assigned to Ellis Island to make a detailed study of the whole situation." Several weeks were spent in this study, which was concentrated on the handling and treatment of the immigrants. As a result, a good many changes in both methods and personnel had been made. There was corruption as well as discourtesy, it had been discovered; these were both chronic problems that grew flagrant with any relaxation of discipline at the island. "In the few cases where it was possible to prove dishonesty," the commissioner-general reported to the secretary, "employees, some occupying positions of trust, were separated from the Service and appropriate action was taken in the case of employees who were shown to be rough and discourteous with the immigrants." [18]

Another step taken by the Department of Labor had been the appointment of a committee to make a study of welfare work among arriving immigrants. The committee was headed by Fred C. Croxton, chairman of the Ohio Council of Social Agencies, and included Julia Lathrop, former head of the Children's Bureau of the department, and Loula D. Lasker, who had been active in Red Cross work in New York City. "I hope to carry this 'cleaning up' work on until we have the Island in as nearly an ideal condition as it is possible to put it," Secretary Davis assured the president of the New York Downtown Chamber of Commerce.

This action was hailed by the *Survey:* "Ellis Island," it said, "provides illustration of the need for such a study." A number of volunteer agencies carried on work of various sorts there. Some of them limited themselves to legal activities, trying to get immigrants their full rights under the law and to secure the admission of deferred cases. Others undertook to get them started right for their destinations and assured of friendly welcome on arrival. Some of them spent "infinite pains" on individual cases, but limited their work to special racial or religious groups. "There are naturally gaps in such a spontaneous coterie on the one hand," the *Survey* pointed out, "and on the other hand there is overlapping." [19]

This committee visited other immigration stations but concentrated its efforts at Ellis Island and held hearings there in the late fall of 1921. Its report, made public in the following year, contained a number of unanimous recommendations: welfare work should be closely coordinated; some welfare workers should be on duty at all times and they should have free access to the immigrants; there should be interpreters trained in social work to serve the immigrants at all times; there should be improved quarters for detained women and children, and day rooms should be provided for all detainees; laundry facilities should be improved; religious services should be provided; milk and crackers should be served to women and children at stated intervals; there should be comfortable reception rooms for immigrants waiting for examination, instead of their being held on the barges; and there should be an information service for detainees. "Heretofore," the report noted, "immigrants have been without service of this kind until their examination was completed, and frequently they have been held apart from the public for several weeks pending their examination by a special board of inquiry." [20]

This formidable program, reflecting some unhappy conditions that had always been present as well as others that were not present when the station had been better administered, was drawn up with the close cooperation of Commissioner Tod. He at once accepted the findings of the committee and set about vigorously to carry out its recommendations as far as he could with the limited funds available to him. There was also a marked improvement in the morale of the staff, which probably had little to do with the work of the committee. Secretary Davis sent his chief clerk to Ellis Island for a check on conditions when Tod had been in office only a few weeks. "As soon as the boat reaches the Island," he reported, "one who has not been on the Island for six or eight months notices certain changes." There was a general improvement in "many ways and many things," hard to define but definitely noticeable. "Employees seem to be more alert and do not seem to treat the immigrants with the authoritarian severity as noted in days gone by." There were a great many physical problems, however, most of which were pointed out to him, along with proposed improvements, but things seemed to be moving in the right direction.

The *Outlook*, having enthusiastically endorsed Tod's appointment, sent a reporter to Ellis Island shortly after the committee's report was made public, to see how he was doing. Tod, she found, was not after personal publicity and preferred action to talk. He did not profess to have mastered the situation and had no ready-made philosophy on immigration, or panacea to cure all its ills. Some real changes had already been made under his administration; and, the *Outlook* said, "this leads one to think that the entire ambitious programme laid out by the Committee on Immigrant Welfare Work will become a reality in the course of time." There had always been some spots on Ellis Island that were a shock, even when it was at its best, according to the reporter who knew the island well, and the Great War had affected conditions there very materially. Commissioner Tod was eradicating "these evil spots" from the Ellis Island routine, and the staff seemed to be pleased. "We had never thought of doing this," said old-time officials as they pointed out changes, "and isn't it an improvement?"

Tod had already fitted up a large room, formerly used for storage, into reception rooms where immigrants were taken directly from the barges. There they could wait in comfort for their turn to be examined. There were water fountains in each section; there was a new cafeteria in the information room for relatives and friends of incoming aliens; and there was a nursery where immigrant women were taught to bathe and properly clothe their infants. A director of information was to be appointed soon to take charge of all welfare work, and there were to be more interpreters, available to immigrants when they were forbidden to communicate with relations and friends. A bigger detention room for women and children was planned ("the author's last visit to the detention room was a horror"), and plans were shaping up for improving living conditions for all detainees. Commissioner Tod seemed aware that Ellis Island was usually called the "Island of Tears" in the foreign language press and was determined to change the name.[21] This, of course, had been tried before with no permanent results.

At the request of the secretary, Albert Bushnell Hart, a distinguished American historian and student of government, spent several days looking into the handling of immigrants. He rode a liner up from Quarantine with the boarding inspectors and visited Ellis Island four or five times. Hart, of course, received red-carpet treatment, and his inspection was made in the winter, when immigration was low. Later he went to Washington and watched in action the secretary's new board of review, set up in an effort to speed action on appeal cases. While he was there, he recorded for his host his impressions of Ellis Island. The existing system of handling immigrants in New York he thought was "a remarkably well organized, well supervised, and efficient system, in which the general principles of humanity and respect for the poor and friendless are well maintained." Ellis Island was "exceedingly well managed. Tod is the right man in the right place." [22]

A little later the results of the previous summer's investigations into graft on Ellis Island were publicized. Dr. Maurice Urstein, Polish emigration expert, the *New York Times* had reported, had traveled from Danzig to New York with immigrants and had studied the workings of the island. He had found much bribery going on. "Emigrants rarely complain about the necessity for bribing," he said. Their first anxiety was "to find just the man to approach." Bitterness came after they realized that they had "bought" the wrong man, or that they could have gotten the same results with no bribery at all. Most tragic were those who spent all their hard-earned cash to buy nothing but deportation. This willingness, even eagerness, of immigrants from some of the European countries to bribe their way, as they had had to do in leaving home, was always a factor at Ellis Island and led to the downfall of more than one official.

Tod had followed up the investigations begun before his arrival, and five persons, four of them Ellis Island inspectors who had resigned during the investigation and the other a concession employee, were indicted by a federal grand jury. There had been a definite conspiracy, U.S. Assistant District Attorney Selig Samson told a *Times* reporter. While the schemes were many and devious, the most common was for one member of the gang to circulate among the aliens and tell tales of the cruel hardships visited upon those detained and of the difficulty of getting permission to land without outside help. This help was promised at various rates, depending largely upon the ability of those approached to pay. The charges apparently rarely exceeded $50 a head and were often much lower, but Samson said that a liner with many steerage passengers sometimes netted the gang as much as $1,500.[23]

But the problems of the island could not all be mastered at once nor while it was under pressure beyond its physical capacity, and the barrage of criticism continued. As the summer came on and the steamship race, which began with each new fiscal year, resumed, Tod's staff was worked to the limit and morale began to decline. The personnel cuts made in the previous year had evidently gone too far, and the pay scale had not been improved. "While I have placed the situation before Mr. Husband," Tod told the secretary in a confidential letter, "he simply states that other stations complain the same way. That settles no problems for Ellis Island, and the fact remains that the eyes of the whole world are centered right here at Ellis Island and only the flaws at this port are printed in the public press. Upon the arrival of every ship protests flood the office because of some occurrence which might have been averted had there been a sufficient force to meet the exigency." The morale had been almost broken among his staff "by the utter lack of consideration shown them. The faithful ones have been furloughed, over-worked and under-paid. . . ." He was anxious to have Davis's administration be a success, he said. "It will not be if Ellis Island is not corrected at once."

Congressman Siegel, veteran member of the Immigration Committee, visited Ellis Island during the summer and confirmed this gloomy picture. He talked with Commissioner Tod, Assistant Commissioner Uhl, and others, and inspected the detention quarters. He found everywhere a lack of guards and other personnel. All the paperwork of the island was woefully behind. Tod "means well," he wrote the secretary, but "conditions since July 1st are even worse than they were at any time with the exception of last October." [24]

Reviewing Tod's first year in office in the fall, the *Survey* found that much had been accomplished, but implied strongly that more could have been done. "Commissioner Tod is an able administrator. He knows the life of his island domain, by day and by night. His orders are issued with precision, born doubtless of his naval experience, and they result in action." Bewildered relatives no longer asked in vain at the information desk for immigrants long since deported. Witnesses called to boards of inquiry were checked by a system of passes which had punctured many previous opportunities for graft. The treasury transmitted money promptly. Records began to approach up-to-dateness. The right of appeal was explained in the alien's own tongue at the first hearing, and all attorneys engaged in such cases were registered and limited to $25 in charges. But more was needed to "evolve, out of an antiquated and architecturally unfit building, the material surroundings for the decent daily reception of a thousand or more prospective American citizens." The year before, an advisory committee had studied Ellis Island and submitted a plan for remodeling and renovation of the island. There had been a special appropriation of $100,000 toward carrying it out. But these funds lay untouched while congestion was as bad as ever. "The plans of the commission for shifts in detention quarters whereby larger and more airy quarters would be available to the detained immigrants are still ignored." Changes such as this took time, but the thought of $100,000 apparently lying idle was hard to reconcile with the desire for more effective administration at Ellis Island.[25]

It is doubtful whether the limited appropriation would have been adequate to make more than a start on all the changes that the committee had recommended, and physical remodeling was difficult while the island was still crowded. Such complaints as that of the *Survey* were taken seriously, however. Commissioner-General Husband proposed a new station on some other site than the tiny island. Secretary Davis asked Secretary of the Treasury Andrew W. Mellon to have the supervising architect make a fresh study of the physical needs of Ellis Island in cooperation with Commissioner Tod. The survey should indicate: "First, What changes could be made at Ellis Island in order to facilitate the work there at an early date; and Second, The possibilities for building a new station as herein outlined at some other point, either for the flow of the normal type of immigration or as a detention station, together with such estimates as to cost of various plans as can be made without great cost." The secretary, who was coming under sharp criticism from British sources about conditions at Ellis Island, gave the substance of his letter to the press. "Three alternative proposals are receiving the attention of officials charged with the enforcement of the immigration laws," the *New York Times* reported from Washington. "One of these provides for the rehabilitation of the present facilities on Ellis Island, a second contemplates the erection of a new station on Governor's Island, and a third would result in the transfer of the entire plant to the mainland."

The project for moving the immigration station from Ellis Island came to nothing. It may be that Davis used it only as window dressing. However this may be, his real objective toward taking the pressure off the island was certainly the solution finally arrived at—the examination of prospective immigrants overseas. This was made clear in the official organ of his Bureau of Labor Statistics, the *Monthly Labor Review*, early in 1923: "With reference to the many hardships arising out of the enforcement of the excluding provisions of the law it should be noted that the Secretary of Labor is strongly advocating the passage of legislation requiring that blood, physical, mental, and character tests be given abroad to prospective emigrants before they have broken up their homes and made the sacrifices necessary for a long journey." The attitude of foreign governments regarding such examinations was, however, "a matter which will have to be reckoned with." Davis had sent Tod on a scouting expedition to look into the possibilities along this line before he entered on duty at Ellis Island, and he never gave up the objective.[26]

Commissioner Tod resigned to return to private business at the end of June 1923. He had done much to improve conditions at the island and took proper pride in the fact; but he had a legalistic attitude toward his duties, and the pressure of politicians to get unqualified aliens into the country wearied him of his office. "It is nothing short of amazing how the friends and relatives of immigrants will pull political strings to get these immigrants into the country," he had told a *Times* reporter months before. "I often have telegrams from Senators and Congressmen on cases that on their face deserve deportation." Politicians and lawyers were "making a mockery of the immigration laws," he declared some months before his resignation. "No one save the man who sits in the office of the Commissioner at Ellis Island can know or understand the great pressure that is brought to bear upon the Department of Labor to allow mental defectives, undesirables and people afflicted with loathsome and contagious diseases to enter this country." Half the stories that were sent out regarding the cases of deportees, Tod asserted, "are regarded from merely a sentimental attitude and the cruel facts are ignored."

The *Times* was editorially sympathetic. "Despite the unwillingness of Robert E. Tod to comment upon his resignation as Commissioner of Immigration for the New York District," it revealed, "it is scarcely a secret that his action was largely in protest against the incessant political pressure used by Congressmen and others intent on violating the provisions of the immigration restriction law." This fire was naturally concentrated on the keeper of the gate at Ellis Island. "Congressmen flatter, cajole, insult or threaten him. Immigrant societies employ skilled agents and lawyers to 'get around' him. The public is stirred by tales of pitiful suffering, of disrupted families, of cruelty and harshness. The brunt of all these attacks is borne by the Commissioner." [27]

It was an old story, but still true as it had been in the days of Williams and Watchorn. Long before his resignation Tod had protested vigorously to his superior in Washington against last-minute stays of deportation, often received by telephone, after deportees had been placed aboard ships. "If an alien has had a hearing, in many cases one or more rehearings, and the record has been reviewed in this office, by the Bureau, by the Advisory Board, and by the Assistant Secretary," he wrote, "it would seem as though he had had his day in court and that if found to be inadmissible to the United States deportation should proceed. If, after all these hearings and reviews, interested parties demand a further stay there can be only one inference." [28]

Tod was succeeded by Henry H. Curran, who had long experience in the hard school of minority New York City Republican politics, had run for mayor, been a magistrate and borough president of Manhattan, and had an excellent war record. Curran felt obliged to accept the appointment tendered him by President Harding, as his Yale classmate, Senator James W. Wadsworth, and New York State National Republican committeeman Charles D. Hilles had jointly recommended him, but he knew that "It would be like walking into a furnace." Curran proved to be an able and kindly administrator, but he had scarcely taken office before the storm of criticism of Ellis Island reached a climax. British immigrants were most sensitive to the conditions on the island, it seemed, or at least most vocal in protesting them. The English press had printed long articles about the inhumanity of keeping British citizens in "cages" with "people of dirtier and inferior nationalities." "The British are continually complaining that they are put in the same apartment as the Continentals," Commissioner Tod told a *Times* reporter shortly before his resignation. "We have eight divisions to make as it is, so you see if we were to subdivide these nationalities the place would look like a honeycomb. We can't give the British separate quarters." [29]

Speeches were made in the House of Commons denouncing Ellis Island. Sir Auckland Geddes, the British ambassador to the United States, visited the island in company with Secretary Davis, at the latter's invitation, toward the end of 1922. He made a thorough inspection and wrote a full report to Lord Curzon, the secretary for foreign affairs, who held it until the following August and then issued it as a parliamentary paper.

This report was probably intended to be objective, but it was taken as a stinging piece of criticism and produced something approaching a first-class international incident. The British press had a field day with the document, which confirmed their worst suspicions of Ellis Island, while American journals, long accustomed to belabor the island themselves, now rallied to its defense. Mr. Tod, Geddes thought, was "a sympathetic, kindly, energetic and efficient man," and "Any country might be proud to point to him as one of its officials." Ellis Island itself was another matter. Starting with the plan of the main building, which "did not impress him favorably," the ambassador discussed the island exhaustively, commenting freely on "locked doors and wire cages" which might be necessary but did "mentally suggest imprisonment," and on such details as corners where there was "impacted greasy dirt that had been there days, if not weeks or months," the "compound smell of old dirt and new immigrant," which it took thirty-six hours to get rid of after he had left the island, badly ventilated rooms, and "make-shift facilities for medical examination."

The essential problem, as Geddes saw it, was the immigrants themselves, many of whom had low standards of cleanliness and consideration for their fellows. General comments included the statement that he would prefer "imprisonment in Sing Sing to incarceration on Ellis Island awaiting deportation" and the opinion that the time-consuming system of appeal to the secretary of labor in Washington in cases of rejection, though probably right in theory, was "nothing short of diabolic" in practice. The buildings, which obviously had not been properly maintained for years, were too small. Ellis Island needed to be relieved of about half of the people poured into it. Increased accommodations, there or somewhere else, were badly needed. "Before seeing Ellis Island," Geddes admitted, "I had imagined that segregation by nationalities might be possible. I am now satisfied that it is not." [30]

The report was "grossly misleading" and "out of date because it comes eight months after his visit to the station," said Commissioner Curran to the *New York Times*. Most of the trouble at Ellis Island lay in the detention cases, "which constitute the one percent of tragedy." These detentions and exclusions he blamed both on the steamship companies for transporting inadmissible aliens and on certain foreign governments for permitting ineligible emigrants to start for America. British immigrants, he declared, his Irish temper roused, were "not very well picked, in spite of the large numbers trying to get in in excess of their quota." The British, he asserted, were "just kicking Uncle Sam's dog around again." The island wasn't a hell hole or a place filled with diabolical cages. "In most instances, the story ends right and they live happy ever after." Curran did agree heartily with some of Geddes's suggestions for physical improvements, he told the *New York Tribune*, and thought it likely that Congress would provide the funds necessary to carry them out. "Actually, there are no great hardships suffered by immigrants at the present time on the island," he insisted. "We are running a pretty good hotel."

Curran's immediate predecessors at Ellis Island were sought out for their opinions of the validity of the ambassador's charges. Former Commissioner Tod admitted to the New York *Evening Mail* that "there is much need for improvement at Ellis Island," while his predecessor, Wallis, repeated his sad tale that Ellis Island was "literally a vale of tears." Curran could accept Tod's comment, but replied with spirit to Wallis's statement that he had "seen as high as 1,100 sleeping on the cold tiled floors in the middle of winter." This was simply an indictment of Wallis's own administration of past years, he pointed out, and had no bearing on his own or Mr. Tod's.[31]

Wallis inadvisedly sent Secretary Davis a letter on the subject, along with a copy of an address he had delivered at memorial services for the late President Harding. Wallis apparently assumed that the Geddes report reflected the existing situation at Ellis Island, Davis replied. "I also note from the *New York Times* that you still refer to Ellis Island as 'the saddest place in the world.' I have also noted from time to time, reported addresses by you as to Ellis Island, describing horrible things." He wished that Wallis would take a look at Ellis Island before he again described to the public what the place was like. He hadn't the slightest doubt that his description reflected conditions as they were when Wallis was there. "It is an evil bird who befouls his own nest." [32]

While the Geddes report was still reverberating through the British and American press, a mixed group of Washington officials visited Ellis Island. Assistant Secretary of the Treasury Eliot Wadsworth, accompanied by Surgeon

General Hugh S. Cumming and Assistant Secretary of Labor E. J. Henning, made the standard tour. At its close, Wadsworth noted solemnly that the facilities for medical examinations were inadequate and that larger detention quarters were necessary. A *Times* reporter, who either had a good memory or had been looking through the old clippings in the paper's morgue, commented drily: "His suggestions for improvements at Ellis Island were the same as those made by Commissioner of Immigration William Williams, who was at the head of the Department during the administration of President Taft." Curran, who escorted the party, said he was pleased to find Mr. Wadsworth in accord with his own views.

Wadsworth gave out his report a few days later. He expressed the view that no one visiting Ellis Island "could fail to be critical to a greater or less degree of the facilities." He took cognizance of the "enormous complexities" of administering the immigration law, and his main criticism was not of the staff but of the accommodations. For example, the intensive individual medical examination introduced during the war could no longer be fully carried out. Only about 800 of the 2,000 now permitted to land daily could receive this examination. With more space, all could be examined. The hospitals were good and well administered but needed better quarters for personnel. The "traffic regulations" for handling immigrants were criticized but could probably not be much improved for lack of space. The report demonstrated that "During Mr. Curran's administration great improvement had been shown," the *Independent* said. Hardship cases had not been eliminated, and there would be too many of them as long as the existing law remained unmodified. "But the comforting thing about the workings of Ellis Island is the thought that Mr. Curran is exercising as much common sense and humanity as he can while still adhering to the spirit of the law." [33]

With all the blistering criticism to which Ellis Island had been subjected in the recent past, it was only natural that the authorities there should make the most of what came their way in letters of commendation. To Commissioner Curran there came a letter from an intelligent and highly educated elderly Frenchwoman, depicting an Ellis Island scarcely recognizable as the same place that Ambassador Geddes had described. It told of a ten-day detention there less than a year after his visit. What most delighted her thrifty French soul, apparently, was that all the service there was free:

GENTLEMEN:

After a life of travel, and study, knowing five languages, it might have been supposed that I had seen everything worthy of interest, yet I had lately an excellent opportunity to study an institution unique in the world, and extremely interesting. I mean Ellis Island.

The construction is vast and imposing tho often crowded by the immense quantity of emigrants, whose absolute ignorance prevents many to appreciate that the short detention is not only imposed for the security of United States, but for their own welfare.

The ladies and gentlemen in charge of the immigrants have inexhaustible patience and kindness. The large admittion hall is (in the evening) used as a concert room (once a week) and cinema once also. Sundays a Catholic, a Protestant and Jewish services are held so any creed can be followed. All this is free. Above, all around the hall, is a balcony. This have white tile walls and floors, porcelaine lavabos and baths. There are two hospital, a kindergarten, medical attendance, all free as well as board logging, entertainment, etc. etc. Interrogation rooms, etc., are on the ground floor. Besides breakfast (coffee, eggs, bread, butter, jam) (lunch–meat, vegetables, cheese, tea) dinner (soup, meat, etc.) there are (morning, afternoon, evening) three distributions of the best of sweet fresh milk and crackers. Many days thirty of those enormous cans are needed (they contain fifty gallons each, I was told). Six hundred and fifty employees are daily in attendance. Eighteen languages are interpreted. From morning till night colored men and women clean incessantly. Towels are changed daily. Sheets three times a week.

I leave to a competent man to estimate of the daily expense of such an establishment, and I should thank heartily an expert to compare Ellis Island to anything of the same sort, any other nation in the wide world has to offer.

This statement is not solicited, but if it can make emigrants understand and appreciate what U.S. does for them, you are welcome to publish it (in any and all of the eighteen languages understood at Ellis Island).

Thanking you for all passed favors, I remain,

Gratefully yours,
F. M. LALANDE.[34]

It seems apparent, however, that Madame Lalande had received special treatment. There were some fairly comfortable detention rooms in the main building, opening off the visitors' gallery. The original dormitories there had been broken up and remodeled into rooms as early as Commissioner Watchorn's administration. Madame Lalande had probably been assigned to quarters in one of them, either because of her age or because she had traveled in the second cabin rather than steerage. While Commissioner Curran had denied to the press that Ellis Island was a place filled with diabolical cages, the bunks then in use in the main dormitories were, in fact, made of wire and did resemble cages. As Curran recalled in his memoirs years later, the great trouble with the island as a hotel lay with the sleeping quarters. "In several small rooms for the detention of special cases there were beds, but in the large rooms, which housed every night nearly two thousand immigrants, there were no beds at all." There were at that time four big dormitories, two for men and boys, two for women and children, each one filled wall to wall and floor to ceiling with "four hundred of these small wire cages." They were in three steel tiers, with narrow aisles between the tiers, joining head and feet with wire between. "On the wire base of each cage was one blanket. Nothing else. No sheets, no pillow —for the latter a folded coat would do." There was little ventilation. "It was a contraption that would make a sardine sick." Curran recalled that he had seen many jails, some of them pretty bad, and that "I never saw a jail as bad as the dormitories at Ellis Island." It took him two years and a special appropriation from Congress to get rid of the wire cages and replace them with real beds.[35]

One of the most persistent complaints about Ellis Island had been the delay in appeals against exclusion. The time lag in this period was often considerable. Pending a decision in Washington, the alien who had been excluded by a board of special inquiry and had appealed to the secretary was held in confinement on the island. When quota limitations were involved, it was often necessary to refer the matter to the Department of State. Some of the ethnic societies which had great influence in Washington could sometimes delay deportations interminably, hoping for an eventual reversal. Ambassador Geddes, in his report, had called the system diabolic. Commissioners at Ellis Island, who bore the brunt of complaint in detention cases, sought to speed the procedure, usually by getting more authority into their own hands. While rulings varied from one administration to another, the department, jealous of its prerogatives, tended to limit the commissioner's discretion, at the same time insisting that it handled appeals with all the expedition possible. The problem was a constant source of administrative friction as well as of adverse publicity and was never settled satisfactorily while Ellis Island functioned as a point of detention. "Always this shuttle service of papers, between Ellis Island and Washington," Curran said later, "made for delay, while the immigrants waited at the island, in an agony of suspense by day, in the wire cages by night. In hot weather their locked-up life on my island was a horror."

Commissioner Curran's correspondence with his superior in Washington on this subject became acrimonious. Shortly after the Geddes report had been made public, he asked for "a special effort at this time toward promptness in deciding appeals," as Ellis Island was "right up to the hilt of decent physical limits" in its detention quarters. He harped on the same theme for many months until the commissioner-general, in exasperation, told him rather loftily that "unlike the field offices and the Bureau the Department's part in handling appeal cases is not a perfunctory one," for "it has a real function to perform, and obviously the cases can not be handled with machine like regularity."

This was too much for Curran. "I hardly think that the successive steps of the actual handling of the various examinations of the aliens are to be tossed off as a matter of such mere routine as your letter would indicate," he replied. Many of the difficulties in these cases, he insisted, were "the result of your systematic withdrawal of discretion from local officials here and every day you duplicate at a disadvantage work already done here, and this you necessarily do in a purely routine way on the basis of reading a piece of paper." He cited a list of recent cases in which he blamed the department for delays of from thirty to eighty-two days. He referred to a Mr. and Mrs. Einsiedler, who had arrived at Ellis Island five months before. They had, he said, "become so indigenous to the soil of Ellis Island that Mr. Einsiedler has mastered the American game of basket ball and is now the leader in alien outdoor sports here. Mrs. Einsiedler has been occupied having a baby at Ellis Island. I do not know what will happen next. But I do know that this case could have been decided before this time." [36]

Another and related point of friction between the commissioner and Washington lay in the lack of explanation by the department of its decisions in appeal cases reversing Ellis Island decisions. "If our Boards of Special Inquiry are too severe or have misconstrued the law," Curran wrote the commissioner-general, "we should know that at once. If the admission is predicated on quota charging or other action by the Secretary of State, we should be apprised of that. In short, we should be enabled promptly in each case to see here through the eyes of the Secretary, in order that our own discretion may be informed accordingly." All the satisfaction he got was a cold reply to the effect that he could not have the information, as "there is no provision of law under which the Secretary of Labor is required to explain his action in such cases to boards of special inquiry or to any subordinate official or employee of the Immigration Service."

Curran was not the man to let the matter drop. By arrangement recently effected, he pointed out, consuls (by this time responsible for most primary examinations) were receiving copies of testimony in exclusion cases before boards of special inquiry at Ellis Island. "Just as the consuls know why we reject, we should like to know why the Secretary of Labor admits. In both contingencies, one government official approves and the other disapproves. Certainly the two disagreeing government agencies should have mutual information for the diversity of action. The consul now has our reasons, and in course of correspondence, we shall have the consul's reasons. You, also, now have our reasons, but we, on the contrary, have not the slightest glimmering of your reasons." [37] Whether it was pure bureaucratic snobbery, the pressure of paperwork, or, as is most likely, reluctance to admit the frequency with which the secretary's office gave in to political pressure in admitting unqualified aliens, the department was most unwilling to explain its reversing decisions to the field.

Ellis Island was to know dark days again, but by the middle of 1924 it was over the worst of its many crises. The quota law, whatever its faults, had served the purpose of reducing immigration to more manageable proportions and the staff organization had been considerably improved. The last serious jam at the station occurred in June. It was caused by a Supreme Court decision declaring that families of aliens in the United States could not be admitted if their country's quota had been exhausted. As part of the rehabilitation program then going forward on the island, one of the older dormitories had been dismantled and there were accommodations for only 1,000 detainees. With over 1,400 immigrants in detention and more waiting on a steamer for accommodations, "400 men were obliged to sleep on wooden benches in the large registry room and many more were quartered on benches in the smaller offices." [38]

Such scenes were done away with by the new law that went into effect at the beginning of July and by the physical improvements then going forward. The Geddes report, resented though it may have been, had made Congress a little more receptive to the needs of Ellis Island. When Commissioner Curran presented a program calling for $2.5 million for the rehabilitation of the existing buildings, new construction, and the enlargement of the island to provide more recreational space, he had gotten at least a part of what was needed—$326,000, or enough to put the old plant in presentable condition. Most of the money had been knocked out by President Calvin Coolidge's director of the budget, but there was no real effort to restore the full amount. As a member of the House Immigration Committee put it, justifying the appropriation, "all of the members of the Immigration Committee who visited the station say that something should be done." The sum requested was "for repairs and alterations at Ellis Island immigration station." When a member inquired whether the commissioner had not asked for more money for additional facilities, he brushed off the question: "Oh, they have plans, but those plans were not before us."

Curran was happy to get the money "to give immigrants real honest American iron beds instead of cages, and larger rooms," but he told a New York church group that "I want $2,000,000 more before I'm through and I'm going to get it." Ellis Island was "not as bad as immigrants going back say it is," but there was much to be done there. Curran never did get the larger amount he wanted, but he put the limited appropriation to excellent use.[39]

In the midst of the furor over the quota law and the horrors of Ellis Island, a basic change in ocean transportation had come about almost unnoticed. After the steamship companies had come to accept the new limitations on steerage traffic, they found that the steerage itself no longer paid. It could be filled only on west-bound voyages at the height of the season, and was little patronized between seasons because of the poor accommodations. The new liners, beginning in 1922, had no steerage quarters, but a new and comfortable set of third-class cabins. "Competition and the Immigration Act have had a noticeable effect on third-class accommodations," an article in the *Nautical Gazette* noted. "Quality and comfort are the watchwords today rather than numbers carried, and the steerage is fast becoming a thing of the past in the North Atlantic service." [40] So passed an institution that had brought more sorrow and discomfort to the immigrant than did Ellis Island at its worst.

The quota law applied to European immigration, but not to immigration from the Americas. There were also a good many classes exempted from the quota limitations. In 1924 there was a large total immigration, 706,896, but

New York's share of it was only 315,587, or considerably less than half. Migration was increasingly across the borders of Mexico and Canada, consisting in part of natives and in part of Europeans seeking entry through softer spots than Ellis Island.[41]

Congress was determined to cut immigration further, and the debate over how it was to be done continued intermittently throughout most of the decade. The first quota law, a temporary measure, had been extended while the debate went on, but in the spring of 1924 a new piece of legislation took its place, effective with the beginning of the new fiscal year. This Second Quota Act retained the basic principle of the first, but changed the quota base from the census of 1910 to that of 1890, to cut down still further the proportion of immigrants from southern and eastern Europe. This quota base was ultimately to be replaced by a similar device based on the national origins of the American people in 1920. The quota admissible from any nation in any one year was reduced from 3 to 2 percent of the census figure, thus reducing the total quota. Annual quota immigration under the new law was reduced from 358,000 to 164,000 per year.

As far as Ellis Island was concerned, the most important single feature of the act was a provision for selection and qualification of immigrants in the countries of origin. All immigrants from the quota countries were required to obtain special immigrant visas, based on examination, from American consuls, and not more than 10 percent of a yearly quota's visas could be issued in any one month. These visas were to expire within a limited period. The overseas examination was intended to prevent, or at least reduce, the tragedy of rejection at immigration stations in the United States after immigrants had expended time and funds in making the crossing. Commissioner Curran, who had had to cope with the almost unmanageable monthly spurts of immigrant flow under the law of 1921, and wanted the traffic spread more evenly, had suggested the 10 percent a month limitation on immigrant visas, as well as the provision for their early expiration.[42]

The idea of having immigrants examined in the American consulates abroad was an old one, more than once proposed by hard-pressed immigration officials and others. The Department of Labor had been exploring its possibilities and propagandizing its principle actively for some time. Now it was to be tried out. Secretary Davis went to Ellis Island in July to see how the new law actually worked. He left "pleased and boasting" over the fact that the island "looked like a 'deserted village.'" He explained that the reason for his gratification was that while at the same time the year before "Ellis Island was choked with immigrants who could not be handled," the new law in operation since July 1 had proved to be all that was expected in relieving the congestion.[43]

At the end of the first year of operations under the new law, its impact was summarized approvingly by the commissioner-general. According to his report, "In no previous year has so even and regular a volume of immigrant travel come to our ports nor has such travel ever before been so carefully and consistently inspected by Government officers." Immigration under the new law was also of a very high order, as was shown by the small percentage of rejections, in spite of the "inspection methods of increased effectiveness made possible by the even flow of travel." Complaints on the part of both the steamship companies and the traveling public had been reduced. This success had been due not only to the inspection at the consulates overseas but, more particularly, to the distribution of the quota over a ten-month period.

The 1924 immigration law was rightly termed "a law with a heart," the report went on. "There is no more midnight racing of immigrant-laden steamers to our harbors; no more congestion of aliens in over-crowded quarters awaiting inspection at ports of arrival; no excuse for hasty or cursory inspection of aliens, or harsh and summary treatment that might result from the efforts of inspectors to facilitate travel and relieve congestion at ports of entry." The Immigration Service had at last "an opportunity to vindicate itself of the charge heretofore made by certain interests that, in its administration of the law, it did not take the human element properly into account." The millennium had come, it seemed, as far as the reception of immigrants at the Atlantic ports was concerned. But the formation in the same year of the Immigration Service's border patrol shows that the problem of immigration control had merely been shifted to new points.[44]

While the new quota law, by ending the congestion there, had most to do with the improvement of conditions at Ellis Island, a good bit of internal house cleaning had been going on as well. "Although conditions at Ellis Island were never as bad as some hysterical people would have the world believe," the *New York Times* commented late in 1924, "the news that a number of much-needed improvements have been made there during the last few months is welcome." Most important, in the view of the *Times*, was the substitution of individual beds for "the old system of bunks in wire cages." Another welcome change was in the arrangement of the reception and examining rooms. The old system was somewhat haphazard. "There was unnecessary climbing of stairs and needless going to and fro. This has been eliminated and the passing of the immigrants from one examiner to another and thence to the rest rooms and transfer station will be more business like." Congress appeared at last to have appreciated "the importance of making Ellis Island as good a reception ground as possible for the incoming aliens. . . . Good-will or ill-will there formed is likely to have a lasting influence on the immigrant's relation to American life."[45]

The *Survey* reported "a remarkably changed Ellis Island." There was still an examination there, even after the examination at the consulate, but "The frightful overcrowding that had been at the root of the worst conditions of the past" was gone. The average number of immigrants being received was about 300, and 500 was considered a heavy day. The new law, "combined with a long needed appropriation and an energetic and constructive administration both at Ellis Island and at Washington," had brought about a general reform. "The housing facilities have been reconstructed; adequate modern plumbing is displacing the ancient exhibits, the iron-pipe two-decker curiosities called 'immigrant bunks' have been scrapped and in their place—wonder of wonders—there now appear beds, real beds, with mattresses, sheets and blankets! Every effort is made to keep together the families who must be detained, while at the same time providing separate quarters for single women and men." There were fewer detentions, and "Ellis Island a gateway, not a hotel," was the aim of the whole staff from the commissioner on down.[46]

The 1924 law required that prospective immigrants applying for visas at American consulates supply testimony of their physical fitness from local medical sources. It was found that the consuls could not depend upon these medical certificates, and a good many physically unfit continued to arrive at Ellis Island. At the suggestion of the surgeon general, the experiment was made of posting Public Health Service examiners in the consulates. This was tried first in England and Ireland and was later extended throughout most of Europe. This went a long way toward making the possession of an American immigrant visa the equivalent of admission to the United States.

What this meant for Ellis Island was that it was rapidly losing the basic function for which it had been created—that of primary inspection of the immigrant. This situation was intensified as immigration inspectors were added to the medical officers at the consulates, so that, in effect, the immigrant was completely "pre-processed" when he reached New York. As the system developed, a final checkup of papers on the steamer coming up the bay normally completed the procedure, and only a small percentage of doubtful cases was sent to Ellis Island to be held for boards of inquiry. As fast as the medical officers and immigrant inspectors were assigned to the consulates in Europe, third-cabin aliens from those countries were discharged at the piers along with the second- and first-cabin passengers. The island, with its massive buildings, was becoming a white elephant on the hands of the Immigration Service.[47] The monster was another thirty years in dying.

Criticism of Ellis Island, naturally, did not automatically cease with the improvements that Commissioner Curran had made and that the 1924 law had brought about. A writer in the *Forum* in 1927, when a good many third-cabin immigrants were still being sent to Ellis Island for examination, could still describe it in detail and call it "a forbidding prison," to which the Statue of Liberty "turns a cold, bronze shoulder." But he was answered in the same publication by a well-informed gentleman who had been startled by this description, had gone to the island to refresh his recollection of the place, and affirmed that "As Americans we need not be ashamed of Ellis Island." [48] The island would never live down its dark reputation, but the abuse was easing and was certainly less deserved.

While Ellis Island continued to handle primary inspections of immigrants from countries where inspection teams had not yet been installed in the consulates, its functions had so diminished that extensive reductions in personnel were under way by 1926. Trained immigration officers were badly needed elsewhere. Two years later the commissioner-general began to speak of the station as "something of an economic problem." It was thoroughly organized and modernized, "the best equipped and operated immigration station in the world," but the buildings were "larger than needful to accommodate present-day immigration." Moreover, the maintenance of "this tremendous plant" was a heavy item of expense. The suggestion of abandoning it for a more modest base was very cautiously advanced. "Where once congestion troubled the officials," the *Survey* commented, "they are now uneasy over the expense of operating an institution that is much too large for present and probably future needs. The tide of immigration now beats upon the land borders—not upon the seacoasts—of the United States." [49]

CHAPTER VII

DETENTION AND DEPORTATION

Any serious proposal to abandon Ellis Island at this time might have had an unhappy effect upon Congress, which had appropriated a good bit of money not long before, at the urgent request of the Immigration Service, for modernizing the station. Some sort of station for the examination and hospitalization of foreign seamen had to be maintained in the Port of New York. There were always stowaways and deserters to be picked up and deported. There were still some immigrants arriving at New York who had not gone through processing at American consulates. There were always some processed immigrants who must be detained for action by boards of special inquiry or for hospitalization. Ellis Island, at the principal port where the transcontinental railroads met the transatlantic liners, was still the most convenient place for the collection of deportees. The island was kept in service.

The long and deep depression that followed the stock market crash of 1929 had significant impact on the station. As the depression wore on, fewer immigrants came. By 1932 there were more aliens leaving the United States than there were arriving. While it is probable that most of the reduction in immigration during the early 1930s was voluntary, it was the policy of the administration of President Herbert Hoover to keep immigration at a minimum. The State Department now to a very large degree controlled immigration at its source through the consulates. In 1930 instructions went to the American consuls to interpret strictly the "likely to become a public charge" clause of the basic immigration law and thus keep down immigrant visas.[1]

Another device for keeping what jobs there were in the hands of Americans was a general roundup of aliens illegally resident in the United States. Secretary of Labor Davis, who had served in the Harding and Coolidge administrations and had been reappointed by President Hoover, entered the United States Senate from Pennsylvania in 1930 and was replaced late in the year by William

N. Doak, an official of the Brotherhood of Railway Trainmen and a stalwart Republican. The new secretary of labor set out early in the following year to clear the land of "every one who cannot prove he is lawfully resident here," and President Hoover sought adequate funds for the campaign. Doak estimated that there were 400,000 deportable aliens in America and planned to corral as many of them as possible. His methods were at first abrupt and brought loud protest. His early campaign was concentrated in New York City, and in a short time more than 500 aliens were rounded up in that city alone. "Ellis Island detention pens are being taxed to capacity by aliens seized by the police and Federal authorities for being in this country illegally," the *New York Times* reported. Doak brushed off protests from the American Civil Liberties Union; "they always object," he was quoted as saying. He seemed to be disturbed, however, the liberal *Nation* noted, when Senator Robert F. Wagner of New York joined the protest. He sought to justify his policy, citing the hard times, alien gangster activity, and "anti-red sentiment which has been prevalent since the war." The drive continued, by April 1,100 aliens had been deported from New York, and at the end of the fiscal year the commissioner-general reported "the greatest number of deportations in the history of the bureau, 18,142." [2]

In August alone a total of 869 aliens were deported through Ellis Island, Acting Commissioner I. F. Wixon there reported when asking for more help in the task of processing such cases. It was the principal operation of the station and required a great deal of paperwork. "Arrivals amount to nothing and hardly enter into the computation of things so far as the work at this Station is concerned," Wixon said. "They are practically all handled by the Boarding Division." There had been "a complete reversion at this Port of immigration work," he wrote the assistant secretary. "Whereas previously it was regarded as the gateway to America, it is now the port of expulsion, and our Law Division and Deporting Division are the two most important at the Station."

A few days later he wrote to the commissioner-general that unserved warrants of arrest were piling up at the island. There were approximately 600 on hand, and the number was increasing daily. Another problem was several hundred communications reporting the unlawful presence of aliens in the United States. "The number of aliens that are reputed to be unlawfully in the United States within this district, appears to be almost limitless," he said, "and, as a consequence of the recent publicity given to the activities of our service in and about New York City, the number of reports from anonymous and other sources of aliens unlawfully here has greatly increased." [3] Doak's policy had given informers a field day; a real witch hunt was developing.

It was in this situation, with the immigration station at Ellis Island functioning primarily as a deportation center, that Edward Corsi was appointed as the new commissioner of immigration at the Port of New York, taking office at the beginning of November 1931. Corsi had himself passed through Ellis Island as an immigrant boy from Italy and had spent most of his adult life (he was still young) in social service work among immigrants in New York City. He had been head of the important Haarlem House settlement for a number of years when the call came.

As Corsi remembered it later, President Hoover had told him, "I think you can clean up the mess down there." The "mess" was a scandal at the island involving a racket that had developed in the issuance of reentry permits. These permits were issued to aliens who had left the country temporarily, certifying that they had originally entered legally. False reentry permits, making admission to the United States or permission to stay here almost automatic, were being prepared with the obvious help of someone with access to Ellis Island files. The situation had developed during the summer as a result of Doak's deportation drive. It was taken seriously. An investigation was under way by Washington office officials, who were temporarily in charge of the island while all the top staff there went on extended leave. Morale was at a lob ebb, rumors were rife, and suspicions were widespread. Commissioner Benjamin M. Day, successor to Curran, resigned in September without returning to duty. He was not accused of having had any part in the reentry racket but felt the investigation was a reflection on his administration. His resignation created the vacancy that Corsi filled. Corsi's first task was to finish the investigation and restore staff morale. He said later that "the investigation proved conclusively that only . . . two minor clerks had engaged in the activities of the racketeers." But the matter flared up again after his departure from Ellis Island and involved a prolonged investigation with wide ramifications.

From the beginning of his administration Corsi realized that the problems of Ellis Island were "in distinct contrast to those of the flood-tide days." The news had gone to all parts of the world that America was no longer the land of promise, discouraging immigration. In the administration of Secretary Doak there was a clearly defined policy of deportation. In some instances he used the "anarchist" or radical clause of the law, but he also made a drive against vagrants and the unemployed. Doak had detailed "ambitious immigration inspectors" to Ellis Island, and, some months before Corsi's regime began, they got the cooperation of the New York City police in raiding a Finnish dance hall in Harlem. All present who could not convince the officers that they were in the country legally were arrested. The performance was repeated at the Seamen's Home on South Street, where many men were jerked from their beds and taken to Ellis Island.[4]

There had not only been vigorous protest at these proceedings at the time, but the strenuous efforts of the secretary of labor to clear the land of unwanted aliens were noted later by the National Commission on Law Observance and Enforcement, popularly known as the "Wickersham Commission." This commission was looking primarily into the lawless activities that had for years accompanied the attempted enforcement of the prohibition laws, but it also prepared a report on the enforcement of the deportation laws. The report called attention to the fact that they were enforced by administrative rather than judicial process. A field agent of the Bureau of Immigration had the whole duty of enforcing these laws within his district. "This makes of such an agent," the commission observed, "a detective, a prosecutor, and a judge—three functions which we have found it safe, in no other phase of life, to intrust to any one individual." While the spirit of the bureau and its agents was believed to be for the most part fair, there were "striking instances of oppression, unfairness, and hardship," which were certainly to be expected under the circumstances.[5]

Secretary Doak managed to have the report held up for some time, and when it was published he contended that the "unconstitutional, tyrannic and oppressive" methods complained of, and the cases cited in the report, belonged to a period prior to his incumbency. Every effort had been made to correct administrative abuses, he insisted, but the right of the American people to deport criminal aliens and aliens illegally in the country was paramount. Practical legislation to strengthen the hands of the Labor Department in this endeavor was needed. The alien gangster, who had thrived under Prohibition, was highly unpopular at the time, and Doak now stressed this aspect of his drive, declaring, "I know of no more important work before the country than to rid it of alien criminals." [6]

In addition to those aliens picked up throughout the country and shipped to the deportation station against their will, there were, in those days, many who went gladly. In the hard times, quite often, "the radical or voluntary deportee left Ellis Island with a smile," Corsi noted. Any alien in the United States less than three years who could prove himself destitute could also be deported at government expense. For some time about 200 a month in this category were applying for deportation. On one ship carrying away nearly 100 deportees early in 1933, about half were volunteers. "Those speaking English were frank about their happiness at the prospect of returning home, explaining that 'on the other side' the lot of the poor was happier," the *New York Times* reported. The tragic cases were the involuntary deportees. The laws were rigid, and Corsi had little discretion in the matter. "We are making every effort to effectively enforce the law as to the expulsion of aliens illegally here," he reported a few months after taking office. But, as he confessed later, "the duties of deportation were never very pleasant to me and often very bitter." This was particularly true when the laws applied to "men and women of honest behavior whose only crime is that they dared enter the promised land without conforming to law." Often, he said, they were forced back to the countries they came from penniless, "and at times without coats on their backs." [7]

Corsi knew the evil reputation of Ellis Island long before he went there to administer it, and he learned more of its causes while he was in office. "Many mistakes blot the record of Ellis Island," he admitted, "and great have been the hardships, the humiliations and the exploitation suffered by the immigrant. Yet, I am sure, there have also been instances of exaggeration in which the vitriol of the public and the press has been unwarrantedly directed at a Service which, in a last analysis, has been more sinned against than sinning." He came to believe that the island's reputation suffered more from the inflexibility of the legal system and from the want of discretionary power on the part of its administration than from willful abuse of authority by officials. The tradition he found at Ellis Island, from which Curran had long departed and which had evidently fallen into an unimaginative routine, was one of the assumed necessity of enforcing the laws to the letter. As a professional social worker, he felt the need of tempering justice with mercy. "Let us carry out the intent of the law, but let us do it as humanely as possible," he said in one of his first official statements.

One of his first efforts was to create better relations with the press than Ellis Island had known in the past. Hitherto, he found, the press had been sharply restricted in its coverage of the island's activities. He called a meeting of New York reporters, had them to lunch, and promised them free entry to the island and access to all its inhabitants. He had a similar meeting with the correspondents of foreign newspapers, which had for years been giving the United States a bad name because of the actual or imaginary conduct of the Immigration Service at Ellis Island. There was a third meeting with the consuls of foreign nations in New York. The result of these meetings, he later believed, was better domestic and international publicity. Following this up, Corsi made numerous radio addresses and platform appearances and urged his senior staff men to do the same, the message being, "We have nothing to hide."

To Corsi, Ellis Island was not a prison, and it was wrong to treat deportees as prisoners. Hitherto they had been allowed to have visitors only on Tuesdays and Thursdays. He issued an order that friends and relatives might come to the island on any day in the week. He found that detained aliens were denied the use of the telephone and, after holding a staff meeting on the subject, had telephones installed in the detention rooms. Hitherto, detained aliens had been allowed outdoors only an hour or two a day. This, it was explained to him, was because of the lack of guards. He requested more guards and got them, "and the immigrants, weather permitting, now spent most of the day playing games or walking in the sunshine." He granted deportees the privilege of going out under guard to visit relatives or to conduct business. He had a special mailbox set up in the detention quarters for mail addressed to him, and he made himself accessible to hear complaints. "Many made valuable suggestions," he noted, "and often these talks were responsible for the prevention of injustices."

Corsi soon gained the support of his staff and managed to hold the confidence of his superiors during the Hoover administration. While the Wickersham report probably had much to do with the easing of the drive against aliens toward the end of Hoover's term, Corsi later believed that he had influenced policy greatly. He invited Secretary Doak to the island, and Doak came on several occasions, "watched the games of the aliens, mingled with them and gradually changed his attitude." His deportation policy softened considerably:

> Such wholesale raids as that on the Finnish dance hall were stopped. The Washington special agents, untrained and overly ambitious, were gradually cleared from the Island. Raids were canceled; arrests were made in orderly fashion and on warrants as provided by law; third degree methods were strictly prohibited; agents abusing aliens, severely punished; hearings on warrants of deportation were orderly, fair and strictly in accordance with law. All this was in direct contrast to conditions which the public had protested vigorously.[8]

Good relations with the Washington office not only influenced deportation policy but also helped Corsi to get the money and authority to make physical improvements on the island. Elaborate plans for expansion and improvement had been prepared long before his time; now many of them were carried out. Early in his administration he obtained $350,000 for a general cleaning and dressing up. Many needed repairs were made; the old marquee in front of the main building was torn down and replaced by a plaza adorned with flowerbeds; and a new room to house the scattered records of the station was built. Larger sums were forthcoming later for more ambitious undertakings, as the new Public Works Administration came into being.[9]

Corsi's policies at Ellis Island blended harmoniously into the New Deal of the Franklin D. Roosevelt administration beginning in 1933. He had known Frances Perkins, the new secretary of labor, in social service work, and on her recommendation he was reappointed. One of the new secretary's early actions was to appoint a nonpartisan committee of prominent citizens, under the chairmanship of Carleton H. Palmer, a New York business executive, to undertake a complete analysis of Ellis Island and to make recommendations for future improvements there. The objective of the inquiry, Secretary Perkins explained, would be "not to find fault with the administration at Ellis Island, but to assist in effecting greater economy in operation and to improve the general amenities in the administration of the immigration law." Corsi worked closely with this committee and had the great satisfaction of finding embodied in its report, issued early in 1934, "practically the whole body" of his own conclusions and recommendations, not only for the improvement of Ellis Island, but also for the reform of the deportation laws.[10]

The committee's report was painstaking and detailed. It reviewed the history of Ellis Island and noted the changing conditions facing the arriving immigrant. In the old days, all immigrants went to Ellis Island as a matter of routine; now they were so thoroughly inspected before arrival, both overseas and on shipboard, that comparatively few were sent there for further examination. Only 4,488 incoming aliens, including both immigrants and visitors, had been held on the island during the previous fiscal year, usually for not more than two or three days. The problem of the outgoing alien was more acute. In the same fiscal year, 7,037 outgoing aliens had passed through Ellis Island. Most of them had to wait there for their passports and sailing arrangements, sometimes for long periods, while foreign consuls carefully investigated their status as nationals whom they should take back.

The report described the physical development of the island and its existing functional use. It noted that "a generous grant" of Public Works Administration funds had already been allocated to Ellis Island and was being used to add new land for recreational purposes. "The committee's recommendations in regard to buildings and grounds," it was observed, "are thus already in the process of being carried out." In other words, the committee had gracefully accepted what was already in part a *fait accompli.*[11]

The administrative organization of the Ellis Island station was described, with complimentary language to the staff and to "the enlightened supervision under which the Island was administered." The report expressed the hope that "for the future the high standards of the past year may be resolutely maintained." The committee found that Ellis Island was now the headquarters of District No. 3 of thirty-two immigration and naturalization districts into which the country had been divided since the immigration and naturalization bureaus had been merged in the summer of 1933. The district included southern New York and northern New Jersey. Separate naturalization offices were maintained in New York and Newark. The district was administered by a district commissioner of the Immigration and Naturalization Service, aided by a district director and an assistant director.

In addition to its executive offices, at this time the Ellis Island station consisted of twelve divisions, their titles generally indicating their functions: Boarding, Inspection, Record, Registry, Law, Bonding, Passport, Treasury, Deportation, Chinese, Night, and Filing. Some of these, such as the Passport Division, were relatively new. The Passport Division was a busy one; its function was to secure passports for aliens to be deported. "Very frequently this involved protracted correspondence with the consulate of the foreign country of which the deportee was a citizen," as in many cases the deportee was no more wanted at home than he was in the United States. The committee found that the Boarding Division, which now did nearly all the actual inspection work, and the Law Division, responsible for investigating deportation cases and handling all related legal matters, were both understaffed. The Chinese Division was a comparatively new one, as the administration of the Chinese exclusion law had for many years been separate from Ellis Island. The total staff at this time amounted to 450, "a much smaller figure than the station had maintained during the height of its operations." No comparable analysis was made of the medical staff at Ellis Island, which was composed of Public Health Service employees, part of the Treasury Department but under the general administrative direction of the commissioner.[12]

The Ellis Island Committee, while generally approving Corsi's administration, pointed out a number of possible improvements, and also made recommendations for improving administrative practices at the consulates abroad. Going far beyond the boundaries of Ellis Island, the committee concerned itself with departmental regulations and made recommendations, generally for the protection of the alien, in connection with reentry permits, certificates of registry, deportation, education, and naturalization. It also drew up a broad program of legal reform, under the heading of "Recommendations Requiring Action by Congress." In general, proposed amendments to existing immigration and naturalization laws were in the direction of greater efficiency and, more especially, more humane and just treatment of the alien.[13]

Accepting Corsi's building program, already under way, the report called for better facilities at Ellis Island for segregating the different classes, both of deportees and of incoming immigrants. To this end it recommended that the large baggage and dormitory building be remodeled for deportees and that a new building be built to hold the incoming immigrants. The new building was to be on a fill (already under construction) behind a new seawall on the northwest side of the island. A number of physical improvements were proposed for the hospital group, and the space between Island No. 2 and Island No. 3, which had been filled during the 1920s, was to be landscaped and used for hospital recreation. There was also to be a new fireproof ferryhouse, and the covered passageways connecting it with the principal groups of buildings were to be rebuilt in fireproof construction. Much detailed repair work was called for throughout all the old buildings.

A large part of this physical development program was carried out within the next two years, the last major construction on the island. Landscaping of the grounds and general repair were carried on with Works Progress Administration labor for several years. The secretary's annual report for 1934 referred to the recommendations of the Ellis Island Committee for alterations and extensions of facilities and said that there were similar needs at other immigration stations. An allotment of $1,422,980 had been obtained from the Public Works Administration for improvements; of this total, $1,151,800 had been given to Ellis Island. "Work on these various projects," the report said, "was started in 1934 but will not be completed until 1935."[14]

The secretary's office had accepted not only the Ellis Island Committee's building program but also many of its administrative recommendations. "The report of the Ellis Island Committee," said the report, "and the recommendations of the district directors, as weighed and considered by the Commissioner and his principal assistants, have been the basis of many of the administrative reforms effected during the past year and of the recommendations for legislation which have been submitted to Congress." Actually, Secretary Perkins had begun to liberalize the regulations affecting arrested aliens as soon as she took office.[15]

Corsi resigned early in 1934, before the Ellis Island Committee's report was released. He found that the routine at the island was so well established that there was little for him to do except sign his name to letters and documents. "Aside from overseeing the functioning of the job," he said, "my daily duties were practically nil. My work there was finished." Fiorello La Guardia, the dynamic new mayor of New York, had asked him to serve as his director of relief. Corsi, who had taken an active part in his friend La Guardia's Fusion campaign for his office, accepted the challenge. Ellis Island's notoriety had faded, the *Literary Digest* commented. "Only occasionally now does this most famous of national gateways appear in the news." It had done so with the recent resignation of Edward Corsi as commissioner of immigration. Ellis Island's major activities were now concerned with deportation. It maintained a detective force whose duties took its members far afield. As the court of last resort for the deportee, it also maintained a large law division. "So altogether it is quite as busy as of yore, but it is now more of a home for a large administrative staff—numbering 450—than a huge clearing house for impatient transients." [16]

Immigration continued at a reduced pace throughout the 1930s. With the growth of totalitarianism in parts of Europe, there was great pressure to relax the immigration laws and regulations in favor of refugees from persecution, especially for Jews in Germany and later in Austria. But the restrictionist bloc in Congress was too powerful to permit legislation, and organized labor strongly cautioned Roosevelt against relaxation of the Hoover visa policy. The Roosevelt administration did finally relax this policy in 1938, after Austria had been absorbed by Nazi Germany, and also promoted an international conference to seek a solution to the refugee problem. But the United States took no lead in accepting more refugees, and little came of the meeting. With 1940 and the fall of Norway and France to the Nazis, the fear of subversion by Nazi agents disguised as refugees brought instructions from the State Department to its consular officers to withhold visas from anyone about whom they had "any doubt whatsoever." Refugees from Nazism taken into the United States during the whole Hitler period have been estimated at not more than 250,000. The tradition of America as an asylum for the oppressed, long under erosion, seemed almost to have vanished. The flow was not on a scale to affect operations at Ellis Island to any marked degree, except for extra paperwork in checking the travel documents of refugees "with particular care." [17]

Deportations also continued, but in a more orderly and generally more humane manner than had been the practice before the time of Corsi and the Ellis Island Committee. Internally, Ellis Island was long racked by a scandal that broke as a result of the consolidation of the immigration and naturalization bureaus. It was found that for years, frauds, involving chiefly naturalization but also immigration cases, had been perpetrated by racketeers acting in collusion with employees with access to the official records stored at the island. In the continuing depression, also, jobs with the Works Progress Administration often came to be highly prized. As such jobs were restricted to citizens, alien applicants who had never bothered to apply for their citizenship papers now sought a short cut, and a whole class of crooks sprang up to meet the need. Commissioner Rudolph Reimer, Corsi's successor, more than once publicly warned aliens against procuring fraudulent citizenship papers for cash, urging them instead to come to Ellis Island where they could get advice and help in making legal application. Fraudulent papers, he admonished them, were subject to cancellation and might lead to the prosecution and deportation of those who used them.

Similar frauds had been exposed in the past, but these were on a scale large enough to justify prolonged investigation. In the first year of the investigation, 5,000 bound volumes of passenger manifests filed at Ellis Island covering the arrival of 4,000,000 individual immigrants were examined for alterations and insertions, and approximately 150,000 naturalization petitions, with files and court records in Manhattan and Brooklyn extending over a period of nine years, were checked. It was revealed that manifests had been altered, official documents were missing, and whole files had been stolen. It was found that "from $300 to $1,200 had been collected for the alteration of manifests to show legal entry and thus safeguard an alien against deportation or enable him to procure citizenship." The investigation continued into 1940 and involved the successful prosecution of over 250 racketeers, island employees, aliens, and steamship companies. The scope of the inquiry was ultimately enlarged to include registry frauds, visa frauds, the smuggling of aliens, seamen's certificate frauds, and other illegal activities.[18]

The fine new immigration building erected on the recommendation of the Ellis Island Committee remained unused for several years. This situation attracted the attention of the Bureau of the Budget, and the Immigration and Naturalization Service was forced to explain. The building had been intended for the use of detained arriving aliens. It had been felt that "a separate building and better quarters should be established for this class of aliens than for the average deportee who is frequently of the criminal or other undesirable type." It had never been used for several reasons. "Principally, the volume of business did not increase, improvements were made in the main building, and, above all, appropriations were never made available for the maintenance of the necessary help to maintain a building of this size." Ironically, while the money could never be had while such a building was really needed, it became available and the structure was erected after the need had passed.

Soon afterward, in 1939, war having broken out once more in Europe, the Coast Guard was directed to conduct extensive patrols to enforce the Neutrality Act. Quarters were needed for training, and the Coast Guard thought that Ellis Island was a likely site. The Labor Department accordingly turned over to the Treasury Department the unused immigration building and the ground floor of the baggage and dormitory building.[19]

The interest of the Budget Bureau in the operation of Ellis Island by no means ceased with the allocation of space there to the Coast Guard. At hearings on Immigration and Naturalization Service estimates a few weeks later, "the Bureau officials objected vociferously to the constant heavy expense involved in operating the Ellis Island ferry-boat and other appurtenances such as the docks and steam boilers on that almost deserted island." Figures supplied to the bureau had shown that maintenance and operation of buildings for fiscal years 1936, 1937, and 1938 had cost $47,820.48, $101,549.16, and $49,598.45, respectively, aside from work done by the Public Works and Works Progress administrations. The operation of the ferryboat *Ellis Island* during calendar years 1936, 1937, and 1938 had cost $79,951.61, $186,222.42, and $81,177.41, respectively. It was suggested that the Department of Labor try to arrange a deal with some other government agency such as the Coast Guard to take over the whole of Ellis Island and secure space and a new building on the mainland.

By this time the combined Immigration and Naturalization Service was carrying on operations at several points in Manhattan. Secretary Perkins accepted the Budget Bureau's suggestion and began seriously seeking a central location which would permit turning over Ellis Island altogether to the armed forces. A project for a $6 million building in Manhattan to house all the local operations of the service was set on foot and approved in the executive office of the president. But no appropriation or allotment of funds was made then, and the building did not materialize until a good many years later.[20]

With the coming of World War II, Ellis Island went through a cycle of use somewhat similar to that which it had experienced in World War I. Before the United States entered the war, however, the island celebrated a birthday party. Commissioner Reimer decided to observe the fiftieth anniversary of the signing of the bill establishing the immigration station, which had taken place on April 11, 1890. Governor's Island fired an eleven-gun salute across the channel and sent over an army band to play for the occasion. The ferryboat *Ellis Island*, which had carried millions of immigrants to Manhattan and a new life in America, was dressed in bunting. The commissioner was host to his staff at lunch, and he reminded them that "fifty years ago President Harrison signed the bill authorizing establishment of the immigration station, which supplanted Castle Garden in Battery Park." [21]

The immigrant had at first been regarded pretty much as a species of import, and the function of immigration control had been assigned to the Treasury Department. Increasingly, he came to be viewed as an addition to the national labor force—a threat or a blessing, depending on the point of view—and immigration control was assigned to the Department of Commerce and Labor (1903). When a separate Labor Department was set up (1913), it was assigned to that agency. Now, with Europe once more ablaze, and especially with the fall of Norway to the forces of Hitler partly through the agency of subversion, the immigrant came to be viewed in still another light. He was considered primarily in the aspect of his potential threat to the national security, and the Immigration and Naturalization Service was shifted to the Department of Justice, effective June 14, 1940.

As part of the same trend, the Alien Registration Act passed in the same month not only required the registration of all aliens throughout the country but also added to the list of deportable classes and called for the fingerprinting of all aliens seeking to enter the United States. This added to the growing bundle of papers that each immigrant had to carry with him and imposed additional duties on the immigration inspector operating from the Barge Office. As always, when the immigration laws were tightened, a few more unhappy immigrants were detained at Ellis Island.[22]

As in 1917, Ellis Island in 1941 and 1942 played host briefly to the crews of captured enemy ships taken over by the government. These men were soon transferred to detention camps elsewhere, as were many other German, Italian, and Japanese nationals picked up by the Federal Bureau of Investigation and temporarily deposited on the island. As the war went on, and immigration through New York almost ceased, Ellis Island became primarily a place of detention for family groups of enemy aliens.[23]

With the detention there of enemy aliens, Ellis Island became again for a time a very busy place. By May 1942, when the Navy Department asked for additional space on the island, the attorney general felt obliged to refuse the request. "The Immigration and Naturalization Service now has in its custody on Ellis Island approximately 1,000 aliens," he explained. "The detention quarters are insufficient for the needs of the Service and it has been found necessary to request the City of New York to permit us to use some of the dormitories on Rikers Island for alien detention facilities." As "numerous complaints of various kinds" came in regarding these detentions, the commissioner began a busy search for quarters elsewhere. Under wartime conditions space was hard to find, and nothing came of these efforts.

Another solution was proposed. The Immigration and Naturalization Service now had some space in the WPA Headquarters Building at 70 Columbus Avenue. It was proposed to rent the entire building (the WPA was now winding up its affairs) and transfer there all the administrative work at Ellis Island, "retaining there only those activities incident to the care and maintenance of detained aliens." This move was carried out in 1943. All the functions of the service in the New York area except detention were concentrated in the Columbus Avenue building, while Ellis Island was kept "solely as a detention station for aliens." [24]

Another important operation began at the island, however, at the same time. An investigation of arrearages in the work of the Record Division there in 1941 had brought a recommendation for the copying of the disintegrating records. The work of microfilming some 14,000 volumes of ships' manifests and other immigration records stored at Ellis Island, covering the years 1897–1942, began in 1943 and was completed in the following year. The National Archives assisted in preparing the material for microfilming, and a negative set of the film record was deposited in the archives, the positive being retained for Immigration and Naturalization Service use.[25]

While a few enemy aliens were kept in internment on Ellis Island into 1948, operations there tapered off rapidly after the end of the war. The Coast Guard station on the island was decommissioned in 1946, leaving the entire immigration building, about half of the ferryhouse, and much of the baggage and detention building untenanted. In this situation the attorney general sought once more to get rid of this expensive installation. "Owing to excessive operating costs," he said, "I deem it imperative that the Immigration and Naturalization Service vacate its quarters on Ellis Island in New York harbor at the earliest possible date." "Ellis Island, the historic patch of land jutting out of the Upper Bay about a mile south of the Battery, which was the port of entry of the great immigrant invasion of the early 1900s," the *New York Herald Tribune* announced prematurely, "is about to be abandoned."

The Public Buildings Administration was sympathetic, but raised the question of what disposition should be made of the property. It appeared doubtful that any other government agency would want it. The National Park Service. which at the time did not have an appropriation adequate to the basic maintenance of its existing holdings, was not prepared to accept it as a historic area on which it would have to spend money. The problem was put under study, and meanwhile Ellis Island, which had lost even the name of an immigration station, was retained in use as a "detention facility" of the Immigration and Naturalization Service.[26]

Describing Ellis Island in 1949, the service's *Monthly Review* had this to say of it:

> Ellis Island, in the Harbor of New York City, is used solely as a detention and deportation center by the U.S. Immigration Service. Once a general reception center for all aliens entering the United States, it has not been used for this purpose for 30 years. No immigrant or visitor whose passport and entry papers are in order now goes to the island. More than 99 percent of all immigrants and visitors arrive with documents and papers in order.

The Immigration and Naturalization Service was making an effort to better the public image of Ellis Island, which had certainly not improved during and after the war. The Communist *Daily Worker* gleefully referred to it as "America's first concentration camp." Edward J. Shaughnessy, recently appointed district director for the New York area, organized a tour of the island for newspapermen, who had for some time been little welcomed there. He insisted that there was nothing secretive about the department that guarded the country's gates; it was no Nazi Gestapo, no Soviet NKVD. "Even more vehemently did he stress in a later informal talk with newspaper men that he planned to explode the myth that Ellis Island was a combination Devil's Island and Alcatraz." He pointed out that the place was not a prison and that the people held there were detainees, not prisoners. They had freedom to roam large areas of the island. There were large sections for recreation, clean dormitories and detention rooms, and the food was ample and wholesome. "The immigration official's statements were borne out," according to the *New York Times* reporter, who seems to have gotten a more favorable impression of the place. On the island that day, Shaughnessy told the newsmen, there were held 330 persons from 65 countries.[27]

In the same year the holding of hearings for detained aliens, which had been done at the office on Columbus Avenue, was returned to Ellis Island, partly on humanitarian grounds. It was pointed out that this move would eliminate the escorting of aliens from the detention quarters on the island by ferryboat and bus to Columbus Avenue, with the accompanying traffic hazards, risk of escape, and "the feeling of being 'herded around' by uniformed officers which no doubt is humiliating to many of the passengers who are held for board hearings." [28]

The cold war with Soviet Russia that developed in the years following World War II brought additional measures looking toward the exclusion of subversive aliens. Liberal forces led by President Harry Truman were able to get two successive measures passed providing for the admission to the United States of several hundred thousand carefully screened "displaced persons," or postwar refugees, but the general trend was still toward exclusion. The "DPs," as they were called, were so to speak washed seven times in the waters of Jordan before they left Europe, and had comparatively little impact on the island. More noteworthy, as far as its effect on Ellis Island was concerned, was the Internal Security Act of 1950. Among its many provisions was one specifically excluding members of Communist and Fascist organizations. This measure was passed over Truman's veto and his vehement opposition. However, with its passage, he directed its enforcement to the letter.

This brought a new flurry of activity at Ellis Island. Aliens arriving at the Port of New York who had received passports before September 23, 1950, and who arrived after that date, had to be carefully screened for membership in the proscribed organizations. They were taken to Ellis Island for the purpose. Those who were or had been members—even if nominal—had to be detained. The Immigration and Naturalization Service, its New York office reported later, "was confronted with the terrific problem of excluding from admission a large horde of aliens who had obtained visas prior and immediately subsequent to the passage of the Internal Security Act. . . . It called for quick and efficient action to relieve the misery, suffering and embarrassment which followed in the wake of this unexpected event." [29]

The *New York Times Magazine* told of the removal to Ellis Island for detention and special screening of 130 immigrants taken from a ship that docked at New York, an experience typical of many. "Believing until their arrival that they had passed the last barrier when they obtained visas and boat tickets, they were baffled and bitterly disappointed." The writer thought that it was high time for Ellis Island to be closed. "It would remove the physical symbol of an institution that for many newcomers means the end of hope, not its beginning." Although conditions were relatively good there and officials sympathetic, it was still "Heartbreak Hotel." "The throngs of immigrants caught in the net of the new security law emphasizes that the nation needs a new gateway."

The magazine *Life* sent a team to Ellis Island and took pictures reminiscent, in their crowded scenes, of those taken by Lewis Hine in 1905. The *American Mercury* proclaimed that many world-famous artists, GI brides, and other aliens had been pulled off ships and planes and sent to Ellis Island after having been issued immigrant visas by the State Department. The *New Yorker* ran a story telling of the detention there of a Czech theatrical producer, George Voskovec, a man with his first papers toward American citizenship, who had been picked up at La Guardia Airport, sent to Ellis Island, and held there for ten months on the hearsay evidence of one witness to his pro-communism.[30]

This was the last serious beating that Ellis Island was forced to take from the press. The situation was eased when Attorney General J. Howard McGrath ruled that "nominal membership" in Nazi, Fascist, or Spanish Falangist groups would not prevent temporary entries. Clarifying legislation was passed in the spring of 1951, making the exclusion dependent solely upon voluntary, and not upon involuntary, membership in totalitarian organizations. Those who had been members of the Hitler Youth in childhood, for instance, or who had been members of a Fascist or Communist labor union in order to be able to eat, were no longer to be regarded as dangerous subversives.[31]

After the detention cases arising from the strict enforcement of the Internal Security Act had been cleared away, a roundup of aliens illegally resident in the district brought another brief period of congestion at Ellis Island. This "so-called free-lance work," somewhat reminiscent of Doak's roundup in 1931, was undertaken on an experimental basis by the local office of the Immigration and Naturalization Service in June 1951. The cold war with Soviet Russia was at one of its numerous peaks, and District Director Shaughnessy no doubt believed that he was doing his patriotic duty in rounding up all the potentially subversive aliens within reach. Officers were sent out "to investigate at docks, restaurants, saloons, hotels, etc. to apprehend any aliens who might be found working there in an illegal status." The central office cooperated by assigning sixty investigators from other districts. In a few weeks approximately 1,500

Waiting at Ellis Island in 1950, during the Internal Security Act flurry of detentions, compared with a similar scene during the high tide of immigration in the early 1900s.

—Courtesy of the New York Public Library

illegally resident aliens in the New York–New Jersey area, were apprehended, including deserting seamen, some stowaways, smuggled aliens, and overstay visitors.

The aliens picked up were held without bail, but their cases were processed as rapidly as possible, with the aid of hearing officers and stenographers from other districts. The island was a busy place for a time, and the drive seems to have been abandoned only because there were not funds to continue it. Senator Pat McCarran of Nevada, author of the Internal Security Act of the year before and then collecting material for the highly restrictive immigration law that was to be passed in 1952, charged that possibly 5,000,000 aliens had poured into the country illegally, basing his statement on secret testimony by immigration officials. These aliens, he was certain, included vast numbers of "militant Communists, Sicilian bandits and other criminals," who would provide an enemy nation with "a ready-made fifth column." The Immigration Service had made little effort to seek them out and deport them, he said, because it was handicapped by lack of funds and staff.[32] Just how militant Communists and Sicilian bandits could be combined in a fifth column McCarran did not make clear.

Ellis Island gradually quieted down again, although increased detentions under the 1950 act and the roundup of illegally resident aliens in the following June for a time raised the population of the island to nearly 1,500. This congestion caused some hurried rearrangement of space and extensive repairs. File rooms had to be cleared and reclaimed as detention quarters. The dining room then in use seated only 300 people, and, as deportees had to be separated from others, this meant that meals had to be served practically all day. Meanwhile, the Public Health Service, which had not been able to obtain funds for necessary repairs, had closed the hospital group on the island, and there was nothing but a small infirmary for the sick. Medical examinations, in many cases, had to be held in PHS hospitals elsewhere in the New York area. A new school was opened for the children of detainees, with as many as 125 children in attendance at one time. The chapel was reequipped, and plans were made for buying new furniture for the detainees' day quarters. The hospital buildings on Island No. 2, abandoned by the Public Health Service, were taken over temporarily by the Coast Guard.

The program of renovation and repair at Ellis Island continued in the following year. A public-address system was installed, providing an "integrated system of surveillance." A thirty-bed infirmary was completed, though serious illnesses were still handled at hospitals elsewhere in the city. Plans were completed and approved for refurnishing the quarters occupied by "passengers," as incoming aliens were now called. At the same time, it was noted that the Ellis Island plant was physically a problem area: "This detention station, with its great, wide halls and corridors, high ceilings, unusable spaces and outmoded utilities, will always present the dual problem of how to utilize it with economy and yet make it serve our purposes efficiently," the annual report noted.[33]

Late in 1953, the commissioner of immigration and naturalization reminded the Senate Appropriations Committee that the recommendations of the service for the construction of a new immigration station in the New York City area had been on file for several years. "However," he added resignedly, "present indications are that it will be necessary for us to continue to occupy Ellis Island indefinitely." The service at the same time issued a short history of the island, emphasizing the improved detention facilities and concluding bravely:

> Today, Ellis Island is a vastly different place from what it was during the exciting bustling days of its youth. However, it still continues to play an important part in the life of this great Nation, and in the minds and hearts of millions of America's foster sons and daughters it will always stand as the "Gateway" to a Promised Land of freedom and opportunity—the United States of America.[34]

Nevertheless, relief was at last in sight. Renewed study of the problem of space indicated that all the operations still carried on at Ellis Island might be housed in the building on Columbus Avenue. The major benefits foreseen were two. "Having all of the functions presently located at 70 Columbus Avenue integrated with the functions now at Ellis Island," the district director reported, "will add tremendously to the efficient operation of the New York District. Also of major benefit will be the tremendous money savings that will be effected by not having to maintain Ellis Island and the ferry." Learning of the proposed move, the *Christian Science Monitor* sent a reporter to Ellis Island to get the facts and pick up some color for a story. District Director Shaughnessy, veteran of thirty-eight years in the Immigration Service, gave a personally conducted tour. "As we walked along the heavily arched masonry corridors," it was reported, "stopping to look into the unused rooms with rows of empty cots ranged under the high ceilings of 1897 architecture, recognizing the scrubbed cleanliness of the tiled floors as evidence of both good housekeeping and little use," Shaughnessy gave a thumbnail sketch of immigration's flood and ebb on the island. That day, he said, there were only 237 detainees on the island; the staff to serve them numbered 250. "Will Ellis Island be given up by immigration?" he was asked. "Certainly," he said, but he would give no date.[35]

The major problem involved was the housing of detainees. That problem was solved, at last, by the simple process of reducing the number of detainees. Attorney General Herbert Brownell, Jr., announced the new policy at mass ceremonies in Ebbets Field and the Polo Grounds in New York on November 11, 1954, at which 16,000 men and women became citizens of the United States. New prearrival inspection procedures at ports of embarkation and on ships crossing the Atlantic, he told the assembled new Americans, would cut possible detentions to a minimum. Furthermore, "henceforth only those regarded as likely to abscond, or who might be risks to national security or public safety, would be detained." Heretofore, many aliens whose papers were not in order were detained at Ellis Island and other facilities. Under the new policy, already being put in force, Brownell explained, most aliens with purely technical difficulties would be allowed to proceed to their destinations under parole.

This simple humanitarian ruling brought the long and troubled history of the Ellis Island immigration station to a close. Within ten days of the change the number of aliens held in New York City dropped to about twenty-five, compared with a usual detention population of several hundred. During the remaining part of the fiscal year 1955, some 200,000 aliens, including immigrants and visitors, entered the United States through the Port of New York, by ship or air, and only sixteen of them were detained. "Ellis Island and other large facilities," the Immigration and Naturalization Service reported at the end of the year, "were closed." The last man detained on the island was Arne Peterssen, a Norwegian seaman who had jumped ship, been held there only three days, and was then released on parole to return to Norway. The ferryboat *Ellis Island*, which had been in service for fifty years, made its last run on November 29 and was left permanently in its slip. The island was vacated and declared excess to the needs of the government; it was determined to be surplus property on March 4, 1955.[36]

Catapulted from insignificance to national and international prominence and notoriety by a set of curious chances, Ellis Island had been for more than thirty years the steadily narrowing gateway to America, as well as the storm center of the national debate, which grew hotter almost by the year, over immigration. For another thirty years it had been chiefly the sad point of incarceration and departure of the unwanted. It had received perhaps 12,000,000 immigrants. A good percentage of these went home again, particularly in depression years. Many came back and passed through Ellis Island two or three times. Many thousands who, for one reason or another, could not meet the increasingly rigid standards of reception and domicile, were barred or later expelled at Ellis Island.

While the permanent addition to the population of the United States that streamed through the island was therefore much less than the number received, the majority stayed and did their part in the building of the nation. Men whom we delight to honor, who came to us by way of Ellis Island, are still with us. Their sons and daughters are legion. There is nothing really fanciful in calling Ellis Island, as has been done, the Plymouth Rock of its day. There is no single point in the country where American social history for a generation and more comes to a sharper focus.[37]

CHAPTER VIII

A NATIONAL MONUMENT

The General Services Administration, responsible for the disposal of unwanted government property, had, in accordance with standing procedures, canvassed federal agencies before declaring Ellis Island surplus. No interest in the aging group of structures on their isolated site developed. According to the prescribed ritual, states and local governments had the next chance at the property, but they were expected to pay 50 percent of fair market value. Varied suggestions developed at this level. The city of New York showed interest in purchasing the site as a home for aged persons and homeless men. Another proposal, from export-import sources, was that the city buy it as an international trade center. Senator Irving Ives of New York introduced a bill for state purchase for use as an alcoholic clinic. New Jersey State Senator James F. Murray, Jr., proposed that his state acquire Ellis Island and develop it as a cultural and recreation center.[1]

New York City negotiations with the GSA for purchase of the island were taken seriously on both sides and went on for some time. Dr. Luther H. Gulick, city administrator, announced in June 1955 that the city was "near an agreement with the Federal Government for acquiring Ellis Island for the treatment and care of aged and alcoholic men." New Jersey now entered into competition. Dr. Joseph E. McLean, New Jersey commissioner of conservation and economic development, prodded by Senator Murray, wrote the regional office of the GSA arguing that the use of Ellis Island as an ethnic museum would be far more appropriate than an institution for alcoholics. He also pointed out that he had a preliminary legal opinion that the island lay within the geographical limits of New Jersey.

State Senator Murray continued to agitate the Jersey claim to the island. Early in the following year he assembled "an expeditionary force of New Jersey officials," which landed there from a Coast Guard cutter and inspected the site. It was reported later that they would have planted a New Jersey state flag if anyone had thought to bring one along. Murray expounded his project for an ethnic museum and recreation center under Jersey auspices, but Mayor Robert F. Wagner's office announced firmly that New York City was "still very much interested in Ellis Island," which it wanted for its departments of welfare and correction. This revival of an ancient dispute formed part of the background in later negotiations for the disposal of the island, and an attempt to heal it was an important factor in the final decision.

As New York City studied the problem further, enthusiasm for the purchase of the island diminished. The property was appraised at something over $6 million and the city would have to put up half the amount. Figures on maintenance cost of the huge array of buildings and the ferry, readily available from the GSA, were discouraging. City employees displayed great reluctance to work on the isolated site with its rather sinister reputation. Negotiations languished, and Walter F. Downey, regional commissioner of the GSA, announced in September 1956 that it had been decided to put Ellis Island up for sale to the highest bidder for private commercial use. Proposals for public use of different kinds had come from both New York and New Jersey, but "None of these proposals developed to the point at which the Government could make an award," Downey said. Nor had any private nonprofit group come forward.[2]

At this point, considerable sentiment appeared in favor of some sort of memorial use of the island, in preference to its commercial use. Telegrams went to President Dwight D. Eisenhower and the GSA from varied sources, urging that the sale be put off to allow time to study its possibilities for preservation as a national historic monument and charging that it would be "cheap and tawdry" to sell it to a private developer. It should be "set aside as a national memorial to America's immigrants." Mayor Wagner issued a statement saying that while his administration could not afford to buy Ellis Island from the federal government, it did not want the property transferred to private ownership. He declared that the government should "retain it as a national shrine or cede it to the state or city." The president obligingly ordered the suspension of plans for the sale, and it was intimated that proposals involving preservation of the island as a national monument might appear in the next Congress.[3]

Here a complication arose. Plans were already far along for memorializing the immigrant in an American Museum of Immigration at the base of the Statue of Liberty, less than half a mile from Ellis Island. The National Park Service, the official agency for administering and developing for public use national historic areas, was deeply committed to this project, which was a combined public and private venture.

The background of the proposal was rather involved. The walls of the famous New York Aquarium in Battery Park had been saved from destruction to make way for the Brooklyn-Battery Tunnel in 1950, after a ten-year battle. The aquarium, which had been built just before the War of 1812 as a fort to guard the point of Manhattan Island, was in that year declared a national monument by presidential proclamation, under authorizing legislation passed by Congress some years before. The American Scenic and Historic Preservation Society, under the leadership of George McAneny, had been instrumental in saving the old structure. Mr. McAneny had been primarily interested in preserving the round masonry building because of its military associations, and the site was now officially designated as Castle Clinton National Monument. But the structure, as "Castle Garden," had also served from 1855 to 1890 as the New York State immigration station, and some 7,000,000 immigrants had been received there.

In 1952 the American Scenic and Historic Preservation Society took up for consideration a project presented by William H. Baldwin, one of its trustees, for an immigration museum somewhere in the Port of New York, where most of the immigrants had landed. The cold war with the Soviet Union had produced a need for national unity, he reasoned, and such a museum would be a strong force to this end. The most appropriate site for it, in Mr. Baldwin's opinion, was Castle Clinton National Monument. The society had been instrumental in saving the structure, he pointed out, and was in a strong position to propose such a line of development to the National Park Service.[4]

The NPS was definitely interested, but had a counterproposal. The Statue of Liberty National Monument had been under its administration for a number of years, and it had done a great deal of planning and accomplished much toward improving and beautifying the area. One of its unfinished projects there was to complete the statue's pedestal in line with the intention of Richard M. Hunt, its architect. Hunt had visualized a stepped terrace around the base of the statue connecting it with the surrounding walls of old Fort Wood. This terrace had never been built, owing to lack of funds, and the intervening space had been filled with a rather unsightly earthen mound. If the terrace were now to be built, it was urged, there would be room beneath it for the proposed immigration museum; and the appearance of the Statue of Liberty, which had been a powerful symbol to arriving immigrants, would be greatly enhanced. As for Castle Clinton, there was not room there for adequate museum treatment of such a broad subject as immigration, and the NPS felt committed to the McAneny plan of restoration as a fort, commemorating the military history of lower Manhattan from early Dutch times. After negotiations culminating in a joint meeting at Castle Clinton, this plan was approved by both agencies.[5]

In accordance with this decision, a private nonprofit corporation known as The American Museum of Immigration, Inc., with Major General Ulysses S. Grant 3rd as its president, was formed to carry on a campaign for public contributions to the building of the museum, similar to the campaign that Pulitzer's *World* had waged many years before to erect the pedestal of the Statue of Liberty. The funds collected would be turned over to the NPS, which would construct and maintain the museum as an integral part of the national monument. The project was by far the most ambitious plan to improve the interpretation of the Statue of Liberty, and would virtually complete the program there. The museum was "intended to harmonize with the basic symbolism of the Statue, stimulating and enlarging the concept of liberty as sought, found, and developed by generations of Americans of diverse origins." [6]

A prospectus for the museum had been prepared by the National Park Service, and the fund-raising campaign was getting into full stride when the movement to memorialize the immigrant at Ellis Island began to gather strength, and when President Eisenhower stopped the proposed sale of the island to allow time to consider this proposal. Mr. Baldwin, who had first proposed the immigration museum, was in charge of the campaign, and the Ellis Island proposal disturbed him. It would, he felt, deflate the drive for funds for the American Museum of Immigration at the Statue of Liberty. "No immigrant," he pointed out in a letter to the *New York Times*, "was attracted to America by Ellis Island or Castle Garden. . . . The lodestar for all of them was the torch of the Statue of Liberty." The National Park Service, equally committed to the project at the Statue of Liberty, also took a negative view of the proposed memorialization at Ellis Island.[7] It had put its immigration eggs in another basket.

The General Services Administration, in accordance with the presidential directive, postponed for some time its efforts to sell the island, but noted that "the proposal to make the island an immigrant shrine was not feasible because the National Park Service had designated Liberty Island as such." New York City had lost interest in the site, and, toward the end of the year, the GSA announced that it would put the island up for auction.

The GSA advertised the forthcoming sale of "one of the most famous landmarks in the world," but when the bids were opened at the middle of February the offers were disappointing. Many bidders had visited the island, but the general view among them was that none of the thirty-five structures could be used for commercial purposes, and that a buyer would have to spend between $8 million and $10 million for demolition alone. There were twenty-one bids, but the highest among them was only $201,000. This was offered by Sol G. Atlas, a builder who had done a large amount of construction in the metropolitan area in recent years. Atlas had plans for what he called "Pleasure Island," which included a 600-room hotel, arcades, canals, a convention hall, a music shed, a school of languages, a marina, swimming pools, a boat-in cinema, helicopter pads, tennis courts, and a "Museum of New Americans." After due consideration, during which protest against commercial use of Ellis Island continued, the GSA rejected all the bids, none of which "was commensurate with the appraised fair market value of the property."

Again in 1959 and in 1960 Ellis Island was twice offered for sale under sealed bids, and twice again all bids were rejected. Sol Atlas remained the high bidder;

he first tripled his bid to $671,000 and then raised it to $1,025,000, but the GSA still held out for a better price. Numerous proposals for public use of the island were also made from time to time, but none of these was considered acceptable. A GSA spokesman stated, when for the third time all sealed bids were turned down, that "the commercial bids were too low and that the non-commercial bids were not adequately developed." [8]

Considerable interest now developed in creating a liberal arts college on Ellis Island. The GSA called on the Department of Health, Education and Welfare to handle negotiations along this line. A large group of educators, with Columbia University heavily represented, formed the Committee on Ellis Island for Higher Education, Inc., and made plans for an unorthodox "college of the future," with an experimental curriculum, high faculty pay, no fund raising, and no endowments. The Department of Health, Education and Welfare was authorized to make the island available without charge. This project was presented to HEW, but, along with several other proposals for use of the island for health or educational purposes, was turned down. None of the proposals, the department announced, "fully meet the requirements as outlined." HEW gave up the effort to dispose of Ellis Island and turned the problem back to the General Services Administration.

Other proposals for public use of the island continued to appear, and several bills in support of these were introduced in Congress. In 1962, New Jersey and New York senators requested public hearings on these bills before the Senate Committee on Government Operations. The subcommittee on intergovernmental relations took up the matter, and the GSA was asked to defer action on final disposal of Ellis Island until it had concluded its review of the problem. There were preliminary hearings in September, and late in the year there were two days of additional public hearings in New York City before the subcommittee, headed by Maine Senator Edmund S. Muskie, Democrat, whose colleagues were Senators Jacob K. Javits and Kenneth B. Keating, Republicans, of New York.[9]

At these hearings many plans were presented. Ellis Island for Higher Education, Inc., renewed its proposal for a liberal arts college, making full use of the existing buildings; Pearl Buck made an eloquent plea for the creation of a center for the comprehensive treatment of the mentally retarded; Jersey City, through its corporation counsel, stated that Ellis Island belonged to New Jersey and that the community "may find it advisable to embrace the island in plans for parks, recreation, residential, commercial and other uses." Other proposals included one for a "self-contained super-modern city" designed by the late Frank Lloyd Wright, a haven for elderly persons, and a training school for Americans going into public and private service abroad. Edward Corsi, former commissioner of immigration, recommended that the island be declared a national monument, stating that "close to half the American people trace their descent to someone who entered this country at Ellis Island."

"This approach met with a sympathetic reaction from all three Senators," it was reported, "and from Mayor Wagner, who testified after Mr. Corsi." At the close of the hearings, the members of the committee commented that several of the proposals had "real merit," but that in each case there were serious drawbacks. The importance of the island as a historic site seems to have impressed the committee. Senator Muskie volunteered the statement that "The problem of disposition has arisen from the fact that Ellis Island, a historic site, cannot be sold offhand and because the Department of the Interior's National Park Service showed no interest in the island in 1957." [10]

Officials in Jersey City and the state of New Jersey had been studying the recreational needs and resources of northern New Jersey for some time, with special attention to the long-decayed waterfront opposite Liberty and Ellis islands. Planning for this area, involving a proposed "Liberty Park," was far enough advanced to make a highly favorable impression on Senator Muskie's subcommittee when it met again to consider the problem of Ellis Island in September 1963. Muskie had called the meeting, inviting New York and New Jersey state and city officials, senators, and congressmen, together with interested federal officials, in an effort to arrive at a consensus on disposal. There was no consensus, but no one present favored commercial development. As a result of the New Jersey presentation, Senator Muskie raised the question of whether the proposed redevelopment of the Jersey shoreline "might enhance the possibilities of using the island for a national park, monument, or recreational purposes." He requested the National Park Service to review its policy toward Ellis Island in the light of New Jersey's redevelopment plans. The service agreed to do so.

Although an Interior Department representative was quoted at the time as telling the subcommittee that "it would not support any proposal for an immigration monument or museum on Ellis Island because there were already two such installations on Liberty Island and at Castle Clinton," the National Park Service had, in effect, yielded. While the point was not stressed in any public pronouncement at the time, it was recognized that New Jersey and New York were at odds over the ownership of the island. If federal jurisdiction were given up, this feud could easily flare up again; while such jurisdiction was retained, both states might be expected to let sleeping dogs lie. The only feasible way to insure this now seemed to be the designation of Ellis Island as a historic site or monument. Furthermore, the park development of the unsightly Jersey City waterfront, highly visible from the Statue of Liberty, was a project well worthy of support.[11]

The National Park Service called its own meeting on Ellis Island in December, at Federal Hall National Memorial in New York City. New Jersey and New York officials were invited, and it was announced that the service had set up a study team, in cooperation with the department's new Bureau of Outdoor Recreation, "to re-evaluate our initial report on Ellis Island in the context of what was happening around Ellis Island." The service asked for comment, saying that it "would cooperate fully with all agencies concerned in this study." In general, aside from some rebellious muttering among its own staff, the announcement was politely received. There seemed to be a disposition among local officials to let the federal government carry the ball. Associate Director George B. Hartzog, who had presided at the meeting, told newsmen after the closed session that "New Jersey's plans, as well as proposals by Jersey City, New York State and New York City, will be considered in the new study." [12]

The study team, headed by NPS Regional Director Ronald F. Lee, conferred at length with New Jersey and Jersey City officials, whose plans for Liberty Park were rapidly shaping up; considered the views of New York officials; visited Ellis Island several times; and submitted its report in the following June. The National Park Service study sought the coordination of the Jersey waterfront plan with development for Ellis Island, without giving up existing plans for the Statue of Liberty National Monument. Its plan for a two-state national historic site on the island, the *New York Times* reported, "would tie in with the American Museum of Immigration now under construction on Liberty Island and with a proposed 500-acre state park along Jersey City's blighted industrial-railroad waterfront." Part of the reasoning back of the plan lay in the fact that summer visitation to the Statue of Liberty was approaching the saturation point. With the development of a park on the Jersey shore, and possible access to Liberty Island from it, the NPS might easily be unable to handle the crowds. "Ellis Island with its proximity and its closely related interest," it was believed, "is a natural area for dispersion of visitors from Liberty Island. The two parks could complement each other."

The report visualized historic site development of Ellis Island, combined with recreational use. The older part of the island would become "an historical sanctuary area," with appropriate interpretation, while the larger and newer part of the island would include day-use park facilities, supporting the green park on the Jersey shore. Ellis Island and Liberty Island would be jointly administered, for efficiency and economy, by the National Park Service. "Any other administration at Ellis Island," it was pointed out diplomatically, "could well result in independent and uncoordinated programs for the two neighboring properties." The project, it was believed, "planned in close relation to the Statue of Liberty and the Jersey waterfront would provide a key public element in this national gateway harbor in the United States." [13]

Edward Corsi hailed the plan for development of Ellis Island as "a national historic site in tribute to American immigrants." It was gratifying to all those who had urged that the island be made a national monument. "For Ellis Island," he said in a letter to the *Times*, "is more than a piece of real estate. It is an important part of our American heritage. For millions of American families it has been a gateway to a new life of liberty and opportunity." Not to use

Ellis Island to honor these latter-day pioneers, Corsi urged, "and to mark the welding of many nationalities, races and religions into a united nation would mean the loss of an important national asset."

Secretary of the Interior Stewart L. Udall, during a conservation tour of the New York area some months later, visited Ellis Island in company with New Jersey and New York officials. He announced that he had accepted the recommendations of the National Park Service for the development of the island as a national historic site with recreational and cultural facilities. Federal development of the island, he commented, would "obviate any opening of hostilities between New York and New Jersey." The president's approval was regarded as a matter of form, a Udall aide told newsmen, and the only question remaining was whether the new park should be created by a presidential order or by Congress.[14]

While there had for some time been bills before Congress toward this end, it was finally decided that the simplest method would be for the president to declare Ellis Island a national monument, as he was empowered to do under the American Antiquities Act of 1906. This was done on May 11, 1965. President Lyndon B. Johnson proclaimed Ellis Island to be a part of Statue of Liberty National Monument, to be administered by the National Park Service. It was stipulated, however, that no funds appropriated for the administration of the national monument should be expended upon the development of Ellis Island except as provided by Congress.

During the ceremonial signing of the proclamation, President Johnson took advantage of the opportunity to call for passage of his immigration bill (which became law a few months later) doing away with the national origins quota system set up in the 1920s. Reform of the immigration laws to abolish this discriminatory system and replace it with a law "based on the skills of applicants" had been a favorite project of the martyred President John F. Kennedy, and Johnson was following it up vigorously. The president also called for funds to rehabilitate Ellis Island and gave his approval to the establishment of a new Job Corps camp, to be situated on the New Jersey shore adjacent to Ellis Island. Job corpsmen would, he said, "transform and restore Ellis Island and help the State of New Jersey create a new Liberty State Park in a blighted section of the Jersey City waterfront." [15]

Shortly thereafter, in a burst of enthusiasm, Secretary Udall designated Philip Johnson—a New York architect who had established a reputation for creating "sophisticated buildings of great polish and elegance," such as the New York State Theater at Lincoln Center—to redesign Ellis Island. The Congress, after a debate in which New Jersey and New York congressmen engaged in some good-natured banter over who really owned the island, passed a joint resolution, approved by the president on August 17, authorizing a maximum of $6 million to be appropriated for the development of Ellis Island as a part of Statue of Liberty National Monument.[16]

The General Services Administration, tiring of the very heavy outlay for maintaining Ellis Island, and feeling that its responsibility for upkeep had ceased, had some time before cut off the heat and other utilities. Only a single guard was kept on the island during the day, assisted by a watchdog who maintained permanent residence. In spite of the dog patrol at night, "harbor pirates managed to sneak ashore and carry off chairs, desks, metal piling and anything else that was portable." The lack of heat in the damp atmosphere of the bay soon showed its effect in falling plaster and tiles. Leaky roofs went unrepaired. Pigeons swarmed in through broken windows, and piles of manure built up here and there in the upper stories. On the lower floors water accumulated in places to a depth of several inches. Vegetation ran wild in the open spaces. The heavy concrete and granite seawall surrounding the island was cracking. Pilferage and vandalism continued. By the time Philip Johnson visited the island to visualize his design problem, the place was rapidly becoming a group of ruins.

Johnson's design plan took this situation into account. The plan was unveiled in the following February with some ceremony at Federal Hall National Memorial, during another visit of Secretary Udall at which he also took part in ground-breaking ceremonies at the projected Liberty State Park in Jersey. The plan, which Udall loyally pronounced "triumphant," called for merely stabilizing the ruins of the principal buildings, including the main building and the older hospital group across the ferry slip. Glass and wood would be stripped off, and vines would be encouraged to grow around and through the buildings. Visitors would view the ruins, creating an atmosphere of nostalgia, from raised walkways. All other structures would be demolished. There would be a viewing pyramid on the point of the original island facing the Manhattan skyline. Not far from it would be a restaurant in the shape of an early fortress. The dominating feature of the design was "The Wall of the 16 Million." This was to be a truncated hollow cone, 300 feet in diameter at the base and rising 130 feet above the harbor on the side toward the Statue of Liberty. It would be ringed inside and out by spiral ramps, along which visitors would see plaques listing the names of the immigrants who had passed through Ellis Island. Behind this monument, toward the Jersey shore, would be a lawn, with picnic facilities and a band shell.[17]

The Philip Johnson plan had a mixed reception. Ada Louise Huxtable, architectural critic of the *New York Times,* thought that it was "a creative, imaginative response to the problem of making a national landmark and shrine out of 27.5 weedy acres that have neither grace nor grandeur, but were the point of entry to a new world for 16 million immigrants." There was less enthusiasm shown on the editorial page of the same journal, where the concept of a wall, to memorialize what had actually been a gateway, was considered of all symbols "the least appropriate." Emily Genauer, in the Sunday *Herald Tribune Magazine,* thought that she had "never read of a project more outrageous." She thought the proposed wall was ugly, and she objected to "the absurdity of preserving and phonying up with vines" a group of commonplace utilitarian buildings of fairly recent construction. She didn't believe that Ellis Island had any significance for the immigrants; only the Statue of Liberty did. Ellis Island was only "a miserable but necessary funnel through which they were poured and processed like cattle." [18]

As National Park Service technicians began considering the Johnson plan, it was soon apparent that its implementation would involve an outlay of probably several times the amount that Congress had authorized to be appropriated for the development of Ellis Island. A study of the island's administrative history had meanwhile revealed that a great many of the names on the ships' manifests, from which the sixteen million were to be copied, were false entries, and that there were not that many Ellis Island immigrants. It did not appear likely, as the Vietnam war heated up, that Congress would soon appropriate even the authorized $6 million. But meanwhile the structures on the island were deteriorating rapidly, and, if any of them were to be preserved, some decision would soon have to be reached. As discussion of necessary planning went on, the conclusion was reached that "The Philip Johnson plan should be deferred indefinitely." When a team was formed in the spring of 1968 to prepare a master plan for Ellis Island, it was informed that "The plans prepared by Philip Johnson should not be an influence on this study." [19]

The master plan team included architects, landscape architects, museum technicians, and historians. The plan prepared by this group, after a proposal for complete demolition to be replaced by simple monumentation had been voted down, followed in general the line of the 1964 study report on Ellis Island, with elaborations based on further study and on close contact with the New Jersey planners. This plan, submitted in June, stressed the close relationship among Ellis Island, the Statue of Liberty, and Liberty State Park on the Jersey City waterfront, and pointed out the need for close coordination in their planning and development. It also recognized the role of Manhattan as a source of visitors, as a transportation base, and as a scenic backdrop for the island. The development concept rested upon retention of the main immigration building as a memorial to the immigrant and as the key to effective interpretation. Other structures, with the possible exception of the older hospital group, were to be removed, except for the ferryboat *Ellis Island*, the existing covered walkways, and three relatively modern buildings which would be useful until development was completed.

Within this framework, three physical units were recognized. The north unit, containing the main immigration building, would communicate the park story. The south unit would serve as a park activity area and a center for ethnic activities, Old World craft demonstrations, and the like. The filled area joining these two units would serve as a transition between them. Access to Ellis Island would be by boat, from Liberty Island until Liberty State Park was developed, and then from both Liberty Island and Liberty State Park. If experience indicated a need for it, access by a footbridge or transportation system from Liberty Park was recommended. The plan provided for interpretive development of the main building, for interpretive and administrative facilities in its west wing, and for a maintenance and residential area. Facilities to support ethnic observances and a concession food service would be provided on the south unit. Space was set aside for a restaurant and for seating for an evening program, if time should prove either to be desirable.[20]

Not all the details of this plan met with full acceptance immediately within the National Park Service, but in due time it was approved in the director's office. Meanwhile, some cleanup work had been done by personnel from the Job Corps camp which had been set up on the site of Liberty Park in Jersey. Unfortunately, the camp was closed before this program had been completed, and the ferryboat *Ellis Island,* which was to have been preserved, sank at her moorings. The decision to save the main building forced early preservation action. Enough money became available to repair the roof, preserving the fine Gustavino arch beneath and preventing further rapid deterioration of the whole building. Plans for limited public access to Ellis Island by boat from Liberty Island had to be postponed for lack of funds to provide the service, to create temporary exhibits, and to provide the necessary protection to visitors.

As funds became available, however, it was the obvious intention of the National Park Service to proceed along the lines of the 1968 master plan.[21] With the completion in 1972 of the American Museum of Immigration at the base of the Statue of Liberty, telling the broad story of immigration, the role of Ellis Island will be that of interpreting in more detail the peak period of that movement, and of preserving the prime symbol of the epic process. Liberty State Park, on the mainland opposite both islands of the Statue of Liberty National Monument, will eventually form the third unit in a splendid group serving the American public at the historic national gateway, combining recreation, historical interpretation, and, it is believed, inspiration of a high order.

NOTES

CHAPTER I
Years of Obscurity

1. I. N. Phelps Stokes, *The Iconography of Manhattan Island, 1498–1909* (6 vols., New York, 1925–1928), IV, 960, V, 1198; James G. Wilson, *The Memorial History of the City of New York* (4 vols., New York, 1892–1893), I, 52–53.
2. Hugh Hastings, ed., *Public Papers of Daniel D. Tompkins, Governor of New York, 1807–1817. Military* (3 vols., Albany, 1898–1902), II, 85–86.
3. E. B. O'Callaghan, *History of New Netherland; or, New York Under the Dutch* (2 vols., New York, 1846–1848), I, 125–126.
4. Mrs. Schuyler Van Rensselaer, *History of the City of New York in the Seventeenth Century* (2 vols., New York, 1909), I, 96–97; Washington Irving, *Knickerbocker's History of New York* (2 vols., New York, 1894), II, 182–183.
5. Van Rensselaer, I, 146; Daniel Van Winkle, *Old Bergen* (Jersey City, 1902), 26–27, 30; Alexander McLean, *History of Jersey City, N.J.* (2 vols., Jersey City, 1895), I, 8–11.
6. Berthold Fernow, ed., *The Records of New Amsterdam* (7 vols., New York, 1897), III, 420; Stokes, IV, 962, V, 1198; *Tompkins Papers*, II, 37–38.
7. Stokes, IV, 370.
8. Murray Hoffman, *A Treatise Upon the Estate and Rights of the Corporation of the City of New York, as Proprietors* (2 vols., New York, 1862), II, 33–34; *Minutes of the Common Council of the City of New York, 1675–1776* (8 vols., New York, 1905), VI, 98, 124–125.
9. Sidney Berengarten, Ellis Island (Civil Works Administration for the Office of National Parks, 1934), 6–7; Stokes, V, 1030, 1141.
10. Stokes, V, 1198; Berengarten, 9–10.
11. *American State Papers. Military Affairs* (7 vols., Washington, 1832–1861), I, 77–81; Proceedings of the Commissioners of fortification for the City of New York and its vicinity, 1794–1795 *passim*, The New-York Historical Society.
12. *Minutes of the Common Council of the City of New York, 1784–1831* (19 vols., New York, 1917), II, 71, 73; *Tompkins Papers*, II, 5–7.
13. Ebenezer Stevens Manuscripts, 1798–1799 *passim*, The New-York Historical Society; Stokes, V, 1375.

14. Maj. Decius Wadsworth to The Inspector of Fortification, February 15, 1802, Jonathan Williams Papers, Lilly Library, Indiana University (hereafter cited as JWP).
15. Irving, I, 281–282.
16. Secretary of War Henry Dearborn to Lt. Col. Jonathan Williams, September 28, 1805, Journal of soundings &c and of surveys made in the Harbour of New York, undated, and Williams to Mr. Van Rensselaer, January 31, 1807, JWP.
17. Outline of a Plan of defence, for the City and Harbour of New York, July 25, 1807, *ibid.*; *Tompkins Papers*, II, 5–7.
18. Williams to Secretary of War, August 28, 1807, May 17, 1808, and Williams to Governor Tompkins, December 3, 1807, March 27, 1808, April 11, 1808, JWP; *Tompkins Papers*, II, 85–86, 89–90.
19. Williams to Secretary of War, November 1808, Capt. Bomford to Williams, November 1, 1811, Secretary of War William Eustis to Williams, March 18, 1812, JWP.
20. Orderly Books, Third Military District, 1812–1815 *passim*, Records of the War Department, National Archives; R. S. Guernsey, *New York City and Vicinity during the War of 1812–'15* (2 vols., New York, 1889–1895), II, 371.
21. Henry H. Pike, *Ellis Island: Its Legal Status* (General Services Administration, Office of General Counsel, February 11, 1963), 9–14; Berengarten, 23–24.
22. Capt. Loomis, Artillery, to Callender Irvine, Commissary General, January 26, 1820, Quartermaster Consolidated Correspondence File, War Department Records, Record Group 92, National Archives; Correspondence, Office of the Chief of Engineers, 1835–1847 *passim*, Record Group 77, National Archives.
23. Records of the Bureau of Ordnance, Navy Department Records, 1862–1875 *passim*, Record Group 74, National Archives; Engineer Correspondence, 1863–1866 *passim*.
24. *Harper's Weekly*, March 14, 1868, 173.
25. New York *Sun*, May 26, 1876.
26. New York *World*, June 18, 1889.

CHAPTER II
The First Immigration Station

1. William C. Van Vleck, *The Administrative Control of Aliens: A Study in Administrative Law and Procedure* (New York, 1932), 5; George J. Svejda, *Castle Garden as an Immigrant Depot, 1855–1890* (National Park Service, 1968), 98.
2. Marion T. Bennett, *American Immigration Policies; A History* (Washington, 1963), 17–18.
3. *Ibid.*, 18; Charlotte Erickson, *American Industry and the European Immigrant, 1860–1885* (Cambridge, 1957), 149–150, 164–165; New York *World*, June 11, 1888; *New York Tribune*, August 10, 21, 1888.
4. Svejda, 124–131; *New York Commercial Advertiser*, April 25, May 28, 1887; *New York Times*, April 15, 17, 1887; *Tribune*, January 27, February 6, 1888.
5. "To Regulate Immigration," *House Report* No. 3792, 50th Cong., 2d Sess., January 19, 1889; *Congressional Record*, 50th Cong., 1st Sess., 6017, 6192; *ibid.*, 2d Sess., 997.

6. *Annual Report of the Secretary of the Treasury*, 1889, LXXVI.
7. Svejda, 138–139; *Tribune*, January 14, February 16, 1890.
8. Walter Hugins, *Statue of Liberty National Monument; Its Origin, Development and Administration* (National Park Service, 1958), 18–19; *World*, March 1890 *passim*.
9. *Congressional Record*, 51st Cong., 1st Sess., *passim; World*, February 20, 21, 1890; *Tribune*, March 11, 1890.
10. *Congressional Record*, 51st Cong., 1st Sess., 3085–3086.
11. *Annual Report of the Secretary of the Treasury*, 1890, 791–792; *Tribune*, May 25, 1890; *World*, May 17, August 3, 1890.
12. Julian Ralph, "Landing the Immigrants," *Harper's Weekly*, October 24, 1891, 821; Rodman Gilder, *The Battery* (Boston, 1936), 215–216; Victor Safford, *Immigration Problems; Personal Experiences of an Official* (New York, 1925), 21–22; *Times*, April 5, 20, 1890.
13. *Annual Report of the Secretary of the Treasury*, 1890, LVIII–LIX, 791–792, 795, 1891, LX; Safford, 84; *Tribune*, April 19, June 8, 1890.
14. John Higham, *Strangers in the Land: Patterns of American Nativism, 1860–1925* (New York, 1965), 63–67, 99–100.
15. *Times*, April 17, 27, May 25, June 9, 1890.
16. Higham, 99–100.
17. D. H. Smith and H. G. Herring, *The Bureau of Immigration: Its History, Activities and Organization* (Baltimore, 1924), 6–7; *Tribune*, June 8, 1890.
18. *American Hebrew*, October 16, 1891, 238; *Times*, January 14, 28, 30, February 1, 9, 1891.
19. "Report of Commissioners Weber and Kempster," *Enforcement of Alien Contract Labor Laws, House Executive Document* 235, 52d Cong., 1st Sess., 1892, 5–140; John B. Weber, "Our National Dumping-Ground. A Study of Immigration," *North American Review*, April 1892, 424–431.
20. *Annual Report of the Secretary of the Treasury*, 1891, LXII–LXIII.
21. *Harper's Weekly*, October 24, 1891, 821.
22. Safford, 22–24; *World*, January 2, 1892.
23. *Annual Report of the Superintendent of Immigration*, 1892, 3, 4–5; *World*, March 13, 1892.
24. *Tribune*, September 2, 1892; *Times*, September 11, 14, November 15, December 9, 29, 1892.
25. *Congressional Record*, 52d Cong., 2d Sess., 290, 2468–2470; *Enforcement of Alien Contract Labor Laws*, 138, 144; Higham, 100; Bennett, 23; *Times*, October 19, November 30, December 1, 1892.
26. *Annual Report of the Commissioner-General of Immigration* (hereafter cited as *ARCG*), 1897, 5, 1898, 3; *Times*, January 6, 1894.
27. Edward Corsi, *In the Shadow of Liberty: The Chronicle of Ellis Island* (New York, 1935), 287; Safford, 13–14; *Times*, March 29, May 17, 18, 1893; *Tribune*, March 29, 1893; *Sun*, April 18, 1893.
28. Joseph H. Senner, "How We Restrict Immigration," *North American Review*, April 1894, 494–499.
29. *Reports of the Industrial Commission* (19 vols., Washington, 1900–1902), XV, *Immigration*, 173, 179.

30. William Preston, Jr., *Aliens and Dissenters: Federal Suppression of Radicals, 1903–1933* (Cambridge, 1963), 11–12; Van Vleck, 6, 42–50, 67–68, 73–74, 77–79, 82; Safford, 192–193; *Times,* December 4, 1898.
31. Superintendent of Immigration to Commissioner, Ellis Island, July 20, 1894, Bureau of Immigration, Press Copies of Letters Sent ("T" Series), 1892–1903, Record Group 85, National Archives; *Tribune,* July 8, 15, 24, 1894.
32. Acting Secretary of the Treasury to Secretary of the Navy, April 17, 25, 1896, Letters Sent, Press Copies ("Immigration"), 1891–1912, Record Group 85, National Archives; Safford, 98–99; *Times,* April 5, 1896; *Tribune,* April 1, 16, 20, 24, 1896.
33. Joseph H. Senner, "Immigration From Italy," *North American Review,* June 1896, 649–656; *Congressional Record,* 54th Cong., 2d Sess., 1219; Acting Secretary of the Treasury to Secretary of State, April 23, 1896, Letters Sent, 1891–1912; *New York Herald,* April 13, 1896; *Times,* April 21, 1896; *Tribune,* April 24, 1896, March 3, 1897; *American Hebrew,* February 5, 1897, 384.
34. *Annual Report of the Superintendent of Immigration,* 1894, 23–24; *ARCG,* 1895, 19, 25–28, 1896, 24–26, 27–33, 1897, 8–9, 11; *Tribune,* June 15, 16, 1897.
35. Telegram, Acting Commissioner-General to Commissioner, Barge Office, June 15, 1897, Bureau of Immigration, Letters Sent, 1892–1903; Commissioner-General Sargent to Gilmore Howard, New York, February 5, 1907, Letters Sent, 1891–1912; *ARCG,* 1896, 33, 1897, 38–39; Safford, 199–200; *Times,* June 17, 1897.
36. Commissioner-General T. V. Powderly to Commissioner, Barge Office, January 17, 1898, Bureau of Immigration, Letters Sent, 1892–1903; *ARCG,* 1898, 40–41; Safford, 200–201.
37. Entries of August 2, 3, 6, 1897, Bureau of Immigration, Record of Correspondence, 1891–1903, Record Group 85, National Archives; Elting E. Morison, ed., *The Letters of Theodore Roosevelt* (8 vols., Cambridge, 1952–1954), III, 171–172; Safford, 201–202, 205; *Times,* August 12, 1897.
38. Erickson, Preface, 104–105, 149–150, 169–171, 175–176; Safford, 83–84, 218–219.
39. *Report of the United States Civil Service Commission,* 1895–1896, 15, 85, 1897–1898, 662, 1898–1899, 435; Henry J. Carman, Henry David, and Paul N. Guthrie, eds., *The Path I Trod: The Autobiography of Terence V. Powderly* (New York, 1940), 299–300; *Times,* June 6, 7, 9, August 31, October 5, 1900.
40. Charges against Assistant Commissioner McSweeney were withheld at the direction of the secretary of the treasury. Notation in ink on letter, Commissioner-General Powderly to McSweeney, August 31, 1900, Letters Sent, 1891–1912; *ARCG,* 1900, 49; *Times,* April 15, 1900.

CHAPTER III
High Tide

1. Safford, 201–202.
2. Edward Steiner, *On the Trail of the Immigrant* (New York, 1906), 79–81.
3. "The Rush for Our Open Door," *Leslie's Weekly,* January 5, 1901, 10–11; *Tribune,* December 17, 21, 1900, July 23, 1901.

4. *Annual Report of the Supervising Architect to the Secretary of the Treasury*, 1897, 25, 1898, 4; Edwin Emerson, Jr., "The Threshold of America," *Harper's Weekly*, February 26, 1898, 210.
5. John W. Harrington, "The New Clearing-House for Immigrants," *Harper's Weekly*, January 19, 1901, 73; *Times*, December 3, 1900.
6. *Annual Report of the Supervising Architect*, 1901, 33–34, 1902, 45–46.
7. "The New York Immigration Station," *Architectural Record*, December 1902, 727–733. Many years later the Ellis Island Committee took exception to the very monumental character of the building that the *Record* had praised. "To obtain a monumental character," it reported, "have been sacrificed not only the flexibility and adaptability of plan needed, but also the abundance of light and air which could have been easily obtained on this site." Helen Arthur, Secretary, Ellis Island Committee, to Commissioner Daniel W. MacCormack, December 8, 1933, File 55, 817/541, General Immigration Files, Record Group 85, National Archives.
8. Wright-Crater Investigation, 1901, File 52,727/4, General Immigration Files; *Times*, August 20, 21, 1901; *Tribune*, September 26, November 21, 1901.
9. Secretary of the Treasury Leslie Shaw to McSweeney, April 28, 1902, Letters Sent, 1891–1912; *Letters of Theodore Roosevelt*, III, 171–172, 221; Carman *et al*, eds., *The Path I Trod*, 301–302; Francis E. Leupp, *The Man Roosevelt: A Portrait Sketch* (New York, 1904), 134–136; *Times*, December 21, 1901; *Tribune*, April 12, 1902.
10. Undated pencil draft, "Introductory," William Williams Papers, New York Public Library (hereafter cited as WWP); *Times*, April 2, 1902; *Commercial Advertiser*, April 2, 1902.
11. *Report of the Civil Service Commission*, 1901–1902, 91; Theodore Roosevelt, *Theodore Roosevelt: An Autobiography* (New York, 1913), 64–68; Leupp, 136.
12. Williams to Shaw, June 16, 17, 1902, Roosevelt to Williams, June 23, 1902, and Williams to Roosevelt, June 24, 1902, WWP; *Letters of Theodore Roosevelt*, III, 280; *Tribune*, June 21, 1902; *Commercial Advertiser*, June 21, 1902.
13. Williams to Messrs. Busk & Jevons, May 1, 1902, to Shaw, May 13, 1902, and to Senator T. C. Platt, May 26, 1902, WWP.
14. Herbert Parsons to Williams, April 3, 1902, WWP; *ARCG*, 1902, 55–57.
15. Acting Secretary to Williams, June 24, 1902, Bureau of Immigration, Letters Sent, 1892–1903; *ARCG*, 1902, 57–58.
16. Commissioner-General Sargent to Williams, July 31, 1902, WWP; *Times*, July 1, 14, September 26, 1902; *Tribune*, September 26, October 30, 1902.
17. T. Williams, "All Immigration Records Broken," *Leslie's Weekly*, August 7, 1902, 126.
18. Ernest H. Abbott, "America's Welcome to the Immigrant," *The Outlook*, October 4, 1902, 256–264.
19. Jacob A. Riis, "In the Gateway of Nations," *Century Magazine*, March 1903, 674–682.
20. Williams to N. J. Sparkling, May 26, 1903, and to John Bell, November 3, 1903, WWP; Williams to Demetrius Christopher, Interpreter (Through Superintendent and Chief of Registry Division), November 30, 1904, District No. 3, New

York (Ellis Island) Letters Sent, Press Copies, 1903–1912, Record Group 85, National Archives.

21. "The Spectator," *Outlook*, March 25, 1905, 730–732; *American Hebrew*, January 20, 1905, 270.
22. "Joseph Murray Affair" file, Roosevelt to Williams, January 12, 1905, Mary Williams to Williams, January 18, 1905, and Allan Robinson to Roosevelt, September 8, 1908, WWP; *Letters of Theodore Roosevelt*, IV, 1077–1078.
23. Secretary of Commerce and Labor Victor Metcalf to Robert Watchorn, January 31, 1905, Letters Sent, 1891–1912; Watchorn to Williams, January 19, 1905, WWP; *Times*, January 17, 1905; *Tribune*, January 17, 1905.
24. Secretary Straus to Commissioner Watchorn, December 30, 1907, Oscar S. Straus Papers, Library of Congress; Mary B. Sayles, "The Keepers of the Gate," *Outlook*, December 28, 1907, 913; Steiner, 89–90.
25. William H. Taft to Herbert Parsons, May 17, 1909, William H. Taft Papers, Library of Congress; Williams to President Wilson, May 6, 1913, and Secretary of Labor William Wilson to President Wilson, June 2, 1913, File 2/2 Immigration Service Records, 1907–1935, General Records of the Labor Department, Record Group 174, National Archives; *Times*, May 19, 1909, June 5, July 1, 1913.
26. Williams to E. I. Hajos, Manager, Home of the Hungarian Relief Society, December 21, 1904, Ellis Island Letters Sent; Safford, 260–261.
27. *Leslie's Weekly*, August 7, 1902, 126; Edward Lowry, "Americans in the Raw," *World's Work*, October 1902, 2654.
28. Sargent to Williams, October 6, 1902, WWP; *ARCG*, 1902, 59.
29. *Tribune*, April 2, 1903; *Times*, May 24, 1903.
30. *American Hebrew*, June 17, 1904, 130.
31. Mark Wischnitzer, *Visas to Freedom: the History of HIAS* (Cleveland, 1956), 41, 54.
32. Williams to Sargent, September 10, 1903, Ellis Island Letters Sent.
33. *Times*, January 19, 1911.
34. *ARCG*, 1911, 146–147.
35. *Times*, May 16, 1911; *World*, May 17, 1911.
36. *Sun*, January 4, 1911.
37. *ARCG*, 1912, 27–28; Safford, 90; Corsi, 285; *Times*, July 18, 1909.
38. Roosevelt to Williams (Personal), January 2, 1903, William Williams Collection, Yale University Library; *Commercial Advertiser*, July 1, 1903.
39. *Times*, September 17, 1903; "The President at Ellis Island," *American Hebrew*, September 18, 1903, 576–577.
40. Hearings before the Commission appointed by the President to investigate condition of Affairs at Immigration Bureau on Ellis Island, under the Administration of Commissioner Williams, Arthur v. Briesen, Chairman, 1903, File 52,727/2, General Immigration Files; "The Ellis Island Investigation," *Charities*, October 10, 1903, 324–325, March 5, 1904, 223–224.
41. Williams to Sargent, February 5, 1904, Williams to Charles Nagel, April 5, 1911, and Nagel to Williams, April 6, 1911, WWP; Robert E. Park, *The Immigrant Press and Its Control* (New York, 1922), 114.
42. *Das Morgen Journal* (New York), April 17, 1911, translation in Charles Nagel Papers, Yale University Library.

43. *New York Evening Journal*, May 24, 1911, clipping in WWP; Jacob H. Schiff to William Sulzer, May 8, 1911, and Edward Lauterbach to Sulzer, May 25, 1911, William Sulzer Papers, Cornell University Library; Nagel to Rev. Theo. Hanssen, May 26, 1911, and Williams to Nagel, June 5, 1911, Nagel Papers; Nagel to Williams, June 6, 1911, WWP; *Hearings on House Resolution No. 166 Authorizing the Committee on Immigration and Naturalization to Investigate the Office of Immigration Commissioner at the Port of New York and Other Places. Hearings Held before the Committee on Rules, House of Representatives*, May 29, July 10–11, 1911, 62d Cong., 1st Sess.; *World*, July 11, 12, 1911.
44. *Slovak National News* (Pittsburgh), November 2, 1911, translation in WWP.
45. *Times*, October 8, 1911; *Das Morgen Journal*, January 20, 1912, translation in WWP; Williams to Commissioner-General, May 9, 16, 1913, *ibid.*
46. William H. Taft to Williams, November 25, 1911, and Williams to Congressman Adolph J. Sabath, September 17, 1912, WWP; Williams to the President, November 27, 1911, Taft Papers; Williams to O. D. Baring, July 25, 1911, Ellis Island Letters Sent; *Times*, October 9, 1911, September 20, October 11, 1912; *World*, February 9, 1912.
47. Moses Rischin, *The Promised City: New York's Jews 1870–1914* (New York, 1964), 95–111; Higham, 124.
48. Sargent to Charles Dushkind and to Williams, January 9, 1903, Letters Sent, 1891–1912; Williams to Roosevelt, January 29, 1903, WWP; *Letters of Theodore Roosevelt*, III, 411–412; *Times*, January 4, 1903; *Tribune*, January 4, 10, 1903.
49. Robert Watchorn, "Gateway of the Nation," *Outlook*, December 28, 1907, 897–911.
50. Assistant Secretary H. A. Taylor to Special Immigrant Inspector Robert Watchorn, Darby, England, July 28, 1900, Bureau of Immigration, Letters Sent, 1892–1903; *American Hebrew*, July 20, 256, October 19, 644, 647–648, October 26, 680–682, 1900; Philip Cowen, *Memories of an American Jew* (New York, 1932), 254–255.
51. Higham, 127–128.
52. *Times*, February 24, May 22, 1907, November 3, 1908; *Letters of Theodore Roosevelt*, VI, 1096–1097; Henry Cabot Lodge, ed., *Selections from the Correspondence of Theodore Roosevelt and Henry Cabot Lodge* (2 vols., New York, 1925), II, 306; Barbara M. Solomon, *Ancestors and Immigrants: A Changing New England Tradition* (Cambridge, 1956), 196–197.
53. Commissioner Watchorn to Secretary Straus, June 5, 1907, File 43/2, Labor Department Records.
54. *American Hebrew*, March 30, 574, July 20, 175, 1906; Cowen, 143–144.
55. "Council of Jewish Women and Immigration," *American Hebrew*, January 31, 1908, 341; *Times*, April 28, 1906, January 11, 1909; *Tribune*, June 14, 1906.
56. Williams to Sabath, July 15, 1909, Ellis Island Letters Sent; *ARCG*, 1909, 133; *Times*, June 5, July 10, 1909.
57. Williams to Commissioner-General Daniel J. Keefe, July 10, 1909, Ellis Island Letters Sent; Acting Commissioner-General Frank H. Larned to Williams, July 14, 1909, Letters Sent, 1891–1912; *Times*, June 30, July 12, 15, 16, 1909.
58. Nagel to Williams, September 17, 1909, Nagel Papers; Max J. Kohler, *Immigration and Aliens in the United States* (New York, 1936), 69; *Reports of the Im-*

migration Commission (42 vols., Washington, 1911), XLI, 160–181; *American Hebrew*, July 23, 1909, 300; *Times*, July 16, 17, 18, 22, 1909.

59. *Sun*, July 27, 1909.
60. Larned to Williams, July 29, 1909, Letters Sent, 1891–1912; Commissioner's Notice to the Boards of Special Inquiry, Ellis Island, July 21, 1909, Taft Papers; *American Hebrew*, July 16, 276, July 30, 320, 1909.
61. Williams to Nagel, July 19, 1911, WWP; Kohler, 69; Louis Adamic, *Laughing in the Jungle: The Autobiography of an Immigrant* (New York, 1932), 41–45.
62. *Globe and Commercial Advertiser*, July 12, 1909; *Evening Post*, July 16, 1909; *World*, July 18, 1909; *Sun*, July 13, 1909; *Times*, July 18, 1909; *Tribune*, July 25, 1909.
63. R. M. Easley to Williams, July 13, 1909, Prescott F. Hall to Williams, July 14, 1909, Superintendent Blatchly of the Charity Organization Society to Williams, July 15, 1909, and Madison Grant to Williams, July 16, 1909, WWP.
64. *Times*, January 24, 1910; Wischnitzer, 60–61.
65. Solomon Shapiro to Williams, May 31, 1910, WWP.
66. *Times*, January 19, 1911; Otto Heller, ed., *Charles Nagel: Speeches and Writings, 1900–1928* (2 vols., New York, 1931), I, 157.
67. Address by Henry J. Dannenbaum, President, District No. 7, B'nai B'rith, January 9, 1912, copy in WWP.
68. Williams to Roosevelt, January 31, 1912, and Jacob H. Schiff to Henry F. Osborn, January 25, 1912, *ibid.*

CHAPTER IV
Problems of the Flood Years

1. Commissioner Watchorn to Secretary Straus, May 14, 1907, Straus Papers; *ARCG*, 1903, 67, 1905, 71.
2. Williams to Secretary Shaw, June 12, 1902, WWP; *Tribune*, July 2, 1902.
3. Ellis Island Office Order, July 16, 1903, WWP; Williams to Supervising Inspector, Ellis Island, September 19, 1903, Ellis Island Letters Sent.
4. Watchorn to Straus, November 11, 1907, Straus Papers; Watchorn to Colin Studds, October 30, 1906, and Williams to Commissioner-General, November 30, 1909, Ellis Island Letters Sent.
5. Broughton Brandenburg, *Imported Americans* (New York, 1904), 215–222.
6. Steiner, 64–76.
7. Paul Knaplund, *Moorings Old and New: Entries in an Immigrant's Log* (Madison, 1963), 147–149; Stephen Graham, *With Poor Immigrants to America* (New York, 1914), 42–47.
8. Safford, 245–247.
9. "Going Through Ellis Island," *Popular Science Monthly*, January 1913, 5–18.
10. Corsi, 72–77.
11. Sargent to Williams, March 25, 1903, Bureau of Immigration, Letters Sent, 1892–1903.
12. Commissioner's Notice, Ellis Island, May 23, 1904, WWP; *Abstracts of Reports of the Immigration Commission* (2 vols., Washington, 1911), II, 309–310.

13. *ARCG*, 1907, 1908, 1911, 1913, 1914 *passim.*
14. Sargent to Williams, December 1, 1904, Letters Sent, 1891–1912; Watchorn to Vasil P. Stephanoff, May 4, 1907, Ellis Island Letters Sent; *Times*, December 18, 1904.
15. North American Civic League for Immigrants: New York–New Jersey Committee, *Report, December, 1909–March, 1911* (New York, 1911), 21–25.
16. *Times*, May 23, 1913.
17. Williams to Commissioner-General, March 9, 1911, WWP.
18. Williams to Commissioner-General, November 17, 1904, Ellis Island Letters Sent; Commissioner-General to Williams, November 18, 1904, Letters Sent, 1891–1912; Williams to Commissioner-General, July 10, 1902, WWP.
19. Fiorello H. La Guardia, *The Making of an Insurgent: An Autobiography, 1882–1919* (Philadelphia, 1948), 66; Safford, 110.
20. Williams to Commissioner-General, July 13, 1909, Ellis Island Letters Sent; Secretary of Commerce and Labor Cortelyou to the Attorney General, December 22, 1903, Letters Sent, 1891–1912; Cowen, 164–165.
21. Williams to Edward Espinosa, January 31, 1911, Ellis Island Letters Sent; Commissioner-General Keefe to Watchorn, March 6, 1909, and Assistant Secretary Wheeler to Watchorn, March 13, 1909, Letters Sent, 1891–1912.
22. *Leslie's Weekly*, August 7, 1902, 126.
23. Williams to Pastor Berkemeier, October 10, 1902; Sargent to Williams, October 11, 1902, Williams to The Home for Scandinavian Emigrants, June 3, 1903, Memorandum of Interview with Baron Karl von Giskra at Ellis Island, February 25, 1904, and Williams to Commissioner-General, April 5, 1904, WWP; *Tribune*, July 25, 1902.
24. Commissioner-General to Hon. D. S. Alexander, October 6, 1906, Letters Sent, 1891–1912; Watchorn to Hungarian Relief Society, November 16, 1908, Ellis Island Letters Sent; *Report of the Commission of Immigration of the State of New York* (Albany, 1909), 88–89.
25. Commissioner Watchorn to the Missionaries at Ellis Island, January 18, 1908, Straus to Watchorn, February 1, 1908, and William Loeb, Jr., to Rev. Dr. Judson Swift, February 1, 1908, Straus Papers; *American Hebrew*, May 10, 1907, 18, January 31, 1908, 334.
26. Williams to Nagel, August 13, 18, 1909, Nagel Papers; Nagel to Williams, August 16, 1909, WWP; *Immigration Commission Abstracts*, II, 312–315; *N.Y. State Commission Rpt.*, 91–93; *ARCG*, 1913, 186–187; *Times*, August 12, 1909.
27. Commissioner-General Sargent to Hon. Herbert Parsons, May 15, 1905, Letters Sent, 1891–1912; Parsons to Alford W. Cooley, May 8, 1907, Watchorn to Parsons, June 25, October 7, 1907, Parsons to William J. Loeb, Jr., April 28, 1908, and Straus to Loeb, May 6, 1908, Herbert Parsons Papers, Columbia University Libraries; Marvin G. Weinbaum, "New York County Republican Politics, 1897–1922," *New-York Historical Society Quarterly*, January 1966, 75–79.
28. Watchorn to Straus (Strictly Confidential), June 22, 1907, File 43/2, Labor Department Records; *Times*, April 12, 1890, January 26, 1893, May 4, 1907; *Tribune*, June 21, 1902, June 1, May 4, 1905.
29. Williams to Nagel (Confidential), March 14, 1911, WWP; *Times*, December 19, 1907, March 28, July 2, 1908.

30. Watchorn to Messrs. Rabiner Bros. & Warner, February 20, 1906, and Assistant Commissioner Murray to Watchorn, May 4, 1907, Ellis Island Letters Sent; Corsi, 78–79, 121; *Times*, January 29, 31, 1911; *Tribune*, May 4, 11, June 1, 1905.
31. William Loeb, Jr., to Straus, July 17, 1908, Straus Papers; Straus to Loeb, November 6, 1908, Letters Sent, 1891–1912; *Times*, May 11, July 2, August 28, October 16, 1908.
32. Watchorn to Straus, January 5, Straus to Watchorn, February 6, and Watchorn to Straus, February 20, March 2, 1909, Straus Papers; Roosevelt to Herbert Knox Smith, January 18, 1909, Theodore Roosevelt Papers, Library of Congress; Straus to The Commissioner of Corporations, January 26, 1909, File 43/2, Labor Department Records; *Times*, January 6, 1909.
33. Nagel to Williams, June 24, 1909, Nagel Papers; Williams to Mr. Fritz Brodt, Ellis Island, July 27, 1909, Ellis Island Letters Sent; *ARCG*, 1910, 136; *Evening Post*, May 28, 1909; *Times*, August 19, 28, 29, 31, September *passim*, October 4, 5, 1913.
34. Williams to Capt. Peter C. Petrie, February 8, 1903, and to Secretary of the Treasury, February 27, 1903, WWP; Williams to Sargent, November 23, 1904, Ellis Island Letters Sent; Acting Commissioner-General to Williams, December 16, 1904, Letters Sent, 1891–1912.
35. Acting Commissioner-General to Watchorn, October 6, 1905, Letters Sent, 1891–1912; Graham, 42–47.
36. Organization of U.S. Immigration Station, Ellis Island, revise of October 23, 1903, File 52,727/2, General Immigration Files; Ellis Island Office Order, April 9, 1903, and Sargent to Williams, April 11, 1903, WWP; Williams to Lawson Sandford, Jr., January 20, 1911, Ellis Island Letters Sent; *Times*, March 5, 1911.
37. Acting Commissioner-General to Williams, September 5, 1903, and Sargent to Williams, September 14, 1903, Letters Sent, 1891–1912; Williams to Commissioner-General, September 12, 1903, WWP.
38. Watchorn to Straus, June 22, 1907, File 43/2, Labor Department Records; "Protecting the Immigrant," *American Hebrew*, June 28, 1907, 208; *Tribune*, January 28, 1906; *Times*, June 21, 22, 1907.
39. *N.Y. State Commission Rpt.*, 74–75; *ARCG*, 1913, 187.
40. Harry Beardsley, "Enormous Flood of Immigrants from Europe," *Collier's*, May 8, 1902, 442–444; *Times*, April 21, 1902; *Tribune*, April 14, May 5, 1902.
41. Williams to Commissioner of Police, New York City, October 19, 1904, Ellis Island Letters Sent; The Society for Italian Immigrants, *Fourth Report, March, 1904 to January, 1906* (New York, 1906), 5–6; *Tribune*, May 30, July 20, 1902, March 3, 1903.
42. Williams to Sargent, January 7, 1905, Ellis Island Letters Sent; *N.Y. State Commission Rpt.*, 71–72; North American Civic League for Immigrants, *Report*, 5–7; *ARCG*, 1913, 186–187.
43. Acting Commissioner-General to Mr. Emil L. Boas, October 24, 1898, Letters Sent, 1891–1912; *ARCG*, 1895, 27–28; *Reports of the Industrial Commission*, XV, 131; Safford, 29–30; "The Detained Immigrant," *Harper's Weekly*, August 26, 1893, 821; *Times*, January 30, 31, 1899, April 6, 1901.
44. Acting Commissioner-General to Williams, May 26, 1902, Letters Sent, 1891–1912; Commissioner-General to Williams, June 6, 1902, Bureau of Immigration, Letters Sent, 1892–1903; *Tribune*, August 21, 26, 1902.

45. Acting Secretary of the Treasury to Williams, June 24, 1902, Bureau of Immigration, Letters Sent, 1892–1903; Williams to Anchor Line, July 26, 1902, and to French Line, December 10, 1902, WWP.
46. *Tribune,* February 22, 24, June 28, 1903.
47. Assistant Secretary Murray to Williams, November 21, 1904, Letters Sent, 1891–1912; *ARCG,* 1903, 66–68, 1904, 104.
48. Williams to Commissioner-General, November 28, 1904, Ellis Island Letters Sent; *Times,* August 14, 1904.
49. *Tribune,* May 4, 1905; *American Hebrew,* June 23, 1905, 104.
50. *Tribune,* October 30, November 1, 1905.
51. *Times,* July 22, August 6, 9, 1906.
52. "Mr. Watchorn on New Law," *American Hebrew,* February 15, 1907, 413.
53. Straus to Watchorn, June 21, 1907, Straus Papers; Watchorn to Straus, June 22, 1907, File 43/2, Labor Department Records.
54. Williams to Commissioner-General, December 28, 1909, January 26, 1912, and Commissioner-General to Williams, November 23, 1912, File 53,438/15, General Immigration Files; Williams to Commissioner-General, May 5, 1910, File 52,519/18, *ibid.*; *ARCG,* 1912, 22–23; *Times,* October 10, 1910, February 16, 1913.
55. *Herald,* February 22, 25, 1908.
56. Watchorn to Straus, February 29, 1908, Straus to Watchorn, March 2, 1908, and Watchorn to Straus, March 7, 1908, Straus Papers.
57. *Times,* March 4, 1908; numerous clippings of approximately same date in Straus Papers.
58. Straus to Watchorn, March 19, 1908, Straus Papers.
59. William B. Howland to the President, September 9, 1908, *ibid.*; *Herald,* April 13, 15, 1908; *Times,* April 5, May 2, 1908.
60. Watchorn to Straus, May 8, 1908, Straus Papers; *Herald,* March 13, 14, 1909; *Tribune,* March 14, 1909.
61. *Evening Post,* November 21, 1902; *Tribune,* November 22, 1902, January 13, 15, 1903.
62. *Tribune,* January 21, 22, 27, February 4, 17, March 11, 13, 1903.
63. Sargent to Williams, July 29, 1903, Letters Sent, 1891–1912; *Times,* March 14, April 27, October 7, 1903; *Tribune,* May 16, December 30, 1903.
64. Henry Cabot Lodge, "A Million Immigrants a Year," *Century Magazine,* January 1904, 469; *U.S. Statutes at Large,* XXXII, 1213, XXXIV, 898; *Times,* December 23, 1905.
65. Watchorn to Sargent, June 9, 1908, File 52,519/18, General Immigration Files; "Importing Women for Immoral Purposes," *Senate Document* 196, 61st Cong., 2d Sess., December 10, 1909; *Times,* August 30, October 5, 1907.
66. Watchorn to President, Board of Magistrates, New York City, August 10, 1908, Ellis Island Letters Sent; Assistant Secretary Wheeler to Watchorn (Confidential), March 3, 1909, Letters Sent, 1891–1912.
67. *Reports of the Immigration Commission,* XXXVII, 68–70.
68. *U.S. Statutes at Large,* XXXVI, Part I, No. 1, 263, No. 2, 825.
69. *Times,* September 10, 1910; La Guardia, 70–74.
70. *Times,* April 10, 1914.
71. *ARCG,* 1901, 40, 1902, 60–61.

72. Acting Commissioner-General to Surgeon General, November 4, 1902, and Secretary of the Treasury to Attorney General, March 27, 1903, Bureau of Immigration, Letters Sent, 1892–1903; Williams to Commissioner-General, September 22, 1903, WWP; Sargent to Watchorn, April 12, 1905, Letters Sent, 1891–1912; *ARCG*, 1903, 65–66, 69–70, 1905, 71, 1906, 69–71; Pike, 61–63; *Times*, July 19, December 18, 1904.
73. Watchorn to Sargent, July 17, 1906, File 50,627/16, General Immigration Files; Acting Commissioner-General to Assistant Secretary, June 19, 1909, and Williams to Commissioner-General, October 19, 1910, File 52,519/18, *ibid.*; Nagel to the President, June 3, 1911, Taft Papers; *ARCG*, 1908, 135–139, 1911, 144–145.
74. Commissioner-General to Williams, March 23, 1903, Bureau of Immigration, Letters Sent, 1892–1903; *ARCG*, 1902, 51–52, 1903, 65–66, 1904, 100–106.
75. Watchorn to Sargent, April 25, June 14, 1906, File 52,519/18, General Immigration Files; Watchorn to Sargent, October 10, 1906, Ellis Island Letters Sent; *ARCG*, 1906, 69–71.
76. Watchorn to Sargent, June 9, 1908, File 52,519/18, General Immigration Files; *ARCG*, 1908, 135–136, 1909, 134.
77. Williams to Commissioner-General, December 3, 1909, File 52,519/18, General Immigration Files.
78. Williams to Commissioner-General, July 1, 1910, File 52,519/18B, and November 22, 1911, File 52,519/18D, General Immigration Files; *ARCG*, 1910, 134–135, 1911, 144–145.
79. *ARCG*, 1911, 145–146; *Times*, January 29, 1911.
80. *ARCG*, 1913, 184–185, 1914, 225–226.
81. James Bryce to Secretary of State, November 29, 1912, copy in WWP; Williams to Commissioner-General, December 11, 1912, File 52,519/18, General Immigration Files; Williams to Commissioner-General, December 16, 1912, Ellis Island Letters Sent; *Times*, July 11, 1911, November 30, 1912.

CHAPTER V
Wartime Interlude

1. *ARCG*, 1914, 35, 1915, 57, 1918, 54; *Times*, August 7, 18, 1914.
2. *ARCG*, 1915, 222–223, 1916, 178; Safford, 91; *Times*, November 26, 1914.
3. Secretary of the Treasury William G. McAdoo to the President, July 8, 1914, Frederic C. Howe to Hon. W. B. Wilson, Secretary of Labor, August 12, 1914, Secretary of Labor, Memorandum for the President, August 18, 1914, and Acting Secretary of Labor Louis F. Post to Howe, August 26, 1914, File 2/288, Labor Department Records; Frederic C. Howe, *The Confessions of a Reformer* (New York, 1925), 252–253.
4. *Times*, August 18, 1914; *Globe and Commercial Advertiser*, August 18, 1914; *Sun*, August 19, 1914.
5. "Turning Ellis Island Inside Out," *Survey*, October 17, 1914, 63; *Times*, September 16, 1914.
6. "For a Better Ellis Island," *Outlook*, October 21, 1914, 402–403; *Times*, March 15, 1915.

7. *ARCG*, 1915, 221; Howe, 254–258; *Times*, January 15, May 20, 22, November 27, 1915.
8. "The New Ellis Island," *Immigrants in America Review*, June 1915, 10–12; Higham, 234–242.
9. *Immigrants in America Review*, June 1915, 12; *Times*, January 15, February 16, 1915.
10. Howe to Commissioner-General, September 24, 1915, File 53,438/15A, General Immigration Files.
11. Commissioner-General Caminetti to Howe, October 9, 13, 1915, Secretary of Labor to Joseph P. Tumulty, October 18, 1915, and Order of the Secretary of Labor, October 25, 1915, *ibid.*; Transcript, Meeting of Committee to Investigate the Question of Bringing Second Cabin Passengers to Ellis Island for Inspection, Held at Ellis Island, N.Y.H., January 24, 1916, File 53,438/15C, *ibid.*; J. B. Densmore to Secretary of Labor, March 6, April 11, 1916, File 53,438/15E–F, *ibid.*; Howe, 260–262; *Times*, October 26, 1915, January 21, 26, 1916.
12. Howe, 262–263; *Times*, July 25, 1915.
13. Commissioner-General Caminetti to Mrs. Kate Waller Barrett, April 15, 1914, Mrs. Barrett to Caminetti, May 9, 27, 1914, Commissioner-General to Secretary of Labor, August 28, 1914, and to Commissioners of Immigration, October 12, 1914, and Amendment of Rule 22 of Immigration Rules, Office of the Secretary, Department of Labor, April 6, 1915, File 53,678/155, General Immigration Files; Howe to Commissioner-General, February 4, 1915, File 19/31, Labor Department Records; Howe, 268–272.
14. "Investigation of Ellis Island Proposed," *Survey*, July 29, 1916, 445–446; "The Bennet-Howe Controversy," *Outlook*, August 2, 1916, 763–764; Howe, 259–260; *Times*, July *passim*, August 8, 12, September 6, 1916.
15. *ARCG*, 1917, XXIX; "Ellis Island Cool Under Showers of Shrapnel," *Survey*, August 5, 1916, 486; Corsi, 117–120; *Times*, July 30, 1916.
16. *ARCG*, 1917, IX–X, 176–177; *Times*, April 7, 8, 15, 1917.
17. *ARCG*, 1917, 176–178; Bennett, 26–28; *Times*, October 17, 18, 19, November 20, 1917.
18. Secretary of Labor Wilson, Memorandum for the Commissioner-General in re Ellis Island, February 15, 1918, File 151/119, Labor Department Records; *ARCG*, 1918, 37–38, 269; *Times*, February 12, 24, March 8, 1918.
19. *ARCG*, 1918, 272, 1919, 28–29.
20. *Ibid.*, 1919, 29; Bennett, 28; Higham, 221; Preston, 182–183; Howe, 266–267, 272–275.
21. "The Deportations," *Survey*, February 22, 1919, 722–724; "Skimming the Melting-Pot," *Literary Digest*, March 1, 1919, 16; Preston, 190–191, 199–200; *Times*, February 11, 12, 13, 20, 1919.
22. Secretary of Labor Wilson, Memorandum for the Commissioner-General of Immigration, March 20, 1919, File 167/255, Labor Department Records; Robert K. Murray, *Red Scare; A Study in National Hysteria, 1919–1920* (Minneapolis, 1955), 194–195; Higham, 229; Preston, 200–201; Howe, 273–275; *Times*, March 14, 16, 18, 20, April 2, 1919.
23. *Times*, March 13, 14, June 5, 1919.
24. *Congressional Record*, 66th Cong., 1st Sess., 1522, 1910–1911; Murray, 176–177.

25. *Times*, May 26, June 3, 4, 1919.
26. Howe, 290–291, 273–275, 326–328; *Times*, September 7, 1919.
27. "Conditions at Ellis Island," *Hearings before the Committee on Immigration and Naturalization, House of Representatives*, 66th Cong., 1st Sess., November 24, 26, 28, 1919; "Ellis Island's Gates Ajar," *Literary Digest*, December 13, 1919, 17–18; Howe, 276; Murray, 205; *Times*, November 22–29, December 1, 1919.
28. *World*, November 25, 26, December 2, 1919.
29. Louis F. Post, *The Deportation Delirium of Nineteen-twenty: A Personal Narrative of an Historic Official Experience* (Chicago, 1923), 4–5, 31–32, 106–109; Corsi, 186, 194–195; Murray, 206–207, 213–214; Preston, 220–221; *Times*, December 21, 22, 28, 1919, January 4, 1920.
30. *New York Call*, January 21, 1920, clipping in File 54,844/54, General Immigration Files; Secretary of Labor, Memorandum for the Acting Secretary, January 23, 1920, and Acting Secretary of Labor John W. Abercrombie, Memorandum for the Secretary, January 31, 1920, *ibid.*; *Times*, January 6, 13, 1920.
31. Secretary of Labor, Memorandum for the Commissioner-General, January 26, 1920, File 167/255, Labor Department Records; "Misleading the Bolsheviki," *World's Work*, February 1920, 326–327; Preston, 221–222; *Times*, February 15, 1920.
32. Higham, 231–232; Murray, 246–249; Post, 187; Preston, 223–224.
33. Memorandum, Assistant Secretary Louis F. Post to The Secretary, July 20, 1920, and Acting Secretary Rowland B. Mahany to Attorney General A. Mitchell Palmer, August 19, 1920, File 19/22, Labor Department Records; Post, 293–296; *Times*, May 26, 1920.
34. Assistant Secretary Louis F. Post to the Commissioner-General, July 21, 1920, File 52,730/40, General Immigration Files.

CHAPTER VI
Revival and Restriction of Immigration

1. "The New Tide of Immigration," *Current History*, July 1920, 704–706.
2. *ARCG*, 1920, 11, 28–29, 87, 316–318; "Immigrants Coming Again," *Literary Digest*, June 5, 1920, 32.
3. "Cool Greetings to Our Immigrants," *Literary Digest*, October 9, 1920, 18–19; Higham, 308; *Times*, July 18, September 24, 25, 1920.
4. "The New Pilgrims," *Survey*, October 30, 1920, 155–156; "The Jaws of the Machine," *ibid.*, 156–157.
5. *Times*, December 9, 14, 1920.
6. Chester H. Lane to Secretary of Labor Wilson, July 7, 1913, File 2/174, Labor Department Records; Frederick A. Wallis to Secretary of Labor Wilson, April 26, 1920, and to Assistant Secretary Post, July 22, 1920, File 2/174B, *ibid.*; "To Halt the European Invasion," *Literary Digest*, December 25, 1920, 14; Higham, 308–309; *Times*, April 30, June 2, August 15, November 17, 1920, January 15, 1921.

7. *Literary Digest,* April 30, 1921, 34, 36; *Times,* February 10, 12, 13, March 24, 1921.
8. Assistant Secretary of Labor Henning to Senator W. P. Dillingham, September 8, 1921, and Commissioner-General Husband, Memorandum for the Secretary, November 16, 1921, File 151/119, Labor Department Records; *Literary Digest,* April 30, 1921, 34, 36.
9. "Where Bad Citizens Are Made," *Delineator,* March 1921, 8–9, 54, 57; *ARCG,* 1921, 26.
10. Kenneth L. Roberts, "The Existence of an Emergency," *Saturday Evening Post,* April 30, 1921, 3–4, 86, 89–90, 93–94; Bennett, 41–42; Higham, 309–311.
11. "Operation of Percentage Immigration Law for Five Months," *Hearings before the House Committee on Immigration and Naturalization,* 67th Cong., 1st Sess., November 10, 1921; *ARCG,* 1921, 16–19; Corsi, 288–289; Higham, 312.
12. "Our 3 Per Cent Immigration Snarl," *Literary Digest,* October 1, 1921, 14–15; M. Gertrude Slaughter, "America's Front Door," *Hygeia,* January 1933, 11–14; *Times,* September 2, October 2, 1921.
13. Commissioner Wallis to Secretary of Labor Davis, October 5, 1921, File 2/174B, Labor Department Records.
14. *House Immigration and Naturalization Committee Hearings,* November 10, 1921.
15. Wallis to Secretary of Labor, May 17, 1921, and Secretary of Labor to Wallis, May 20, 1921, File 2/174B, Labor Department Records; Secretary of Labor to Robert E. Tod, May 31, 1921, and Tod to Secretary of Labor, October 6, 1921, File 151/98, *ibid.*; Frederic C. Morehouse to Secretary of Labor, January 17, 1922, File 151/119, *ibid.*; *Times,* May 12, October 12, 1921.
16. Wallis to Secretary of Labor, October 5, 1921, File 2/174B, Labor Department Records; Secretary to Tod, October 11, 1921, and Tod to Secretary, October 25, 1921, File 151/98, *ibid.*; *Outlook,* November 2, 1921, 333–334; *Times,* October 23, 1921.
17. Secretary to Tod, October 28, 1921, File 151/98, Labor Department Records, and Tod to Secretary, October 29, 1921, File 151/119, *ibid.*
18. Commissioner-General Husband, Memorandum for the Secretary, November 16, 1921, *ibid.*; *Times,* July 15, 17, 1921.
19. Secretary of Labor to Harry H. Schlaht, November 2, 1921, File 151/119, Labor Department Records; "A Light on Arriving Immigrants," *Survey,* August 1, 1921, 560.
20. "Ellis Island," *Survey,* January 14, 1922, 585–586; "Immigrant Aid," *Monthly Labor Review,* February 1923, 28–32; *Times,* November 3, 1921, January 3, 1922.
21. Chief Clerk, Memorandum for the Secretary, December 15, 1921, File 151/119, Labor Department Records; Natalie de Bogory, "Practical Americanism at Ellis Island," *Outlook,* February 8, 1922, 223–224.
22. Albert Bushnell Hart to Secretary of Labor Davis, February 8, 1922, File 151/119A, Labor Department Records.
23. *Times,* January 2, April 4, 5, 1922.
24. Commissioner Tod to Secretary of Labor (Personal and Confidential), July 8, 1922, and Congressman Isaac Siegel to Secretary of Labor, August 1, 1922, File 151/119A, Labor Department Records.
25. "Ellis Island Stuck Fast," *Survey,* October 15, 1922, 75–76.

26. Secretary of Labor to Secretary of the Treasury Mellon, December 15, 1922, File 151/119A, Labor Department Records; *Monthly Labor Review*, February 1923, 31–32; *Times*, December 19, 1922.
27. Telegram, Geo. B. Christian, Jr., to Commissioner Tod, June 18, 1923, File 151/98, Labor Department Records; *Times*, November 14, 1922, April 1, June 12, 14, 1923.
28. Tod to Commissioner-General, January 23, 1922, File 52,730/40A, General Immigration Files.
29. Henry H. Curran, *Pillar to Post* (New York, 1941), 285–287; *Times*, August 17, 1922, June 13, 21, 1923.
30. A. Geddes, British Embassy, Washington, to Secretary of Labor Davis, December 30, 1922, File 151/119A, Labor Department Records; Great Britain, Foreign Office, *United States, No. 2 (1923). Despatch from H. M. Ambassador at Washington reporting on Conditions at Ellis Island Immigration Station* (London, 1923), 1–12; *Times*, December 8, 17, 29, 1922.
31. "Ellis Island Stirring up the British," *Literary Digest*, September 1, 1923, 17–19; "Ellis Island a Red Rag to John Bull," *ibid.*, September 22, 1923, 23–24; *Times*, August 16, 17, 1923; *Tribune*, August 17, 1923.
32. Secretary of Labor to Frederick A. Wallis, August 21, 1923, File 151/119, Labor Department Records.
33. "Ellis Island," *Independent*, September 29, 1923, 125–126; *Times*, September 18, 21, 1923.
34. "Kind Words for Ellis Island," *Literary Digest*, March 8, 1924, 46–47; *Times*, February 17, 1924.
35. *ARCG*, 1908, 135–136; Curran, 293–294.
36. Commissioner Curran to Commissioner-General Husband, October 9, November 20, 1923, File 52,730/40B, General Immigration Files; Curran to Husband, October 6, 18, 1924, and Husband to Curran, October 8, 1924, File 52,730/40C, *ibid.*; Curran, 296–297.
37. Curran to Commissioner-General, December 29, 1924, January 24, 1925, and Commissioner-General to Curran, January 21, 1925, File 52,730/40C, General Immigration Files.
38. *Times*, June 5, 1924.
39. Curran to Commissioner-General, December 17, 1923, File 55,640/558F, General Immigration Files; *Congressional Record*, 68th Cong., 1st Sess., 4107–4108; *Times*, December 22, 1923, January 23, March 17, 1924.
40. "The Passing of the Steerage," *Literary Digest*, January 21, 1922, 20.
41. *ARCG*, 1924, 34.
42. Bennett, 50–52; Higham, 316–324; *Times*, February 8, 1924.
43. *Times*, July 20, 1924.
44. *ARCG*, 1925, 1–2, 8–9, 34.
45. *Times*, December 23, 1924.
46. "How the Immigration Law Works," *Survey*, January 15, 1925, 441–444; Curran, 304.
47. *ARCG*, 1927, 5, 9, 1930, 17; U.S. Department of State, *The Immigration Work of the Department of State and its Consular Offices* (Washington, 1932), 2;

Ralph C. Williams, *The United States Public Health Service, 1798–1950* (Washington, 1951), 108–110.

48. John W. Harrington, "Ellis Island, by Liberty Darkened," *Forum*, March 1927, 331–340; Oscar W. Ehrhorn, "Not So Bad," *ibid.*, August 1927, 309.
49. *ARCG*, 1926, 15–16, 1928, 26–28; "The Eclipse of Ellis Island," *Survey*, January 15, 1929, 480.

CHAPTER VII
Detention and Deportation

1. *Annual Report of the Secretary of Labor*, 1932, 73–74; *Immigration Work of the Department of State*, 3–4; Robert A. Divine, *American Immigration Policy, 1924–1952* (New Haven, 1957), 77–79.
2. *ARCG*, 1931, 35; Gardner Jackson, "Doak the Deportation Chief," *Nation*, March 18, 1931, 295–296; *Times*, January 6, February 10, 16, 24, April 11, 1931.
3. Acting Commissioner I. F. Wixon to Asst. Sec. of Labor W. W. Husband, October 2, 1931, and to Commissioner-General, October 9, 1931, File 55,630/4A, General Immigration Files.
4. Corsi, 30–31, 64–65, 93–94; *Times*, July 31, September 3, 24, October 9, 1931.
5. National Commission on Law Observance and Enforcement, *Report on the Enforcement of the Deportation Laws of the United States* (Washington, 1931), 5–6.
6. *Times*, August 9, 1931.
7. Commissioner Edward Corsi to Commissioner-General, March 23, 1932, File 55,630/4A, General Immigration Files; Corsi, 94–95, 97; *Times*, January 5, 1933.
8. Corsi, 187, 296–297, 300–301, 308–309.
9. Commissioner-General Harry E. Hull to Commissioner, Ellis Island, April 1, 1931, File 55,728/709, General Immigration Files, and Corsi to Commissioner-General, March 24, 1932, File 55,728/709E, *ibid.*; Corsi, 309–310.
10. Corsi, 310–312; *Times*, June 23, 27, August 10, 1933.
11. Ellis Island Committee, *Report of the Ellis Island Committee, March 1934* (New York, 1934), 10–13, 17.
12. *Annual Report of the Secretary of Labor*, 1934, 47; *Report of the Ellis Island Committee*, 48–53.
13. *Ibid.*, 132–137, 140–146.
14. *Annual Report of the Secretary of Labor*, 1934, 72; District Director Byron H. Uhl to Construction Engineer Paul H. Heimer, Treasury Department, January 10, 1935, and to Treasury Department, Procurement Division, May 10, 1939, File 55,952/287, General Immigration Files; *Report of the Ellis Island Committee*, 137–140.
15. *Annual Report of the Secretary of Labor*, 1933, 53–54, 1934, 49.
16. "At the Observation Post," *Literary Digest*, February 24, 1934, 14; Corsi, 314; *Times*, February 2, 1934.
17. Arthur D. Morse, *While Six Million Died: A Chronicle of American Apathy* (New York, 1967), 146–149; David S. Wyman, *Paper Walls: America and the*

Refugee Crisis, 1938–1941 (Amherst, 1968), 43–51, 155–156, 172–174, 217–219; *Annual Report of the Secretary of Labor,* 1939, 89–90.

18. File 38/170, Parts I–XII (1931–1938), General Immigration Files; *Annual Report of the Secretary of Labor,* 1935, 82, 1936, 91, 1937, 94, 1940, 122–124; *Times,* August 11, 1937.
19. Memo, Mr. Shaughnessy to Mr. Saunders, March 8, 1939, File 56,034/475, General Immigration Files; Asst. Secretary of the Treasury Herbert E. Gaston to Secretary of Labor, September 29, 1939, and Secretary of Labor to Asst. Secretary of the Treasury, October 14, 1939, File 55,912/699, *ibid.*
20. Marshall Dimock to Secretary of Labor, December 20, 1939, Secretary of Labor Perkins to Commissioner of Public Buildings W. E. Reynolds, March 15, 1940, and Report on Plans and Estimates for Construction Projects, Executive Office of the President, Approved November 18, 1940, File 56,034/475, *ibid.*
21. *Times,* April 12, 1940.
22. Bennett, 65–67; Divine, 106–107.
23. *Annual Report of the Attorney General,* 1941, 236; *Annual Report of the Immigration and Naturalization Service* (hereafter cited as *ARINS*), 1942, 3–5; 1945, 46–47.
24. Attorney General to Secretary of Navy, May 2, 1942, File 55,912/699, Commissioner Earl G. Harrison, Memorandum for Mr. Charles Fahy, Solicitor General, October 26, 1942, File 56,116/657, and W. H. Wagner, Administrative Assistant, Memo for Mr. Oliver, December 19, 1942, File 56,034/475, Immigration and Naturalization Service Records (continuation of General Immigration Files); *ARINS,* 1943, 26.
25. Ralph W. Gorton to Lemuel B. Schofield, Special Asst. to Attorney General, February 18, 1941, File 56,067/183, I. & N. Records, File 56,134/715 (1943–1944), *ibid.*
26. District Administrative Services Officer to Commissioner, Central Office, August 22, 1946, File 56,297/928, Attorney General to Commissioner of Public Buildings, November 22, 1946, and R. O. Jennings, Public Buildings Administration, to Mr. Rigsby, Bureau of the Budget, February 26, 1947, File 56,034/475, *ibid.*; *ARINS,* 1948, 19, 1949, 23–24; *New York Herald Tribune,* May 25, 1947.
27. Frances W. Kerr, "Ellis Island," *Monthly Review,* May 1949, 144–145; *Times,* March 18, 19, 1948, April 8, 1949.
28. Memo, Acting District Enforcement Officer Trent Dozer to Acting District Director Edward J. Shaughnessy, April 27, 1949, and Assistant Commissioner W. F. Kelly to District Director, May 16, 1949, File 56,177/103, I. & N. Records.
29. District Director Shaughnessy to Commissioner, August 24, 1951, File 56,319/503, *ibid.*; *ARINS,* 1951, 13, 52; Divine, 163; *Times,* October 16, 23, 1950.
30. "New Role for Ellis Island," *New York Times Magazine,* November 12, 1950, 20; "Ellis Island 1950," *Life,* November 13, 1950, 123–127; "Isle of Detention," *American Mercury,* May 1951, 556–563; "A Reporter at Large," *New Yorker,* May 12, 1951, 56–77.
31. *ARINS,* 1951, 13; *Times,* November 29, 1950, March 29, 1951.
32. District Director Shaughnessy to Commissioner, August 24, 1951, File 56,319/503, and July 30, 1952, File 56,333/898, I. &. N. Records; *Times,* July 14, 18, August 21, 1951.

33. District Administrative Officer to District Director, March 23, 1950, File 56,297/928, I. & N. Records; *ARINS*, 1951, 52, 54–55, 96, 1952, 48–49; *Times*, December 28, 1950.
34. Commissioner of Immigration and Naturalization to William J. Kennedy, Jr., Senate Appropriations Committee, November 6, 1953, File 55,812/450, I. & N. Records; *History of Ellis Island, New York* (Immigration and Naturalization Service, November 1, 1953), 3–6.
35. District Director Shaughnessy to Assistant Commissioner, August 10, 1954, File 56,358/200, I. & N. Records; "Last Days of Ellis Island," *Christian Science Monitor*, September 1, 1954.
36. *ARINS*, 1955, 6; Pike, 7; *Times*, November 12, 14, 30, 1954.
37. Popular estimates of the number of immigrants who passed through Ellis Island have ranged all the way from 16,000,000 to 30,000,000. An analysis of the statistics now available indicates that the number was actually somewhere in the neighborhood of 12,000,000.

CHAPTER VIII
A National Monument

1. "Disposal of Ellis Island," *Senate Report* No. 306, 89th Cong., 1st Sess., June 9, 1965; *Times*, January 9, May 5, June 6, 1955.
2. "Disposal of Ellis Island"; *Times*, June 29, July 21, 1955, January 5, September 14, 1956.
3. "Disposal of Ellis Island"; *Times*, September 16, 20, 23, 25, 1956.
4. Minutes of Board of Trustees Meeting, January 16, 1952, Files of American Scenic and Historic Preservation Society, Federal Hall National Memorial; *Report of New York City National Shrines Advisory Board* (New York, January 31, 1957), 13–14.
5. Assistant Director Ronald F. Lee, National Park Service, to Alexander Hamilton, American Scenic and Historic Preservation Society, April 11, 1952, ASHPS Files.
6. Minutes of Board of Trustees Meeting, December 15, 1954, ASHPS Files; Hugins, *Statue of Liberty National Monument*, 82–83.
7. Thomas M. Pitkin, *Preliminary Draft Prospectus for the American Museum of Immigration* (National Park Service, 1955), 1–110; *Times*, September 26, 1956.
8. "Disposal of Ellis Island"; *Times*, November 17, December 29, 1957, January 2, 17, February 15, April 3, 1958, February 17, March 10, May 9, November 3, December 3, 1959, January 14, 1960.
9. "Disposal of Ellis Island"; *Times*, April 17, August 10, 29, November 29, 1960, March 8, 1961, February 16, March 9, December 7, 1962.
10. "Disposal of Ellis Island"; *Times*, December 7, 8, 1962.
11. "Disposal of Ellis Island"; *A Study Report on Ellis Island* (National Park Service, June 1964), 1; *Times*, September 5, 1963.
12. National Park Service Meeting at Federal Hall, December 3, 1963, Subject: Ellis Island Disposition, File L58, National Park Service Files; *Times*, December 4, 1963.

13. *Study Report on Ellis Island,* 2–15; *Times,* June 16, 1964.
14. *Times,* June 26, October 22, 1964.
15. Presidential Documents. Title 3—The President. Proclamation 3656 Adding Ellis Island to the Statue of Liberty National Monument, May 11, 1965; *Times,* January 7, 1965; *Herald Tribune,* May 12, 1965.
16. Public Law 89–129, 89th Cong., H. J. Res. 454, August 17, 1965; *Staten Island Advance,* July 13, 1965; *Times,* June 8, August 19, 1965.
17. Personal observation—this writer accompanied Mr. Johnson on his inspection tour of Ellis Island; *Times,* July 16, 1964; *Time,* March 4, 1966, 78.
18. Emily Genauer, "The Hazards of Patronage: Venice and Ellis Island," *Herald Tribune Magazine,* March 13, 1966, 31; *Times,* February 25, 26, March 27, 1966.
19. Memorandum, Regional Director, Northeast Region, to Director, October 13, 1967, Subject: Master Plan Team-Ellis Island, File D18-APC, NPS Files; Memorandum, Deputy Assistant Director, Cooperative Activities, to Chief, Office of Resource Planning WSC, February 14, 1968, Subject: Master Plan Study, Ellis Island, File D18-CAM, *ibid.*; *Times,* March 5, 1968.
20. *A Master Plan for Ellis Island, New York* (National Park Service, June 1968), 4, 14–23.
21. "Statement: Ellis Island," National Park Service, January 1970.

BIBLIOGRAPHICAL NOTE

For the earlier history of Ellis Island the several collections of published sources and standard secondary works on New York colonial history are adequate. The material is well summarized in an unpublished report, "Ellis Island," by Sidney Berengarten, prepared under the Civil Works Administration for the then Office of National Parks in 1934. There are copies in the files of the National Park Service. There is also a copy in the New York Public Library, where authorship is incorrectly attributed to Rudolph Reimer. Another valuable report, constituting a legal history and covering the whole period from early Dutch times to the 1960s, is Henry H. Pike, *Ellis Island: Its Legal Status*, prepared for the General Services Administration in 1963. The National Park Service has copies of this report.

For the history of Ellis Island as a military installation, from 1794 to 1890, there is a relative abundance of source material. The building of the first fortifications there is treated in the Proceedings of the Commissioners of fortification for the City of New York and its Vicinity, and in the Ebenezer Stevens Manuscripts, both in The New-York Historical Society. The rebuilding of the little fort in the years just before the War of 1812 is described in the Jonathan Williams Papers at the Lilly Library, Indiana University. This material is supplemented by Hugh Hastings, editor, *Public Papers of Daniel D. Tompkins Governor of New York, 1807–1817. Military* (3 vols., Albany, 1898–1902). The later history of the fort, and of the navy's munitions depot that it became, can be traced in manuscripts in the National Archives, notably Correspondence, Office of the Chief of Engineers, Record Group 77, and Records of the Bureau of Ordnance, Record Group 74.

The sources available for a study of Ellis Island as an immigrant station are without visible limit, but have disconcerting gaps. The story of the great migration that funneled through the island after 1891, reached a peak in the years before World War I, began reviving after the war was over, and was then largely cut off, is an absorbing one. Much has been published about it from the immigrant's point of view, and much more lies fallow in family letters and foreign language newspapers. The material is in many tongues and scattered in a thousand places. There are still survivors of the experience available for interview. A beginning is now under way at collecting this type of material on tape at the American Museum of Immigration, Statue of Liberty National Monument. Willard S. Heaps gathered a considerable amount of such material for his book for young adults, *The Story of Ellis Island* (New York, 1967). The whole great movement from Europe to America has been described from the immigrant's point of view in vivid terms and from a scholarly base, but without documentation or much specific reference to Ellis Island, in Oscar Handlin, *The Uprooted: The Epic Story of the Great Migrations that Made the American People* (Boston, 1951). The rise of the restrictionist movement that finally brought mass immigration to an end has been treated in detail in John Higham, *Strangers in the Land: Patterns in American Nativism 1860–1925* (New Brunswick, N.J., 1955, and reprint, New York, 1965).

Something has already been done along the line of administrative history. George J. Svejda, *Castle Garden as an Immigrant Depot, 1855–1890* (National Park Service, 1968), covers the period preceding the establishment of the federal immigration station on Ellis Island and serves as an excellent introduction. Ann Novotny, *Strangers at the Door: Ellis Island, Castle Garden, and the Great Migration to America* (Riverside, Conn., 1971), has chapters on Ellis Island drawn in good part from this writer's "Report on Ellis Island as an Immigrant Depot, 1890–1954," prepared for the National Park Service in 1966.

Autobiographies and published letters of men who had to do with Ellis Island and its administration are fairly numerous. Victor Safford, *Immigration Problems; Personal Experiences of an Official* (New York, 1925), is a thoughtful book of reminiscences by a medical officer who served at the island during the late 1890s and early 1900s. There are highly illuminating bits in Elting E. Morison, editor, *The Letters of Theodore Roosevelt* (8 vols., Cambridge, 1952–1954), including not only letters but also detailed and thoughtful notes. This work is especially useful on the reform of the Ellis Island administration in 1902. Fiorello H. La Guardia, *The Making of an Insurgent: An Autobiography, 1882–1919* (Philadelphia, 1948), has good chapters on Ellis Island operations during the later 1900s, when La Guardia was an interpreter there. Philip Cowen, *Memories of an American Jew* (New York, 1932), has useful facts on the administration of Robert Watchorn from 1905 to 1909, when Cowen, former editor of the *American Hebrew*, was serving at Ellis Island on the boards of special inquiry and in other capacities. Frederic C. Howe, *The Confessions of a Reformer* (New York, 1925), relates rather emotionally the tribulations of Ellis Island's administrator during World War I and the Red scare that followed that conflict. Henry H. Curran's attractive book of memoirs, *Pillar to Post* (New York, 1941), has a vivid chapter on the administration of the island at the end of its period of mass reception of immigrants. Edward Corsi, *In the Shadow of Liberty: The Chronicle of Ellis Island* (New York, 1935), describes conditions there after the great rush of immigration had been stopped and the island had become primarily a deportation center, but has many colorful forays into the earlier history of the station. Corsi had access to much material that has since been destroyed.

Official manuscript sources for an administrative history of Ellis Island exist in bulk, but are badly broken up or are in cumbersome form. The General Immigration Files, and some of the succeeding Immigration and Naturalization Service Records, in Record Group 85 at the National Archives, were withdrawn and largely destroyed in 1960, making the evolution of organization and policy difficult to trace.

Illuminating fragments remain and have been used. There are also hundreds of volumes of letter files to 1912 in this record group, very poorly indexed and in good part illegible or nearly so. They include Letters Sent, Press Copies ("Immigration"), 1891–1912, 340 volumes; Bureau of Immigration, Press Copies of Letters Sent ("T" Series, 1892–1903), 14 volumes; and District No. 3, New York (Ellis Island) Letters Sent, Press Copies, 1903–1912, 340 volumes. These have all been broadly sampled. There is a Bureau of Immigration, Record of Correspondence, 1891–1903, 27 volumes, in the same record group, which offers a rough cross-index to the letter files within its period and has some information within itself not found elsewhere. There is also a collection of Early Immigration Records, 1882–1906, 140 boxes. This consists of folded original correspondence from state and later federal immigration stations, with brief notations of replies. This material has not been used in the present work. For the period after 1912 no letter files have been found and the numbered files are badly broken up. This lack has been supplied to a limited degree from Immigration Service Records, 1907–1935, General Records of the Department of Labor, Record Group 174. Access to the numbered General Immigration Files and succeeding Immigration and Naturalization Service Records, such as survive, can be had at present only through the Immigration and Naturalization Service. It is understood that these records for the period 1903–1952 will have the restriction removed in 1977.

Official records are richly supplemented by the William Williams Papers in the New York Public Library for the years 1902–1905 and 1909–1913. Williams, as commissioner of immigration at Ellis Island during two terms and under two presidents, saved a large body of both official and private correspondence and related material dealing with his administration. There is also a small William Williams Collection in the Yale University Library. His relations with the Washington office during his second term are further clarified by the Charles Nagel Papers in the Yale University Library, and by the illuminating Folder 1579, Ellis Island; William Williams, in the huge collection of William Howard Taft Papers in the Library of Congress. For the intervening period, 1905–1909, marking the peak of immigration, when Robert Watchorn was commissioner at the island, no Watchorn papers have been found, but the Oscar S. Straus Papers in the Library of Congress are very helpful. Some material on the end of Watchorn's administration has been gleaned from the vast bulk of the Theodore Roosevelt Papers in the same repository. Exhaustive investigation of this rich collection was not possible. Some light on the impact of politics on the administration of Ellis Island during this period is found in the Herbert Parsons Papers, Special Collections, Columbia University Libraries. Commissioner Frederic C. Howe, unfortunately, burned his personal papers relating to Ellis Island (1914–1919), intended for a book, when he resigned in 1919.

There are extensive published records, and they have been heavily drawn upon in the preparation of the present work. These include the annual reports of cabinet officers and subordinates charged with the administration of the immigration laws. Most important of these for Ellis Island are the reports of the commissioner-general of immigration (1895–1931). These cover the high period of immigration and often include the reports, or extensive extracts therefrom, of the commissioners at the island. Reports of a number of special commissions include reference to Ellis Island, and several of these have been used. Probably the most detailed and illuminating of these for the purposes of this study is the *Report of the Ellis Island Committee,*

March 1934 (New York, 1934). There is abundant material in congressional publications. Debates on immigration and immigration policy, with frequent references to Ellis Island, are scattered through the *Congressional Record*. A few extracts have been made. A number of published hearings and reports from committees of Congress have also been used. Perhaps the most interesting of these, certainly the most emotionally charged, is "Conditions at Ellis Island," *Hearings before the Committee on Immigration and Naturalization, House of Representatives*, 66th Cong., 1st Sess., November 24, 26, 28, 1919. These hearings covered the administration of Commissioner Howe at the time of the big Red scare.

The New York newspaper and periodical press showed active interest in Ellis Island during the years when it was receiving immigrants in great numbers. Much use has been made of such contemporary material. At many points, because of serious gaps in the official records, it must be relied on heavily to produce a coherent narrative. Newspapers have been used largely in the order of their accessibility. For most of the period the *New York Times* has a published index, with a disconcerting gap in Ellis Island's busiest years. This newspaper has been combed for the years 1887–1968. The *New York Tribune* is indexed to 1906; it has been searched for the years 1887–1906, and many items have been taken from it for later years. There is an index to the New York *World* for several years in the 1880s and early 1890s, and it has been examined for these years. Later use of the *World* has been made here and there as leads were followed up. Other New York metropolitan newspapers are occasionally cited.

For Ellis Island in the latter nineteenth century and the beginning of the twentieth, the most useful periodical is *Harper's Weekly*. There are also good articles on Ellis Island in *Leslie's Weekly* and the *North American Review*. For the whole period from the establishment of the Ellis Island station to the outbreak of World War I, when immigration was sharply reduced, the *American Hebrew* showed active interest in the problems of its Russian coreligionists arriving there and kept a close watch on its operations. The magazine *Charities*, which became *Charities and the Commons* and then the *Survey*, had much comment on Ellis Island in the years from 1903 to 1929. The *Outlook* was actively interested in Ellis Island throughout its peak period of operations and during its postwar tribulations. For the early 1920s the *Literary Digest* is most useful. Many other periodicals published occasional articles on Ellis Island, and these have been used as they have been found helpful.

There are a number of useful monographs on the subject of immigration policy and practice during the period when Ellis Island was the chief immigrant receiving station. Among these are Marion T. Bennett, *American Immigration Policies: A History* (Washington, 1963), and William C. Van Vleck, *The Administrative Control of Aliens: A Study in Administrative Law and Procedure* (New York, 1932). Roy L. Garis, *Immigration Restriction: A Study of the Opposition to and Regulation of Immigration into the United States* (New York, 1927), has been largely superseded by Higham's detailed study of the restrictionist movement. Robert A. Divine, *American Immigration Policy, 1924–1952* (New Haven, 1957), covers the period when Ellis Island had lost its primary importance. Some of its interpretations have been sharply challenged in David Wyman, *Paper Walls: America and the Refugee Crisis, 1938–1941* (Amherst, 1968). Barbara M. Solomon, *Ancestors and Immigrants: A Changing New England Tradition* (Cambridge, 1956), tells of the rise of the Immigration Restriction League in Boston, and has a number of pertinent references to Ellis Island. Charlotte Erickson, *American Industry and the European Immigrant, 1860–1885* (Cambridge, 1957), provides the background for the attempted enforcement at Ellis Island of the almost unworkable contract labor laws. William Preston, Jr., *Aliens and Dissenters: Federal Suppression of Radicals, 1903–1933* (Cambridge, 1963), is essentially the story of the suppression of the IWW during and after World War I, but illustrates the general lack of concern for the Bill of Rights in the handling of immigrants and has useful references to Ellis Island. Another scholarly study bearing on Ellis Island during the period of the big Red scare is Robert K. Murray, *Red Scare: A Study in National Hysteria, 1919–1920* (Minneapolis, 1955). Still of interest in this connection is Louis F. Post, *The Deportation Delirium of Nineteen-twenty; A Personal Narrative of an Historic Official Experience* (Chicago, 1923).

For the period after the closing of the detention station at Ellis Island, the efforts to dispose of the property and the decision to make it a part of Statue of Liberty National Monument are well summarized in "Disposal of Ellis Island," *Senate Report* No. 306, 89th Cong., 1st Sess., June 9, 1965. Supplementary material has been found in the files of the American Scenic and Historic Preservation Society, Federal Hall National Memorial, New York City, and in those of the National Park Service. For narrative continuity, the *New York Times* has been chiefly relied on.

INDEX